S0-BWW-180

THE AZTECS AT INDEPENDENCE

MIRIAM MELTON-VILLANUEVA

THE AZTECS AT INDEPENDENCE

Nahua Culture Makers in Central Mexico, 1799–1832

THE UNIVERSITY OF
ARIZONA PRESS
TUCSON

The University of Arizona Press
www.uapress.arizona.edu

We respectfully acknowledge the University of Arizona is on the land and territories of Indigenous peoples. Today, Arizona is home to twenty-two federally recognized tribes, with Tucson being home to the O'odham and the Yaqui. Committed to diversity and inclusion, the University strives to build sustainable relationships with sovereign Native Nations and Indigenous communities through education offerings, partnerships, and community service.

© 2016 by The Arizona Board of Regents
All rights reserved. Published 2016
First paperback edition published 2022

ISBN-13: 978-0-8165-3353-4 (cloth)
ISBN-13: 978-0-8165-4697-8 (paperback)
ISBN-13: 978-0-8165-3463-0 (ebook)

Cover design by Leigh McDonald
Cover photo by Miriam Melton-Villanueva

Publication of this book is made possible in part by funding from the University of Nevada, Las Vegas, College of Liberal Arts, and by the proceeds of a permanent endowment created with the assistance of a Challenge Grant from the National Endowment for the Humanities, a federal agency.

Library of Congress Cataloging-in-Publication Data
Names: Melton-Villanueva, Miriam, author.
Title: The Aztecs at independence : Nahua culture makers in central Mexico, 1799–1832 /
    Miriam Melton-Villanueva.
Description: Tucson : The University of Arizona Press, 2016. | Includes bibliographical references
    and index.
Identifiers: LCCN 2016008674 | ISBN 9780816533534 (cloth : alk. paper)
Subjects: LCSH: Nahuas—Ethnic identity. | Nahuas—Writing—Sources. | Nahuatl imprints—
    Sources. | Nahuatl language—Social aspects—Sources. | Nahuas—Religion—19th century. |
    Nahuas—History—19th century—Sources. | Nahuas—Social life and customs—19th century—
    Sources. | Nahuatl-Spanish dialect—Mexico—Sources.
Classification: LCC F1221.N3 M45 2016 | DDC 305.897/452—dc23
LC record available at https://lccn.loc.gov/2016008674

Printed in the United States of America
♾ This paper meets the requirements of ANSI/NISO Z39.48-1992 (Permanence of Paper).

In memory of my father and dedicated to my mother and son who traveled with me to the Huasteca Veracruzana to learn more than Nahuatl

CONTENTS

ILLUSTRATIONS

FIGURES

TABLES

ACKNOWLEDGMENTS

THIS BOOK WOULD HAVE BEEN IMPOSSIBLE without the kindness and support of many. The National Academy of Sciences Ford Foundation's Postdoctoral Fellowship at UCLA's Chicano Research Center gave me a precious year to craft this narrative and a network of scholars and editors to whom I am forever indebted. Field research and language training were sponsored by the families of my *tía* Hortensia and *tío* Luis who sheltered me in their homes in México; the Doris G. Quinn Foundation Dissertation Fellowship; the National Academies Foreign Language Area Studies Summer Grant; the Andrew W. Mellon Summer Institute in Spanish Paleography at The Huntington Library; the University of California at Los Angeles (UCLA) Latin American Institute; the UCLA History Department; the University of Nevada, Las Vegas (UNLV) College of Liberal Arts; the California State University Student Research Competition in Behavioral and Social Sciences; the UCLA Center for the Study of Women; and the National Research Council's Ford Foundation Dissertation Competition.

I would not have become a historian without the inspiration, support, and training of Kevin Terraciano and James Lockhart. James patiently corrected my translations, but all errors are mine. Stephanie Wood, Susan Schroeder, Catherine Komisaruk, Robin Derby, Lise Sedres, William Weber, Teofilo Ruiz, John Sullivan, Lisa Sousa, Claudia Parodi, Martha Ramírez-Oropeza, and John Pohl served as culture-transmitters, helped me find my bearings and navigate.

I thank the Nahua teacher-scholars of Sullivan's Zacatecas Institute for Teaching and Research in Ethnology (IDIEZ), especially Delfina de la Cruz, who opened her home to me—not only in ritual, song, and dance with the grandmothers but also in preparing food and in the boisterous play of my own child with his new friends, navigating three languages.

I am forever grateful to the vicar of the Ex-Convento de San Juan Bautista in Metepec for entrusting me with permission to research and photograph documents in the parish archive. I thank Maritzella, guardian of the archive, who supervised my long hours of work. Their care, caution, and dedication, despite meager resources, have protected the patrimony of local communities in ways other institutions have not. The late municipal historian of San Bartolomé, don Pedro Valdez Martínez, helped untangle puzzles in the sources by sharing his knowledge of the geography and community of San Bartolomé. Heartfelt thanks belong to him and his wife for bringing to life many landmarks with which I had only worked in two dimensions. I thank the *fiscales* and *topiles* who today continue the work of our ancestors, creating community in San Bartolomé.

Mine are the hardest-working editors in the business; I notice they are the last to leave at all the conferences. Thanks to Kristen my shepherd, Natasha the visionary, and the whole crew at Arizona. Liam Frink, Stephanie Wood, and David Tanenhaus generously read early manuscript drafts, kept me sailing ahead into the unknown. And to the anonymous peer reviewers of this book, I give heartfelt thanks for their endorsement, insight, and expertise.

The research and support of Teresa Jarquín Ortega at El Colegio Mexiquense prepared the foundation from which I could find the Independence archive; I am indebted for her kindness with an inexperienced student on her first research trip. Thanks also to the maestros Marco Aurelio Chávezmaya, Bertha Balestra Aguilar, and Eduardo Osorio for their invaluable introductions in Toluca. I also thank my cohort and colleagues at UCLA and UNLV. And deepest gratitude to the gentle mentors who encouraged my voice.

Las Vegas, Nevada, November 26, 2015

THE AZTECS AT
INDEPENDENCE

INTRODUCTION

MY MOTHER'S fingers pressed the embroidered flowers on my neck-line, *"Este se llama quexquemitl*, Miri." I had called the shawl she put over my shoulders a *poncho*; she replied, "This is called a quexque-mitl," teaching me the Nahuatl for the Pre-Columbian shawl still used today. She interpreted the world for me with words. I learned from her the power of naming. If you know the true word for something, no one can take it away. Well, the object or person could leave, but kinship remains as a guide to find its heart again. The word itself pulses, a beacon. A little girl, feet firmly planted on both sides of a border I didn't know existed, my Mexico counted on the sound of summer rain and a horned toad that would come out from under my grandmother's roses every yellow morning to play with me. Church and prayer and food and music, always music. I didn't learn that some people used "Mexican" as a derogative until college. My mother's world protected me so entirely; each song a charm. Every word, said or sung, resonated with in-trinsic values that crossed geographies of time, in sacred languages. Even my accountant uncle, once greatly urged, could stand up and recite poems that would make everyone cry. It's this slippage, this flight to and from language-anchored ideas, that reminds us that many worlds are possible.

"In the beginning was the Verb," begins my grandmother's leather-bound Bible, in Spanish. Life itself, birthed by verse. How I constructed this project, my method, is anchored by words. Words liberate; without a commitment to indigenous records, this story would not have fledged. The birth is hard. Not just the getting of access, but the finding, transcribing, translating, and analyzing in context with what we already know—this path is for hearts dedicated to a new world in which quiet voices are valued. New Philology: it sometimes feels like a sleepy sermon, but I like to think of the craft as a process akin to investigative journalism. It's an adventure to track down local records. And if the stories are treasures, then indigenous documents are the maps; each word holds the imprint of people's ideas that leads us to how, where, and when they change and persist over time. I do not yet understand everything I have encountered in these manuscripts; I offer this work to stimulate further discussion and encourage future research with the Independence archive.

In daily interactions we all take the colonial story into independence. My parents kept Spanish in the home; even as a schoolgirl in Alta California they encouraged me to learn the contradictory rules and choose among conventions. One day I came back from school confused. Someone had accused me of being Spanish, because I spoke Spanish. I knew that was wrong; does this mean I speak Mexican? My mother first pointed me in the direction of indigenous languages "more complex than Spanish"—in fourth grade. Chapter 2 attempts an answer.

THE HISTORICAL NAHUAS: A STORY OF ETHNIC ENCOUNTERS

The impulse to rename, to erase, reflects a territorial strategy. Many people are not taught that we stand on native land, that national borders continue to divide first nations, that migrant labor existed before the United States. Indigenous histories represent the missing pieces to our contemporary identities, allowing us to recognize the far-reaching historical reasons behind contemporary social patterns, from migration to food sovereignty. Ancient practices understood as cues to modernity make us whole.[1] This study is offered as an antidote to the colonial nose wrinkle that relegates indigeneity to impolite behavior, thinks diversity is something new, discourages language acquisition, and doesn't want students with Spanish and English surnames to speak Zapotec or Tagalog, Diné Bizaad or Squamish, respectively.

First, let me situate this story. We know the Sierras; the Rocky Mountains don't recognize national boundaries. As they reach down into the heart of Mexico

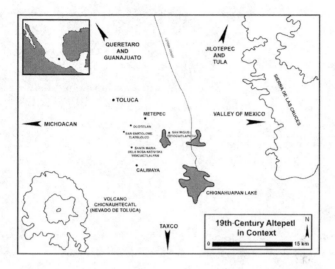

FIGURE 1. Map of the Metepec-region altepetl studied. (Map by Aaron R. Woods.)

they join with the transversal volcanic range, as if creating the bottom of a cup. This story begins here, in the protection of the high valley once called Matlatzinco, after the most numerous ethnic group established here.

The topography situates the various *altepetl* (Nahua city-states) in this story below the eastern foothills of the valley's volcano, one of the highest peaks in the country. Metepec, the pueblo that still houses Nahua documents, at Mexican Independence served as home base for the itinerant priest who rotated his service among the altepetl represented herein: *San Bartolomé* Tlatelolco, Santa María de la Rosa de Nativitas *Yancuictlalpan*, Santa María Magdalena *Ocotitlan*, and San Miguel *Totocuitlapilco* (italics represent the truncated form used within, in lieu of the full altepetl names).[2] They existed then as they do today: between a volcano at lower left and the range that separates them from Mexico City to the right. Standing on the volcano looking eastward into the sunrise, the mountains to Michoacán are behind us, to the west. Straight ahead, in the middle ground, rises the range of Las Cruces mountains that divides this valley's altepetl from Mexico Tenochtitlan in the Valley of Mexico. Yet farther behind these nearer mountains appear Popocatepetl and Ixtlacihuatl, the boundaries of the next valley beyond Mexico, the valley of Puebla-Tlaxcala. Presided over by weepy volcanoes, this dramatic geography forms the heart of a larger central Mexican region to this day.

Long before Iberians (Spanish and Portuguese from the Peninsula of Iberia, in advance of consolidating their national boundaries) trudged up from Veracruz, indigenous communities negotiated extreme geographic diversity both in terms of culture and language groups. The archeological record goes back three thousand years.[3] Extensive trade crisscrossed not only within and between these separate valleys but also to Teotihuacan in the north. Especially in the eleventh century, an unidentified drama played itself out in Teotihuacan that brought waves of migration into the Valley of Matlatzinco, the early name for Toluca Valley. It was during this time that the Matlatzinca also forged alliances with nomadic Chichimecs through marriage, which involved welcoming them into the sedentary agricultural traditions of their fertile valley.[4] This phase saw northern Chichimec communities migrate into the Otomí-Mazahua-Matlatzinca zone and settle along the Lerma River. Each ethnic group retained its distinct language and identity, even when joining into political alliances of neighbors with distinct languages and customs. Metepec, described in chapter 4 as the altepetl that now houses the Independence archive (the testament sources for this study, which date from the Mexican Independence era), originally incorporated one of these Chichimec communities.[5]

Intense contact between distinct culture and language groups characterize the Matlatzinco/Toluca Valley, but ethnic diversity was not unique to this basin. Across the Las Cruces range and into the Valley of Mexico, in the altepetl of Azcapotzalco, the same mix of languages was spoken, and the political principal in Azcapotzalco spoke Matlatzinca.[6] Otomí speakers permeate the Mexica landscape too, appearing in altepetl records throughout the Valley of Mexico, even forming their own ethnic *tlaxilacalli* (units of the altepetl city-state) in Nahua Coyoacan.[7] The Otomí, now the group with the largest population, inhabits the center and north of the Toluca Valley. The Matlatzinca, the oldest group in the valley, lives in the center and south. The Mazahua live mainly in the north and west. And thanks to Stephanie Wood's research we know that the Mexica, the dominant group, lived in most areas as an ethnic minority.[8] Thus, at the moment when Iberians first arrived speaking Castilian, at least four large indigenous ethnic groups cohabited the Matlatzinco Valley.

Then who are the Aztecs, if late arrivals to the valley? Aztec, Mexica, and Nahua all refer to the same culture group, with each term favored by different disciplines. For clarity, it is the language of the Mexicas, Nahuatl, that leads many language scholars to use the word Nahua to describe Mexica society, even if Nahuas never used the term themselves. Beyond its root in the widely used language of trade at the time of Iberian migration, *Nahua* speaks to a larger-than-politically-Mexica heritage, including people who were not part of the Aztec sphere, such as the people of Tlaxcala. *Mexica* tends to carry that same larger meaning and has become the most widely accepted term by many scholars across disciplines, based on the influential urban polity Mexica of Tenochtitlan that gave the geographic region its name: Mexico. I found a death register in which a Nahuatl writer refers to *Mexica* and other ethnic communities in Metepec (referring to distinct ethnic settlements within the altepetl and their death rites), thus settling the question as to whether Nahuas ever used the term *Mexica* to refer to themselves in the colonial period.[9] Further, in early colonial sources the leaders of San Bartolomé Tlatelolco and Totocuitlapilco claim their land was given to them by Mexicas, back when Tenochtitlan was the colonizing entity, as spoils of war, apparently the reason why the Nahuatl language predominated in the altepetl studied here.[10] Yet *Aztec* remains the most well-known term, a rather unfortunate twist, because they never called themselves by that name, either. This study generally follows the convention established by four generations of New Philologians in using the term *Nahua* for Mexicas who lived during the colonial period.[11]

The people of the Matlatzinco/Toluca Valley were not strangers to conquest—nor to challenging it. Two waves of Mexica colonization hit the valley. From 1474 to 1476 the Mexica, aided by Texcocanos and Tepanecas as allies, subjugated the Matlatzincas of this valley, but two powerful local altepetl resisted their allotted tribute in wood, on the grounds that the Mexica's appeal felt like a demand to them, as opposed to a request. By consensus the two altepetl decided that they did not have enough wood on their mountains to provide the Mexicas with the amount they requested.[12] During this period Axayácatl and his son Moctezuma appointed Mexica *calpixque* (overseers),[13] later also deployed by the Spanish monarchy during the colonial period. Essentially tax collectors and bureaucrats, calpixques did not just tax. They not only enforced what the locals considered environmental degradation but also imposed Nahuatl as the official language.[14]

The well-known painted cloth called the Lienzo de Tlaxcala (figure 2) shows how the locals viewed the "conquest." In their eyes, it was the return of the Mexica alongside an army of Otomí, Tlaxcalteca, and Iberians. Subjugation to the Mexica for tribute was not new, only now as they returned with weapons to the Matlatzinco Valley, it was with some new friends.[15] That event, now commonly called the Spanish Conquest, happened in 1521, a century after the first

FIGURE 2. From Lienzo de Tlaxcala, plate 40, sixteenth century.
The Matlatzinco Valley is now called the Toluca Valley.

subjugation by Mexicas described above. The Mexica had originally subjugated the Matlatzinco Valley and made the Nahuatl language compulsory.[16]

So the tables turned, and the Aztecs of the central basin of Mexico became intimately familiar with some of the same forms of subjugation they themselves had perpetrated in the Valley of Matlatzinco *before* the Iberians. When Spanish was imposed as the new lingua franca in the sixteenth century, Nahuas adapted by maintaining their language and local ways, regardless of the colonial encumbrance of Spanish and the stated aim to eradicate indigenous tongues.[17] This study furthers this colonial story into the early nineteenth century; in this region, Nahua political and ritual lineages persisted beyond the expulsion of Spanish rule.[18]

Diverse ethnic communities coexisted in this valley before Iberian migrants; just because this study shows that altepetl were practicing Nahua cultural traditions, it does not mean they became ethnically homogenous. Census figures from the late colonial period illustrate this complexity. Mark Mairot's analysis of the Revillagigedo census of 1791 noted that while no Europeans lived in pueblos, San Bartolomé had the second largest number of Hispanic families in Toluca's region.[19] The balance of Toluca's overall "Hispanic" population numbers fell into imprecise ethnic groupings, categories without clear boundaries; 66 percent were marked down as *españoles*, 8 percent as *castizos*, and 26 percent as mestizos.[20] That means nearly half of the census sample of "Hispanics" who lived in pueblos appear to be indigenous not just because of residence in a pueblo but also at least partially by birth heritage. Because the census listed place of birth, we know that nearly half of the "Hispanic" men in San Bartolomé were actually native to indigenous pueblos: seven were born in Metepec, and one each was born in San Antonio la Isla, Santiago Tianguistenco, and Zumpango.[21] Just like today, people didn't fit neatly into census categories.

A MEXICAN CULTURE OF WRITING

Pre-Columbian Aztec writing, one of the hallmarks of Mesoamerican culture, continues to arouse much interest. *Tlacuilos* (painter-writers of Aztec books), called *escribanos* in the colonial context, quickly adopted the Roman alphabet, a writing form encouraged by the Christian bureaucracy. Chapter 3 shows guilds of escribanos still active in the nineteenth century using Nahuatl. The written word is presented herein as a successful strategy in cultivating Nahua lifeways, as an integral support for ritual and bureaucratic lineages. In the earliest hours of the colony, writers in many native communities continued keeping the records of their lives in their own languages, and they did so for centuries.[22]

Aztecs thus adapted the new alphabet by springing forth like Huiztilopochtli—nearly fully formed.[23] Because of the widespread culture of writing, lineages of writers existed prior to Spanish introductions. In the Mexican experience, before contact with the barefoot Franciscan friar-scholars who taught them Spanish, the highly trained tlacuilos kept records of events, generated almanacs, maintained tax records, and calculated multiple (365¼-day, 260-day) agricultural, astronomical, and divinatory calendars, while guarding the stories of peoples, their festivals, and their social values. In central and southern Mexico, these specialized groups of writer-painters used what Elizabeth Hill Boone calls semasiographic writing, generating volumes of graphic manuscripts.[24]

The advantage of Mexican graphic writing systems is that historians from radically different language groups could read each other's books and share basic ideas in writing; their pictography was not language dependent.[25] Colorful texts conveyed meaning directly, without isolating words, similar to the way we interpret signs found at an airport today. To comprehend why we do not yet fully understand Mexican codices, note how symbols we today consider universal when seen over a doorway, like the symbol of a human figure overlayed with a triangle, actually carry intangible meanings that might be difficult to discern. In the case of the triangle figure, we expect people to sort themselves according to gendered human bodies (triangle to mean skirt; skirt to mean female) and walk into the doorway to take care of the human body's excretory processes in a room removed from the public—abstract understandings which are not even hinted at in the symbol on the door. Semasiographic writing similarly combines abstract meanings with literal, or pictorial, symbols and then adds phonetic marks. In an airport, one might not fully decipher the triangle figure: symbols are in no way actually "universal" but learned, shared between speakers of different languages. Today, we may not fully parse the Mexican books of fate, but when the precolonial codices were written, Nahuatl, Otomí, Mixtec, Zapotec, and myriad other distinct languages in Mexico held iconography, visual conventions, and graphic style in common.[26] A remarkable strategy for literacy, unintelligible language groups could read each other's texts. The striking continuities at Independence in this sense do not represent an anomaly for the development of Nahuatl but rather an extension of a larger Mexican culture of writing—not an isolated practice among one language group nor within one principal altepetl.

IDENTIFYING HOW ALTEPETL STRUCTURES SUPPORT LOCAL CULTURES

Aztec civil society formed complex horizontal networks. Women and men might walk to their altepetl marketplace from various suburban tlaxilacalli to buy, sell, and mingle; the roads were so well maintained they provided public bathrooms.[27] In the altepetl they might pick up street food, like *tecuilatl* (spirulina "cheese" algae) tacos and little fish cooked up right before your eyes.[28] Here they contributed their time to labor drafts to help fulfill larger obligations of their altepetl and joined together on broad public works projects or to celebrate seasonal festivals.[29] They shared common leader-ancestors, ritual symbolisms, land, and language—and considered their main political loyalty to be to their own local altepetl not necessarily to the altepetl that exacted their tribute and labor. Many scholars have long theorized that strong subregional ethnic institutions allowed altepetl to insulate themselves after the colonization of Tenochtitlan; this study supports this understanding, further identifying specific groups and people, like the *fiscalía* of chapter 1, a governing body larger than just *fiscales*, at work within their respective altepetl. Self-contained

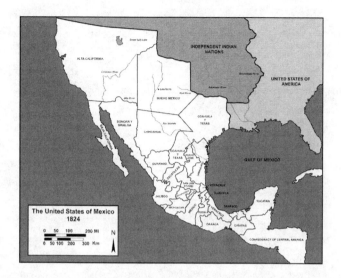

The United States of Mexico
1824

FIGURE 3. The changing boundaries of the new nation after Independence. In Florida and much of the vast region called Alta California (which includes today's Nevada, Utah, and Arizona), these claims remained actively contested by indigenous nations and city-states. (Map by Aaron R. Woods.)

groups, allied in local, decentralized cellular structures, allowed distinct altepetl to adapt to colonialism, literally and figuratively, on their own terms.

The fall of Mexico Tenochtitlan in 1521 marks the imposition of Christianity. Within one generation, recordkeeping shifted into Roman script but remained in indigenous tongues, especially Nahuatl, the supra-regional language of trade. The theological imperatives of monotheism, articulated as a legal justification for murder, theft, and political conquest, allowed indigenous archives to be burned—in the effort to stamp out "devil worship."[30] Few native books dating before colonialism survive, yet this study presents the recordkeepers, indigenous escribanos who survived into the nineteenth century, not as isolated individuals but as still part of vibrant identifiable associations with distinct altepetl formulas. Independence struggles in Mexico are considered to have begun in 1810 with the freedom cry of a priest who spoke Nahuatl, calling out in Spanish to cast off the rule of Spain.[31] The year 1821 generally marks the end of the Independence period; the establishment of the Mexican nation under a federal constitution came in 1824.

Aztecs and their descendants preserved, as Stephanie Wood described, "a heritage of active participation and a native orchestration of crucial events."[32] Life in altepetl has been a central research question for ethnohistorians studying the Mexican colonial period. My challenge was to carry this inquiry into the nineteenth century. By looking at the careers of escribanos, I began to describe another layer of altepetl organization, as seen in chapter 1. Then the conservative nature of Nahuatl texts described groups of escribanos so faithful to their formulas that I distinguished between notarial schools in chapter 3. In chapter 2, finding Nahuatl influences within Spanish-language texts still astonished me: Nahuas continued to express their ideas with an indigenous framework, in Spanish.[33] One would expect by this time that Spanish would function as the normative structure. Instead, I came face to face with an "unusual" Spanish, one that unexpectedly retained Nahuatl notarial models—even though the language itself had already transitioned to Spanish. Chapter 2 describes the escribanos working in Spanish and chapter 3 those working in Nahuatl; it was their work in continuing centuries-long traditions that led me to feel certain that their notarial organizations did not exist in isolation. Given escribanos' exceptional success in adapting their own worldview to the homogenizing pressure of colonialism, I looked for and found evidence of additional groups involved in culture making. These people, actively participating in local practices, are described in chapters 1, 5, and 6. After all, Metepec functioned before contact as the bureaucratic seat of calpixques; the precedent of institutional support of Nahua escribanos in this area is long.

Confronted with their own texts, the depth of civic engagement in the Independence archive astounds: the bilingual literacy; the training of escribanos and other public servants; the adherence to precedent; the number of Nahua men called to serve in a local government body that I identify as the fiscalía; the number of Nahua women bequeathing land to fulfill ancestral ritual requirements; the geographic diversity of saints' cults . . . the data spills quietly, relentlessly, to carve their own concepts into the foundation of history.

AMENDING HISTORICAL VIEWS OF THE NAHUAS

Early colonial accounts tend to consider American people (if they mention indigenous people at all) as insignificant—or an impediment—to building society. The journals written by Spaniards, even the few that describe native settlements as impressive civilizations, extoll their own Christianizing and "civilizing" deeds to the Crown. Broadly, Latin American colonial history is considered to have begun with early epic narratives, chronicles, and biographies, all offering the point of view of migrant Europeans. These narratives variously exoticized or scorned the few *indios* (Indians) they mentioned.[34] Not until the twentieth century did academics, most from the World War II era, begin to look at varied aspects of life in the colonies, its groups, and its institutions. This approach became possible because scholars added archival materials in their studies. Archival sources, sought for and found mainly in Spain, reflected the extensive correspondence between the Crown and its subjects, with a focus on ecclesiastical correspondence and a dash of the familiar memoirs.[35]

But the essential turn in the story came when Sherburne F. Cook and Lesley Byrd Simpson, demographers at Berkeley, crunched the numbers, estimating the native population at four points in the early colonial period.[36] The population for 1519 came in at 11,000,000, falling to 2,014,000 people by 1607, figures that caused much debate because it meant that more people lived in parts of central Mexico at first contact than they did at the time of publication.[37] Rousing debate followed, with other scholars showing evidence for areas with even greater population density at the onset of colonialism than the Cook-Simpson estimates.[38] Woodrow Borah joined Cook to revise and extend the Cook-Simpson monograph and in 1960 published new evidence from a newly found tribute register, as well as tribute data from "fiscal materials" in Tlaxcala.[39] These figures revealed the context for "Spanish" colonial society: an indigenous one.[40]

Simultaneously, historians influenced by anthropology began looking at indigenous communities from the inside, using their own records, applying (reluctantly at first) a narrow ethnographic, or microhistorical, focus on settlements.[41] When local altepetl records are analyzed, the data can look different than when the lens is wide and regional. It's not that either is wrong; it's that the scholars are careful and true to their sources, and the situation is complex. So when Osowski's meticulous regional study finds a "sharing of religious culture," this is absolutely true, even as this book shows a geographic diversity of religious practices among neighboring altepetl.[42]

This cross-pollination of anthropology's narrow, physical-local lens with history's long sweep led historians to begin analyzing the native-language historical record abundant in Mexican archives, stirred by the scent of microhistory.[43] This trend developed into a prominent school of ethnohistory, devoted to the contribution of native people in the development of society in the Americas.[44]

Ordinary people left land sales, contract agreements, last testaments, complaints, municipal records, financial vehicles, and more in Nahuatl, the primary indigenous language of trade in central Mexico.[45] The Nahuatl words in these documents were used to identify indigenous practices and concepts underlying what previously were considered simply Spanish introductions. American communities adjusted to Spanish demands, yet in many cases the indigenous structures gave colonial society its patterns, lifeways found today. A limitation in Mexican ethnohistory is that Nahuatl sources become scarcer, with little known from beyond the 1780s. This left ethnohistorians unclear about how local indigenous society was evolving during that time.[46] The Independence archive, described below, fills this gap, providing the first ethnohistorical study of the Nahuas in the early nineteenth century.

I also engage another trend in the literature, the study of women. Like other branches of history, the Latin American field has focused its analysis on men as actors.[47] Meticulous archival studies mentioned the presence of women, for the simple reason that women appeared in local records far back before the medieval period.[48] But to many prominent scholars, women's presence in the historical record is mentioned as an afterthought, finding women's status only in relationship to a male relative.[49] Within the rising of philological ethnohistory, a strong current formed to study women with the Nahua notarial records that documented the lives in this under-researched class.[50] One could say that the two branches, ethnohistory and women's studies, in synchrony with the objectives of new cultural historians, have been among the most progressive, prominent, and fruitful in early Latin American studies since the 1980s.[51] Notarial records, known for being rich sources about women's lives, include wills, also known as testaments. Testaments document a cross-section of society, regardless of economic status. These data specify the participation of women in rites both within their local church and in the household context, for this little-studied time period. Chapters 5 and 6 bring this new data about indigenous women to the fore. The predominance of women is treated in chapter 5, in which I argue that the Independence archive offers a new perspective of differentiation in practices at the altepetl level. Accounting for divergent local traditions, the full participation of indigenous women in the testamentary tradition can now be understood for the colonial period too. While the sheer predominance of women active in owning and bequeathing property at Independence surprises, it also allows us to look back and see these numbers in the context of established precedent.

METHODS

The words of our ancestors as studied here spring from the Independence archive—a collection of testaments that were not supposed to exist. Consisting of more than 150 Nahuatl-language, and some Spanish-language, wills, all the main sources for this study were written by indigenous escribanos, Nahua notaries, from four altepetl in the Metepec region of the Toluca Valley from 1799 to 1832.[52] Until now, it was generally assumed that substantial writings by Nahuas ended before the colonial period, by 1800.[53]

Sometimes, we set out on a journey without a destination. This project, born within a broad search for Nahuatl-language documents in local archives, almost didn't happen. While the cache of Nahuatl-language testaments I tracked down in a provincial parish spoke clearly of the local society in several altepetl (and therefore of great interest as ethnohistory), my first impulse was to devalue their importance based on their lateness. Colonized notions of authenticity colored my understanding of their value; early material, which shows less cultural exchange, is greatly prized. Without the intervention of senior scholars, advisors who confronted me with disbelief about their timing, I would not have understood that these documents fundamentally change the periodization of Nahuatl ethnohistory.

A basic axiom of the New Philology dedicates scholars to an indigenous point of view.[54] Some readers may find this focus narrow; my training expects one to use a culture's own words and compare these to their own writings across time to establish change and continuity within a cohesive conceptual system. Every chapter is based on original research and analysis of the wills from main altepetl represented in the Independence archive, data which is then compared with other sources. The goal is to glimpse an understanding of the world as lived by the people who left us their ideas, instead of comparing them to outside concepts (especially of European hierarchies, so commonly assumed). In each research trip to central Mexico looking for documents written in Nahuatl, I specifically sought sources housed outside the reach of central Spanish administration, documents made by and for indigenous people. In local archives, texts retain their local context and relationship to each other, original demographic percentages not affected in any way by being plucked out and tucked into the countrywide Spanish legal system. The Independence archive retains this local character, maintaining the quantitative trends and proportions presented herein, as well as the data for qualitative analysis of social change and continuity over time.[55]

In my search for Nahuatl documents I met a vibrant network of writers, poets, municipal historians, bookdealers, and archive directors in Toluca; one introduced me to another, and so on, until I met Theresa Jarquín Ortega.[56] On the storied grounds of the Colegio Mexiquense, she confirmed the probability of Nahuatl documents in a box that I found listed in her published index of the parish archive of Metepec.[57] Many people along the way warned me about limited access to the parish archive. With the support of the vicar of the convent in Metepec, I located and identified the uncataloged Nahuatl texts and was given the unprecedented permission to photograph them.[58] Without photographic collection of the dated texts, this project would not have birthed, because no one would have believed me. I was asked to provide the photographs to the father of my field as proof; the more usual handwritten copies would not have provided unequivocal evidence of the existence of this collection of Independence period wills.

With a large corpus of material collected, virtually unintelligible to any but a few experts, and difficult even for them because of its newness, I was faced with the challenge of reducing the material to order before I could make sense of it. Organizing the material from different research trips immediately became my fundamental concern, especially cross-referencing my growing transcriptions against so many original digital photographs. Winnowing out duplicates, I generated lists and charts, compiled large binders of the primary documents, and indexed them, eventually building rosters of the individual testaments by date and place of origin.

San Bartolomé's large collection proved the most complex, yielding the most quantitative evidence. Careful reproduction and indexing were essential, a daunting task that took much more time and effort than working with material from archives with indexed material. Because I found the Independence texts uncataloged, I developed a numbered reference system; appendix 1 contains rosters for the code I use in endnotes. For example, SBT#89 refers to will number 89 from San Bartolomé Tlatelolco, while Oco#11.2 refers to the second bequest in will number 11 from Ocotitlan. This allows quick groupings for analysis unfathomable from long lists of names. I hope these will continue to serve researchers, for those who would use this data.[59] As I copied each letter from every word of all the wills onto my keyboard, I retained the original capitalization and punctuation, but as described in chapter 2, I standardized the spacing.[60] At this stage I blessed the precise, steady hands of Nahua escribanos illustrated in chapter 4. Compared to Spanish escribanos, indigenous writers' manuscripts appear as if printed; clear and legible.

One by one, I began to translate the nearly one hundred Nahuatl wills from San Bartolomé, at first taking rather blind stabs at what can best be described as an art.[61] My first testament took a week of ten-hour days. At the end of each day I would electronically send off my work and start again the next morning, reconciling the corrections given overnight by senior Nahuatl scholars James Lockhart, Kevin Terraciano, and John Sullivan. The formulaic nature of testaments makes them ideal sources for a nonlinguist like myself. I would encourage all researchers to use Nahuatl-language parish records not only for their rich content about ordinary people but also for their formulaic structure, which can be easily learned. And because the parish texts all related to each other in the Independence corpus, forming a geographic pool, I learned the main escribanos' handwriting and quirks; eventually I got to the point where I could translate one testament a day.[62]

This book, focused on presenting the altepetl of the Independence archive as distinct cultural entities, used other sources for comparison and context. I compared Independence data with the previous century by using the Testaments of Toluca, an invaluable regional collection of testaments that emanate from the same geographical region.[63] The Toluca collection offers a wider regional sample: more altepetl are represented, but fewer from each place. Fortunately, the Toluca collection holds testaments from San Bartolomé, the best documented Independence altepetl, allowing for comparison with the immediately preceding time period. Further, I continue the direction of Caterina Pizzigoni's excellent monograph based on Toluca wills, which identified the need for new work about local communities—into the next century.[64] The three-volume Rojas collection of wills offers the broadest geographic and temporal sample.[65] The sixteenth-century testaments from Culhuacan offer the only comparisons from a whole in situ altepetl collection.[66] Unpublished wills from the Puebla area that should prove a fruitful future comparison are being currently translated by Erika Hosselkus. I also used Alanís Boyso's election lists from Toluca to interpret associations of officers in Independence wills.[67] Sources from private collections, Spanish legal code, Metepec's bilingual death records, and various notarial records from the notarial archive of the State of Mexico add dimension.

Native-language ethnohistorians endure the added difficulty of finding, transcribing, and analyzing native-language documents because the voices of indigenous women and men carry a unique historical perspective that otherwise is not heard or included in history.[68] Entire communities left wills ostensibly to confirm the transfer of property, but their words also declare their intergenerational devotions, opening a small window onto the organization of daily life.

ANOMALOUS TEXTS, STRANGE IDEAS, AND TENSILE CULTURES

The Independence archive was not supposed to exist, but other "anomalous" texts from this period can now be understood as part of a larger and varied institutional transition experienced by local associations. The strangeness of a Nahuatl-language testament from Metepec published in 1976, strange because it was dated 1795, can now be seen in a larger cultural context, a continuity instead of inconsistency.[69] Cross-cultural assumptions about indigeneity remain limited by what Kerwin Lee Klein calls idea frontiers, feeding national hungers for a wild and strange uninhabited (un-Indian, un-Mexican) West.[70] When the popular imagination intersects Mexico, it revels in describing Aztec culture singularly in terms of ancient public blood rites, as if capital punishment was an exotic and unfamiliar ritual no longer practiced in the United States. The equally sensational Aztec systems of public education, social codes, astronomical calculations, art, architecture, aquaculture, poetry, botany, and continental trade alliances do not merit mention. The logical conclusions students reach about indigeneity dehumanize the American culture that, like Rome, gave its language to vast regions, facilitating trade—and this culture still lives today. History books don't offer the public spectacles of killing from the Roman era as the sole cultural feature, yet that tends to be the only thing many students know about the Aztecs when they enter my classroom—except that they've also heard of their "disappearance." Sigh.

Devoid of the drama of Inquisition records, lacking the tension of criminal proceedings, the nineteenth-century testaments recount the whispered things that Nahuas expected to last beyond their last breath: rituals, organizations, community. As Eric Van Young puts it, "Crisis might actually be *lived* in a very circumscribed way, without much obvious connection to macropolitical events or formal ideologies."[71] Not that the people of San Bartolomé, Ocotitlan, Yancuictlalpan, and Totocuitlapilco did not engage larger structures—for we know they did for centuries—rather the way they engaged connected them to their own local context. Nothing illustrates this more poignantly than the ability, through centuries of colonialism, to continue to evolve one's traditional systems of writing, ritual, and self-organization: Nahuatl remained normative. Even with this close lens, Van Young's[72] argument holds: Nahuas in this period remained conservative in the sense of retaining local lineages and identities yet tensile-strong rather than static.

In sum, every chapter is based on new research. Chapter 1 presents the fiscalía as an institution that, despite the context of crisis, trains the majority of available men to serve their communities in producing important life events, and making and keeping the records. Chapter 2 demonstrates, with examples from the Independence archive, how to approach and interpret Spanish-language texts written by Nahuas and how escribanos used Nahuatl to shape Mexican Spanish. Chapter 3 documents escribanos writing in Nahuatl, how they continued crafting their manuscripts according to ancient practice, like a father and son whose two generations of work are compared. In closely contrasting their individual styles, lineages and alliances among the escribanos emerge. Chapter 4 describes the paper, ink, adobe walls. A philological analysis of the wills over time identifies local "standards," presenting a view of culture making that operated at the level of the altepetl: neighboring communities developed and recorded distinct testament practices. In Chapter 5, women enter the picture as testament issuers and property owners in surprising proportions; rites on church grounds become a way to see glimpses into a fuller social life, one in which women predominate. Chapter 6's research on how household folk practices intersect with land use shows "how something as ordinary and discrete as land inheritance, in the name of household saints, fostered cultural resilience." A ritual for All Saints' Day is documented and linked in phrasing to the sixteenth century's Día de los Muertos (Day of the Dead), answering contemporary cultural critics' questioning of the folk practice's lineage. People don't tend to share in the sponsorship of saint festivals, at least in the sense that each household produces rites for unique saints that generally do not overlap between neighbors. And interesting phrasing pops up—supporting the king at Independence. Chapter 7 concludes by leaving our heart at the foot of the *chichicaztle* (nettles) at the crossroads of past and future. The epilogue weaves distant strands into a paragraph of unfinished cloth, with the hope that many other hands will find new patterns and pick up the thread.

1

INSIDE THE ALTEPETL OF SAN BARTOLOMÉ

MY FIRST SIGHT OF SAN BARTOLOMÉ'S PARISH came with twilight, the towers surrounded by storm clouds, the bells ringing. I traveled with family on cobblestone streets, slick with mist. We stepped into the sanctuary's light. Every wall sparkled with high domes, white and gold. Our footsteps echoed. The church was empty save for six men in slacks and crisp button-down shirts gathered in front of the altar, dressing a life-sized saint. They were the fiscales, though I didn't know it yet, and they prepared the saint for a celebration at another parish, in another town. When I approached one of the men about local history, he suggested I ask to speak with "el fiscal Eduardo," whom I promised to locate the next day.

Our children ran outside just as it began to sprinkle. Then something exploded, making us jump out of our shoes: the fiscales set off fireworks below the bell towers.

Then they set off more *cohetes*. When we approached, one of the men explained they were engaged in a battle with the clouds, chasing off the approaching storm. He said that it was a very old tradition, that lightning struck the church not too long ago, causing major damage. Humbling to think of a job description that includes negotiating with lightning.

The bells and explosions receded to silence. "Ay, chiquitos, ya se acabaron los cohetes" (My little ones, the fireworks are over), I said to the kids, ushering them along verbally. But something kept us glued to the church. We were quite

FIGURE 4. My first sight of San Bartolomé's parish. Photo by Melton-Villanueva.

entranced with the place, the moment. The fiscales lit off extra fireworks, just to please the kids. I couldn't help myself; the parish of San Bartolomé will forever be etched in my memory as a Harry Potter castle, equal parts European architecture and local magic.

The next day I met the officers at the church. The storm had passed, and the narthex gave a clear view to the snow-capped volcano. This time the officers worked in the courtyard, covered in a thick layer of masonry dust, helping with the construction of future living quarters on church grounds. The whole group of them turned to greet me; each one shook my hand. I recognized the eyes of the man who had told me about their tradition to keep away the lightning. When I asked him if he was the fiscal, he deferentially motioned to himself and his co-workers and said, "We are all fiscales." Last, I was introduced to the *topile*, a literally giant man. The parish of sleepy San Bartolomé still has a topile and fiscales. They still plan, produce, and lead the logistics surrounding major life events in their community. We can see subtleties in how they disburse power. Today the fiscales work together without a visible hierarchy yet with deliberate consciousness about their status. Their organization holds heritage as a way to respond to changing local needs and continues to reflect Nahuatl titles (such as *topile*).

My work in the archives mirrors much of what I still see on the ground. At Independence, the fiscal, *alguacil*, and topile, and each of their assistants, occupy a governing body located in the parish identified in this study as the fiscalía.[1] This cabildo-style administration differs from the official indigenous town council cabildo in many ways, though they share members. The bulk of this chapter describes evidence of a fully functioning parish government (fiscalía) by illustrating its connections to the town council (cabildo) and by presenting the meticulous training, rotation, and succession of fiscalía members.[2] These careers in the fiscalía illustrate why the Independence archive exists: a large community of people participated in the bureaucratic functioning of San Bartolomé's parish administration. The long-standing written traditions described in subsequent chapters did not exist in isolation: in this section I describe specific people and organizations working with great autonomy, supporting the scholarly sector of Nahua society into the Mexican national period.

What brought me to explore the inner workings of San Bartolomé was the question of how they retained impressive escribano lineages beyond the colonial period: 115 testaments survive from San Bartolomé and 95 are in Nahuatl. The Independence archive surprised the field of Latin American ethnohistory because indigenous writing had been shown to have an inverse relationship to the march of the colonial period: the longer the colonial system lasted, the rarer native writing became. This suggested inquiries around one key event: the support and/or destabilization of indigenous escribanos. Though outlawed, people still wrote in Nahuatl; they were supported by social structures that subtly but effectively defied outside attempts to undermine local control. These social structures, housed in the local parish and described in this chapter, illustrate how Nahua communities protected and re-created themselves with representative *buen gobierno* (good leadership). To appreciate these local networks, I begin with a larger context.

HEALTH CRISIS IN THE ALTEPETL

The Independence archive weeps. Indigenous populations, decimated by foreign illnesses in the first century of the colony, continue to suffer epidemics of disease unknown to their communities in the nineteenth century. Person after

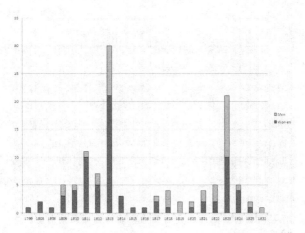

FIGURE 5. Known deaths in San Bartolomé, 1799–1832. The largest epidemic visible in the Independence archive data occurred in 1813. Due to the drop-off in recordkeeping, the 1833 pandemic is not chronicled.

person on their deathbeds asks for an intercessor, witnesses, and an escribano to record their last wishes because they know death approaches.

The graph in figure 5 points to an ongoing health crisis confronting the altepetl of San Bartolomé. The spike in 1813 represents another epidemic, an event difficult to appreciate without its colonial context. Silva Alejandra Gutiérrez Hernández and Pedro Canales Guerrero have identified that the disease that left this mark in the Independence archive correlates with the typhoid scourge that raged through the Mexican countryside, a widespread regional outbreak.[3] Previously, waves of *viruela* (smallpox) mostly killed children (a change from the earliest colonial period), but in 1813, adults succumbed to typhoid in greater numbers.[4] To interpret epidemic figures it helps to understand that diseases target people without antibodies (a state indicating less exposure to illnesses); when plagues strike and people bemoan the death of many children, we can infer that the adults have acquired immunity to the disease. Adults survive because previous exposure created antibodies and thus resistance. But the death rate in 1813 includes a majority of the adult population, so we know that something else was going on.[5] Because adults in San Bartolomé did not hold antibodies, this strain of typhoid was likely new to the area.

Thus, despite the seeming remoteness of Nahua altepetl, evidence shows indigenous communities regularly succumbed to the disease consequences of contact and the movement of people to and from international trade routes.[6] What this tells us is that people are starting to move in overland routes with north-south trajectories in greater numbers. We know this because when the 1833 cholera pandemic hit San Bartolomé, it was the first time European disease arrived into central Mexico from the north. Until 1833, disease spread horizontally, along the usual trade routes from Spain via Cuba and the Gulf Coast, across Mexico to the Philippines and back. But the 1833 cholera pandemic traveled down to San Bartolomé from Louisiana (a U.S. state since 1812) via land. When we think of Mexican Independence, death by violence and revolt may take center stage.[7] But in the Independence archive we are faced with additional challenges, the tragedies of colonial epidemics that never really stopped—regardless of a baseline rise in indigenous population in the previous century.[8] A persistent background of epidemic cycles clarifies a larger context of this chapter: the need of Nahua civil society to constantly reinvent itself, to adapt and change in the face of demographic disaster.

CELLULAR LEADERSHIP STRUCTURES

Given that Nahua officials attended every person on his/her deathbed, the logistics surrounding epidemics stretched the limits of local governing bodies. Their work, documented in the Independence archive, expands what we know about the cellular hierarchies of Nahua civil society. The division of labor between governing bodies, as presented below, depended on local needs.

When people in San Bartolomé described their town at Independence, many still use the word *altepetl*.[9] This Nahuatl word for city-state signals the continuity of a civic structure that allows individual communities to change, literally and figuratively, on their own terms. The word, used before colonization, is well-known for the colonial period, most famously in the early colonial period town council cabildo minutes of the altepetl of Tlaxcala, where men took turns to deliberate contentious issues and lead discussion.[10] The idea of altepetl as a decentralized cellular structure has corollaries throughout Mesoamerica; the word *altepetl* in Nahuatl corresponds to *cah* in Mayan, *ñuu* in Mixtec, and *inpuhetzi* in Matlatzinca.[11] Communities' use of the term at Independence means that despite population loss, destabilization, and simplification of altepetl (tlaxilacalli subunits could achieve altepetl status), the Nahua practice of representative government remains solidly founded within a long tradition of indigenous self-governance.

Self-organizing groups are difficult to describe using familiar linear structures. Whether in biology or politics, complexity feels like chaos. But the strength of cellular decision-making bodies resides not in rigid monarchies of power-over (that when overthrown, their lineage breaks) but in the flexibility of grassroots that share knowledge and power. Pruned or transplanted, they adapt to people's changing needs. When Charles Gibson first described these indigenous political structures, they formed a representative government that stretched across the Nahua social landscape.[12] Its composition included not just the members of the indigenous cabildos but also a diverse and outlying kinship network. Gibson, however, saw the numerical schedules of cabildo-style representation, succession, election, and rotation as adoptions of Spanish tradition. Then James Lockhart identified the representative cellular hierarchies of the altepetl as a preexisting Nahua governmental form.[13] Given a hereditary structure in precolonial leadership, Chimpalpahin Cuauhtlehuanitzin clarifies how Mexicas abandoned the idea of a monarchy even before the founding of Tenochtitlan, saying they adopted participatory governance, "By common consent among themselves they elected and placed [in office] a captain general and chief magistrate to govern."[14] The way San Bartolomé governs itself at Independence furthers our understanding of cellular representative bodies in the altepetl, identifying the fiscalía as an institution, not just a fiscal and his assistant.[15]

The importance of the altepetl as a unifying entity does not negate its component, independent sociopolitical organizations—within or outside—the altepetl center. Rather, altepetl by definition are formed by subgroups of people that build (and dissolve) their particular organizations based on local needs. Together they governed the altepetl; parallel groups entwine in terms of membership with the cabildo of record. Like subgroups that formed self-organizing tlaxilacalli, fully functioning administrative bodies coexisted inside the altepetl. To quote Rebecca Horn, these subunits of the altepetl form the "primary site of identity beyond the level of the household."[16] These complex arrangements mark the Nahua countryside: subgroups found representation in altepetl, which in turn could form confederations. Like a compound flower, where many smaller blossoms combine to give the appearance of a single whole, Nahua society can best be described as cellular as opposed to hierarchical.[17]

LOCAL OFFICEHOLDING: DIFFERENTIATING CABILDO AND FISCALÍA MEMBERS

Intermittently, the Nahua town council (cabildo) of San Bartolomé would send someone out to deliver their election results, carrying them by hand to the Spanish governor for endorsement. Perhaps the election lists got delivered more regularly than known, but lists survive in the Spanish colonial archive for the years from 1775 to 1791, 1802, and from 1807 to 1809.[18] A priest helped submit the results by signing off as a witness to the election report. These election lists, because they name the members of the cabildo alongside each member's title, enabled me to begin to distinguish the public cabildo in San Bartolomé from a parallel administration in the altepetl: the fiscalía.[19] It's well known that indigenous parish officials existed.[20] Their function is less well understood, especially in the context of the whole altepetl. For even though the fiscal is not part of the cabildo or the *oficiales de la república* (officials of the republic), Pizzigoni describes how in sources the fiscal gives the impression of "being as important as an alcalde."[21] Fiscalía ranks look cabildo style, but it is not the legal cabildo; it exists in addition to it.

One reason the difference between officers of the fiscalía and those of the cabildo remained unclear for so long is that nominally, the jurisdictions fall into exclusive spheres: the Church (fiscalía) and the secular municipal town council (cabildo). But in practice, they overlap in terms of membership and jurisdiction. While the fiscalía falls under the jurisdiction of the Church—which might prevent indigenous autonomy—San Bartolomé is a *visita* (visit) of Metepec, which means that there is no full-time priest, only one that would stop in once in a while when you needed him (apparently the priest is booked for celebrations and to sign off on local recordkeeping). Spanish bureaucratic overseers of both political bodies (secular and ecclesiastic) do not live in San Bartolomé. And while the cabildo fell under secular jurisdiction of the distant Spanish governor, a priest witnessed their election reports. Clearly, the two distinct administrations did not operate in mutually exclusive contexts.[22] One difference is visibility: the cabildo operates as the body that interfaces with the colonial administration and enters the records of the colonial bureaucracy. The fiscalía operates under the radar in that sense; their membership does not appear on the lists sent to be approved by the Spanish governor.

Men in the municipal cabildo hold specific positions and may additionally act as administrators of social subunits of their altepetl.[23] Cabildo officers include alcalde (head arbitrator), *juez* (judge), mayordomo (city majordomo), *regidor* (council member), *merino* (ward leader), alguacil (constable), topile (a Nahuatl term translated literally as "holder of a staff"; another officer sometimes called constable), and escribano (notary). The three most basic positions of the cabildo are mirrored in the fiscalía but not in the upper ranks. Sometimes an altepetl would be big enough to have its own *gobernador* (governor) too. In 1801 a Nahua gobernador was finally added to the elected ranks: a move generally associated with population increase. In a significant turn of events, the Nahua topile gets dropped from the list of elected cabildo officers sent to the Spanish governor in 1809, though this uniquely Nahua role does persist in this period within the fiscalía.[24]

The existence of a separate fiscalía, a well-functioning governing body parallel to the cabildo, shows great continuity with the colonial period. To quote Lockhart, it is known that in Nahua colonial municipalities, "a second Spanish-style organization" coexisted with the secular cabildo members and took care of coordinating altepetl religious practices and attendant logistic duties.[25]

But the fiscalía does not exist to this measure in all altepetl. In the neighboring altepetl of Yancuictlalpan, people mainly relied on their cabildo; the fiscal works with cabildo officers.[26] In Ocotitlan, the fiscales do form a fiscalía like San Bartolomé; their titles also designated them as *de la santa iglesia* (of the church). The reason for this variation appears to be the flexibility with which subunits could dissolve or combine into representative confederations. This deserves much study. In these cases it appears that interdependent tlaxilacalli now functioned as autonomous altepetl, and the layers of preexisting governing bodies that represented their distinct tlaxilacalli barrios were incorporated into the altepetl based on representative (and therefore variable) population figures.

In San Bartolomé, men started their careers in the cabildo first and then moved into the fiscalía, overlapping three roles including the escribano.[27] And a significant amount of time separated the two career tracks.[28] It's not a revolving door, where you hop from one administration immediately into the other; the offices in both bodies appear to operate independently of each other. Santos Manuel served first in the secular cabildo, as regidor mayor, in 1802. Eleven years later, in the epidemic year of 1813, he served as fiscal mayor—an officer in the fiscalía.

Despite these independent administrations, with separate tenures, the larger question about the boundaries, or division of labor, between these entwined public cabildo and Church fiscalía sectors remains yet unanswered. The overall impression supports the reality of local differences in structures while at the same time holding similar goals (and therefore maybe doing some of the same things) of representing their districts.[29] I would venture to say that the differences actually supported their shared goals, for in this flexible and ever-responding way, they best served their constituencies. Geographic variation between the representative structures of adjacent altepetl shows that some altepetl had an active fiscalía while others did not.

Every year, like clockwork, the fiscales celebrated the new year by leaving (for outgoing officers) or accepting commitments to serve in the following calendar year. They rarely served in the same post beyond one year, within clear term limits. It's conceivable that recordkeeping was more spotty for the cabildo election lists, but if we take the data at face value, cabildo officials rotated less regularly. Either way, the rapid turnaround of fiscalía officers means a significant percentage of the male population was trained to take part in their altepetl's sociopolitical ritual life. The implications of this aspect are discussed below in terms of the effect of the fiscalía on civil society.

It must be noted that in both the cabildo and fiscalía, Spanish gender expectations played a significant factor in terms of who was allowed to serve. There is a reason women have not yet been mentioned. As described in chapter 5, Nahua women's official political careers begin to disappear from the record very early in the colonial period while Nahua men continued many careers at the local level within the colonial system. It is not until we look at the workings of people in local parishes that women (and the fiscalía) appear in the written record. In the case of the fiscalía, men's roles were sanctioned by the Church, and archives housed in the places of worship they and their ancestors built.[30] In this way, work in church shows how ritual practices remain a central activity for the creation of indigenous status and identity and allows us to see hitherto unseen actors. However, until I describe ritual practices (not just leadership) within the colonial Church, men inhabit these earlier chapters almost exclusively.

FISCALÍA: ROTATION AND SUCCESSION

Officers and escribanos in the fiscalía come to the bedside of the dying, which is how they enter the Independence archive as witnesses. Unlike other altepetl, witnesses for people's last testaments in San Bartolomé are drawn exclusively from the fiscalía. This not only gives the impression of a particularly powerful parish-based fiscalía but also suggests that San Bartolomé was originally an interdependent tlaxilacalli that now functions as an autonomous altepetl.[31] In this case, the secular government for a "full" altepetl was apparently grafted into a community with a preexisting political organization that was based in the Church.[32] The Independence evidence points to fiscalías as the main administrative body for smaller units to the altepetl. As subunits became a formal altepetl, requiring a cabildo, the newly inserted oficiales de república existed independently yet fluidly with the preexisting fiscalía, in cellular fashion, and in some cases drawing from the same community members but at different times.[33]

Ordinary people participated in Nahua leadership. The most striking aspect of the fiscalía is the percentage of the population of San Bartolomé involved in its membership; it was common for men to contribute to their altepetl as members of the fiscalía. Over the Independence archive's three decades, six positions that rotate every year mean that about 180 different positions came available in this period, and that number does not include the 14 escribanos attested from the same period. In 1746, San Bartolomé had 89 families.[34] With an estimated 22 percent population growth of 20 families over 54 years, we could assume 109 families averaged 2 adult males able to serve.[35] We are looking at 218 possible candidates for 194 different administrative terms. That means 89 percent of the adult male population served in the fiscalía. Most of the estimated 218 adult male population would have had to participate to fill 194 available offices, even if some careers took more than 1 position.

These numbers reflect a fiscalía that was not run by a handful of powerful men or hereditary rulers who controlled decision-making. Nahua men who became fiscalía officers rotated yearly through six positions: the fiscal, alguacil, topile, and three *menor* (minor) assistants, one to each office. The institution is not new for the Independence period. The fiscalía in San Bartolomé can be confirmed for at least a century before.[36] Comparing early eighteenth-century testaments, the same fiscalía officials appear: titles and rank remain the same in the nineteenth century, also always listed with the fiscal mayor mentioned first.

Spanish fiscales, in the colonial Spanish context (outside indigenous altepetl), function as city attorneys and prosecutors, but in the indigenous context fiscales were also associated with financial stewardship and described as a church steward, "the highest of all indigenous church-related officials."[37] Lockhart found that the indigenous fiscal would be the person in the altepetl to receive people's payments for Mass.[38] Alguaciles act as municipal constables, yet

Officers unique
to fiscalía

Officers found

in both

Officers unique
to cabildo

fiscales

alguaciles

topiles

escribanos

alcaldes

juezes

mayordomos

regidores

merinos

FIGURE 6. Officials of the cabildo and fiscalía in San Bartolomé.

all three positions appear associated with justice.[39] Note that governors and alcaldes, found in colonial altepetl, commonly populate the secular cabildo, and
this also differentiates the cabildo at Independence. Governors and alcaldes are
entirely missing in this Church-based fiscalía. Let's look at figure 6, which illustrates the differentiation and similarity between cabildo and Church officials.

The Venn diagram in figure 6 illustrates how the post of fiscal is unique
to the fiscalía and cannot be found among the members of the cabildo. Further, the fiscalía functioned as a much smaller governing body than the cabildo,
including only six people plus the escribano—each of the three posts had an
assistant with the same title and "deputy" (menor) attached. For comparison,
the cabildo officers, plus their assistants, numbered about sixteen.[40] Just as the
cabildo does not use the word *cabildo* in the election records—they call themselves *officers of the republic* (de la republica)—the fiscalía officers call themselves
of the church (de la santa iglesia). This is the method to distinguish if an alguacil
belongs to the fiscalía or the cabildo: look at their full titles.

To identify if an altepetl has a functioning fiscalía, and you have enough
documents from one locality, look at the titles of the witnesses in testaments.
If the officer's title is fiscal, alguacil, or topile, and called *de la iglesia*, they belong to the fiscalía. When I first understood this pattern, it became clear that I
needed a new term that would differentiate the "fiscales" referred to in Spanish

documents, one that would encompass all the members of the organization in my descriptions of the administrative body as a whole. Clearly, these men were not simply assistant priests. When I read that Tlaxcala's contemporary municipal historian calls the archive of the fiscales a *fiscalía*, it seemed an appropriate word for the organization that makes and works in the archive: *fiscalía*.

The story behind my adoption of this term begins with the article in which Delia Annunziata Consentino interviewed the community historian of Tlaxcala, Luis Reyes García. She mentions a contemporary usage of the word *fiscalía*.[41] A contemporary Nahuatl speaker, Luis Reyes García identifies the fiscalía as a place, overseen by the fiscal, that continues to house their historical archives. This study uses the term *fiscalía* to indicate all the governing members of the administrative body (not just the fiscal and his assistant) of the parish that generated the documents, not just the archive.

Because the fiscalía works directly in their own barrios at Independence, sometimes those who ask them to witness their last testaments are close family members. The fiscal's assistant, or second-in-command, was called a menor, who would work alongside the first-in-command, the mayor, of that same position.[42] In a literal translation to English, you could say each position in the fiscalía had a "minor" and "major" role. When the lead fiscalía officers couldn't make it, their deputies filled in for them. In 1803, don Luis Isario filled in as fiscal mayor for don Pedro Martín.[43] During the typhoid epidemic of 1813, don Hilario Dionisio filled in for the fiscal mayor five times.[44] In 1819, don Lucas José filled in for don Juan Crisóstomo during the making of Lucas Florentino's will.[45] In this way, deputy officials experienced many possible scenarios for a job description—before they were given the lead charge in the position. This leadership structure values experience and ensures that officers are well trained and can help each other. This predictable sequence of temporary ascension points to a stable political organization.

Unlike fiscal and alguacil, the official called the topile derives its title from the Nahuatl and is commonly found as a loanword into colonial Mexican Spanish. Recognizing *topile* as an indigenous term, we can identify it as a preexisting concept and distinct position of leadership.[46] Topiles are said to have acted as minor officials or constables.[47] But something about this role did not have correspondence in the Spanish hierarchy, or the word itself would not have been adopted into Mexican Spanish. *Topile* literally means one who holds the staff, referring to the staff of office which in precolonial times symbolized leadership and was also associated with music.[48] The IDIEZ dictionary, compiled by native speakers, says the topile is today known in the Huasteca area of Veracruz as a community official who goes from house to house calling people to a community meeting. It is this sense of an "official of the people" that Rémi Siméon attests with *nuestro oficial* for *topilecauh*.[49] Thus, though the topile carries the lowest rank in order of appearance in the sources, this official may have most closely served in the community, and based on the word's persistence, he was certainly considered vital to Nahua society.[50]

In a first impression of the record, it looks like the head topile worked alone without an assistant, but this is not the case. Because mayor topiles in this period, with one exception, never missed work, rarely did the deputy topile get an opportunity to exercise the role as witness and appear in the record as having existed. When Santos Venacio stepped in once as the only attested deputy topile (topile menor), the deputy position was located and confirmed as a formal office.[51]

In terms of career advancement, alguaciles and topiles become fiscales mayores at nearly the same rate. Even though alguaciles are considered higher in the hierarchy, men who enter the fiscalía at this level do not appear to have an advantage over topiles in terms of promotion. As seen in table 1, this pattern appears in contrast to the invariable ranking found in the corpus: first fiscales, second alguaciles, and third topiles. The fiscales are always listed first and the topiles last. On its face, the supposed lowest-ranked topile position operates as the stepping-stone to fiscal mayor, so the ascension patterns of topiles represent an interesting insight into complex cultural meanings associated with horizontal promotion that I am as yet unable to discern.

TABLE 1. Fiscalía Titles in San Bartolomé (ranked in the invariable order given in sources)

1. FISCAL	2. ALGUACIL	3. TOPILE
fiscal mayor (lead)	alguacil mayor (lead)	topile mayor (lead)
fiscal menor (deputy)	alguacil menor (deputy)	topile menor (deputy)
-both fiscales called *don*	-alguaciles not called *don*	-topiles not called *don*

NOTE Executors and notaries also participated as witnesses; executors were not officers but were closely allied with testator and expected to carry out testator's last wishes. Sometimes *teniente* replaced *menor* as deputy rank designation.

CAREER PROGRESSION IN THE FISCALÍA

Looking closely at career progress, it becomes clear that ascending rank is not a haphazard process. Ascension in rank usually takes a significant amount of time, especially considering that the post only lasts one year. Bernabé Antonio served as both topile mayor in 1819 and fiscal mayor in 1832: the intervening years numbered thirteen before he was promoted.[52]

It takes don José Felipe seventeen years to be promoted to head fiscal—certainly not a hurried process. He worked as deputy fiscal in 1806. Seventeen years later, in 1823, he moves into acting as lead fiscal mayor. In the intervening years, between serving in the two fiscal positions, he appears named as executor in 1813 by Victoria María and in 1822 by Gerónima Antonia.[53]

Don Mariano Martín's career similarly represents a significant amount of time and breadth of experience. He worked in 1810 at his earliest position, as topile mayor. He then skipped alguacil and served as lieutenant fiscal before becoming lead fiscal mayor in 1825.[54] A decade and a half capture his movement from lower-ranking officer, a time when he is known as Mariano Martín (without the honorary *don*) to fiscal mayor, when he is known as don Mariano Martín. In fact, he starts to be known by *don* toward the end of his work as topile mayor, as evidenced in his appearance as the executor for Miguel Antonio in 1813.[55] His promotion took a watchful fifteen years.

After the 1813 epidemic, a change in this practice of very slow career ascension appears, though it is unclear if this is primarily due to the decline in available adult men to serve. Specifically, one cohort served twice, though not in succession. Because members of the fiscalía only serve in a position once, when I saw that don Juan Crisóstomo served two nonconsecutive year-long terms as fiscal mayor, it flagged my attention. After two years of being off the job, he came back to work in the same position of fiscal mayor.[56] Significantly, his deputy, don José Lucas, served as *fiscal menor* in those same two years, implying that their whole fiscalía cohort class of 1816 was called upon to serve twice. In an interesting aside, don José Lucas (the deputy fiscal menor) served once as fiscal mayor in 1819—subbing for don Juan Crisóstomo, an eventuality for which his position as menor prepares him.[57] Though not immediate promotions, the fact that only two years intervened appears to testify to unique social demands following the epidemic.[58]

One other exception to the rule that members of the fiscalía have strict term limits and do not serve twice is don Luis Isario, who also served two terms as fiscal mayor.[59] Compared to don Juan Crisóstomo's relatively quick career turnover of two intervening years, don Luis's ascension happened within a more expected timeframe for promotions.[60] Seven years intervened between the time in 1802 when he was elected to fiscal mayor to the point when he served again in 1809.

Don Mariano José's career also stands out for its unique pattern, perhaps suggesting a mistaken identity. First of all, he is the only fiscal mayor to move backward in the typical career sequence.[61] He serves as fiscal mayor before he becomes alguacil, so the career move might be considered a regression not a promotion. Three years in-between the two positions span from 1815 to 1818. Yet notably, he does not carry over the *don* of fiscal mayor as alguacil, when normally he would keep the honorary title for life, after serving once in a position that conferred the *don*; in this case the role of fiscal mayor earns the honorary title. While this decaying of status and retrogression of rank may signal social and political simplification, another scenario is possible. These unlikely events could mean that two different people named Mariano José worked in the fiscalía. If don Mariano the fiscal mayor was a different person than Mariano (without the *don*) the alguacil, then the anomaly of regression and demotion disappears.[62]

Despite working in a cohort, not all officers advanced into top fiscal mayor positions; promotion was not automatic. Twenty-four different alguaciles mayores served from 1799 to 1832. Nineteen of these men who served as lead alguaciles never moved higher up the ranks; one-fifth moved up into the position of fiscal mayor.[63] Topiles, however, are proportionately nearly as likely to progress to the top job of fiscal mayor, which is interesting in that topiles are lower ranked than alguaciles. Of the twelve different topiles mayores attested in this period, one-half of them moved up into alguacil or fiscal positions. Of these six topiles, two reached fiscal mayor, one-sixth of the total of twelve. Officers in the fiscalía still worked within a broad system of rotation and advancement, but since promotion did not happen uniformly, it appears that merit and/or financial capacity factored into men's continued service.

In all, this complex organization, commonly perceived in Spanish ecclesiastical texts as "the fiscales" or assumed to be simply the "priest's assistant," implies that there were just one or two favored men appointed by Spanish priests; in San Bartolomé, this is not the case.[64] Officers of the fiscalía retain self-governance, replicating themselves every year in deliberate patterns of ascension.[65] Loss of religious autonomy could have in many places been accelerated by Bourbon reforms that placed schoolteachers into pueblos to supplement the teaching of Church doctrine, but one schoolteacher lived in San Bartolomé, and the fiscalía at Independence remains strong.[66] Mark Christensen shows, by analysis of ecclesiastical documents once assumed to be written by Spanish priests, that fiscales worked autonomously on many levels in writing and teaching doctrine.[67] He describes fiscales in terms of being "surrogate priests" who negotiated Catholicisms in their local context.[68] This observation appears to closely describe the fiscalía in this place and time.

EXECUTORS: HONORARY TITLES AND STATUS

Serving in the fiscalía or cabildo of San Bartolomé was not the only avenue to serve the altepetl and acquire social prestige; these are just the easiest career trajectories to document. One alternate type of service to the community came in being the personal executor of someone's will. On their deathbeds, people named a family member or close ally to trust with their last wishes; choosing a fiscalía member as the executor made them advantageous allies as executors not only for their extended social ties but also for their civic/ecclesiastic authority and ability to negotiate official channels of power in their name.

Sometimes men earned the honorific *don* outside the cabildo-to-fiscalía track. This timing can be discerned by their appearance as executors at the side of people on their deathbeds. Just as witnesses were expected in the Nahua context to lend integrity to the proceedings (beyond simply attesting to events, as expected in the Spanish context), the fact that others (not officials) could administer wills meant that the role of executor may have had complex social meaning.[69] The language used for executors implies this, giving another angle with which to view internal networks of social status in the altepetl.

One change can be tracked over time by looking back for comparison to the previous century: the number of executors chosen by women and men leaving their last wills. In two of the three known eighteenth-century testaments also from San Bartolomé, testators name two executors, whereas in the Independence period this becomes rare, with naming only one executor becoming the convention.[70] In an exceptional request for the Independence archive, in 1812 Florenciana María named two executors.[71] But given the altepetl's earlier preference for two executors, her "exceptional" request actually represents a carry-over of an older pattern. In this case Florenciana María named both an intercessor and an *albacea* (executor), following the eighteenth-century form. The reason I mention her case is that it points us to language use that could eventually help us understand the complex social meaning of executors.

Significantly, the Nahuatl term for "executor" still exists into this period, despite the widespread and long-standing use of the Spanish loanword albacea in Nahuatl-language texts. While we have no way of yet understanding many aspects of what it was like to serve as an executor in this time and place, a sense of the role comes in the manner that many people, and their escribanos, use two different words to describe the task. Most people at Independence choose one person to be their executor and are expected to do the job of both—*tepantlato* and their albacea.[72] While the latter term is a Spanish loanword that literally translates to *executor*, the term *notepantlato* comes from the Nahuatl and means *intercessor* (the one who speaks for me).

The implication is that *tepantlato* carried a different meaning, beyond executor, or there would be no need to reiterate a word with the same meaning. As just mentioned, Florenciana María went so far as to ask separate people to act for her.[73] She asked don Gregorio Martín to act as intercessor and José Anselmo to act as executor, strongly suggesting that each aspect of what we typically tend to lump into one term, *executor*, carried a distinct and more nuanced meaning. This tactic, unique in the Independence archive, actually represents a continuity of an older tradition; in previous periods people commonly chose two Nahua "executors,"[74] though by the time the nineteenth century arrives, both roles become fused into one "executor" expected to speak for the testator in the execution and protection of the terms of their will.

What caught my eye in Florenciana María's case was that the men she chose for each role carried different social rank. That don Gregorio was asked to act as the intercessor, and José Anselmo (without the honorific title) was asked to be the executor, indicates that the role of tepantlato might be more associated with earned community status than albacea and directed me to inquire further.

After making many charts, I could see that community members always associated head officers (fiscal mayor and alguacil mayor) with the term *intercessor*, but not *albacea*. Using the Nahuatl *–tepantlato* (intercessor), people ask their fiscalía head officers to be their "executor," blending the meanings, perhaps signaling a change in function as both positions became consolidated into one job.[75] As illustrated in table 2, eleven lead (as opposed to deputy) officers served

TABLE 2. *Mayores* as Executors: Terminology for Fiscalía Lead
Officers Named Executors in the Nahuatl Language

DOCUMENT	*MAYOR*	EXECUTOR NAME	TERMS FOR EXECUTOR*
SBT#2	fiscal	don Lucas Florentino	i
SBT#3	fiscal	don Isidro Ignacio	i & e
SBT#8	fiscal	don Pedro Martín	i & e
SBT#12	fiscal	don Martín Pedro	i
SBT#15	fiscal	Bernabé Antonio	e
SBT#29	fiscal	don Martín Pedro	i & e
SBT#33	fiscal	don Andrés Martín	i & e
SBT#35	fiscal	don Mariano Martín	i & e
SBT#37	fiscal	don Martín Pedro	i & e
SBT#47	fiscal	don Martín Pedro	i & e
SBT#54	fiscal	don Martín Guillermo	i & e
SBT#56	fiscal	don José Lucas	i & e
SBT#58	fiscal	don José Felipe	i & e
SBT#74	alguacil	Mariano José	i & e
SBT#88	fiscal	don José Felipe	i & e
SBT#91	alguacil	Mariano José	i & e

NOTE Overall, among the ninety-five Nahuatl wills, fourteen use *albacea* (executor) exclusively, ten use *tepantlato* (intercessor) exclusively, and sixty-seven use both terms for their executor(s).
* abbreviation of terms for executor: i = *tepantlato* (from the Nahuatl, meaning "intercessor"); e = "albacea" (Spanish loanword, meaning "executor"); i & e = both (terms used simultaneously)

as executors on nineteen occasions, each time by a different testator. Twice they were called by the term *tepantlato* exclusively, thirteen times both terms are linked together, and three times they are called *albacea* (executor), but these wills are written in Spanish.[76] Thus, with one exception, in the sixteen Nahuatl-language wills where fiscales mayores are called to be executors, the word *tepantlato* is connected with them.[77] While this distinction makes no sense in the Spanish context, Rebecca Horn found that early Nahua executors were typically municipal officials in Coyoacan, which indicates that at least early on in some places, local meanings associated executors with Nahua social authorities, despite the early adoption of *albacea*.[78]

The one exception to this rule (of asking fiscales mayores to be executors by always calling them *tepantlato* [intercessor] and not *albacea* [executor]) is the career of Bernabé Antonio—but he served as executor long before he became head fiscal. He served as fiscal mayor in 1832, so when he was named executor in 1811 he had not yet acquired the honorific title of *don*.[79] In the year 1811, without yet having acquired the status of don (as head fiscales typically receive the title; see table 1), Bernabé was called executor, using *albacea* not the common *intercessor/-tepantlato* for men with official rank.[80] This usage further supports the idea that the role of *-tepantlato* signified earned community status because before Bernabé Antonio rose in political rank, he was just *albacea*, no *don*. Thus, the only time a fiscalía officer, who in his career had become a fiscal mayor, was called an *albacea* (when named as executor) was twenty-one years before he actually became fiscal mayor. In other words, this exception actually further establishes the link between political status and the role of tepantlato, because in this case the executor had not yet earned the *don*.

If *intercessor* is associated with high status in the Nahua system of fiscalía leadership and ascension, then we can say that even early in his career don Isidro Ignacio acquired or carried prestige in a way that Bernabé Antonio did not, and we are left with another cultural enigma. When don Isidro Ignacio becomes a fiscal mayor in 1814, he is addressed with the honorific *don* due to his position. But eleven years earlier, in 1803, when he was named executor by Marcela Martina, he did not carry the *don*, yet his role is described as both intercessor and executor, even though his formal status as fiscal mayor was a decade away. The dual nature of how Isidro's status was conceived by Marcela Martina (the person who appointed him) points to many other avenues of civic participation available: he in fact later served as deputy governor (a secular official) in 1811.[81] It would be a beneficial line of future inquiry to discover if his earlier status as tepantlato was influenced by family lineage in order to understand the broader influences on the inheritance and/or acquisition of status in this period. If we could determine the social meaning of being called *intercessor* in Nahuatl, it might illumine why people resisted the sole use of the loanword *albacea* for so long.

Despite the noteworthy change in the number of executors that people requested, the fiscalía officers appear as they did—a century before. As noted, the common tradition in San Bartolomé during this previous era was for testators to name two executors (usually called *intercessor* and *albacea*) and three witnesses. These witnesses were members of the fiscalía, de la santa iglesia (as opposed to members of the cabildo, clearly called *de la republica*). And in the fiscalía, two positions acquire the title *don*, precisely the same two fiscales who carry the *don* in the Independence period. The "lower" alguaciles and topiles lack the honorific title, as they do at Independence.

Thus, it can be said that the widely constructed political structure of the fiscalía is not new. The fiscalía continues into Independence in the altepetl of San Bartolomé.[82] María Bernardina's words illustrate the local form as it adapts to the Independence period:[83]

> And I say that the one who is my intercessor and executor is my brother don Florencio Bernardino, if he does it well, our lord God will reward him on my behalf. I have concluded my testament in the presence of my fiscal mayor of the holy church don Isidro Ignacio, and my fiscal menor don Juan Crisóstomo, and my alguacil mayor Martín Tiburcio, and notary of the holy church Cipriano Gordiano. Today Sunday the 25th of September of the year 1814.
> —Testament of María Bernardina, 1814, translated from Nahuatl, SBT#64

However, five men who become fiscal mayor cannot be found within the fiscalía system of advancement, meaning that status could be acquired outside the fiscalía. Don Pedro Nicolás appears as fiscal mayor without a track record in "lower" positions, but his case is just a function of his timing within the sources.[84] He appears in the first record from the Independence archive, thus his previous work would not be recorded. However, don Rafael Angel, don Juan Carmen, don Silverio Basilio, don Santos Manuel, and don Andrés Teodor also worked as fiscal mayor without confirmed work within "lower" fiscalía offices. These fiscales mayores had not previously served as topile or alguacil in the fiscalía.[85] But I can say that they were most likely not outsiders to San Bartolomé's Nahuatl-speaking community who somehow had managed to insert their way into leadership. Given the indigenous naming patterns of these men, and their appearance in Nahuatl-language testaments, even if they were from outside the altepetl, it's conceivable they worked within the same advancement system of neighboring altepetl.

More likely, because these men enter the ranks of officers without previous experience within the ranked cohort of officers, it looks like the avenues of advancement were much broader than the service of the ranked fiscalía and cabildo bureaucrats, especially when a common career path begins in the cabildo.

Though few other alternative opportunities to political participation and development (aside from executor) were actually spelled out in the sources, because of the short terms in office, we know that fiscalía officials did not spend the majority of their life in these formal positions. Thus it's safe to say that in the complex hierarchies of their community and subgroups, men and women gained status and performed authority in other ways not circumscribed by the formal ranks of officers.

In sum, the language people used to describe the people they chose to administer their wills points us to interesting methods of unpacking complex social ranking. Though the fiscalía was shown to have existed over time, it was not the only method of acquiring social capital.

FISCALÍA: OFFICIALS AND HONORARY TITLES

Returning to a close analysis of the fiscalía officials, though they continue with the same rankings found in the previous century, small changes in the way their honorary titles are recorded suggest changes in the way the community is viewing their status. This changing nature of status may eventually be linked to the effects of Independence struggles and potential changes in Church structure; the evidence hints at some change in prestige. The long-standing tradition seen in table 1 shows how the fiscales are the only fiscalía representatives who carry the honorific title of *don*.

In central Mexico, it is widely known that the title *don* becomes an important social marker for the contact period called Stage 3,[86] essentially associated with men who held higher local office, either in the cabildo or fiscalía. However, looking at the descriptive labels written in Spanish by priests as they catalogued the testaments of the Independence archive, one might think that the *don* had faded from use because it is absent. In fact it is only the Spanish colonizer's worldview that no longer recognizes the title when writing about indigenous people. Evidence shows that the *don* retains exactly the same meaning and importance at Independence as it did in the eighteenth century.

A few times, the escribano (notary) deviated from this system of earned honorific titles. Twice fiscales mayores were not conferred an honorary title at the moment the notary recorded the presence of officials of the fiscalía. Once, when Bernabé Antonio acted as the fiscal mayor, the highest position, he was not granted the title *don*, which was highly unusual and may have been a small sign of a larger political upheaval in which he lived.[87] Bernabé Antonio previously performed as topile mayor, which does not confer the *don*; he does not appear in the record as having served as alguacil.[88] Thirteen years after his turn as topile mayor, he worked as fiscal mayor in 1832, which adds to the mystery as to why he was not conferred the *don* because one would assume much more experience and status could have been earned in the intervening years. Because the collection of testaments ends in this last year, I posit that in the next attestations, beyond the limits of this archive, he could have acquired the *don*, but for now, the question remains unanswered.

In the only other example, Hilario Dionisio's formal title also slipped off once. His term as fiscal mayor occurred in the middle of the 1913 epidemic, during which he officiated as witness for eight people during the dictation of their last testaments. In one of these times he was not called *don* by the escribano while in his term as fiscal mayor, though the other seven times the escribano called him by the corresponding honorific. In a parallel occurrence, this happened one other time during Hilario Dionisio's term as deputy (fiscal menor), a rank which also always confers an honorific *don*.[89] Both instances with Bernabé Antonio and Hilario Dionisio being denied the *don* while in their posts as the highest-ranking indigenous officer could represent something as trivial as notarial oversight or imply some measure of degradation of the status of local officials in the national period.

Inspecting the honorary titles of fiscalía officers offers a method to view what may be particular changes in prestige. These changes could be attributed to myriad social-political factors related to epidemics and changing demographics within the crisis of Independence and deserve further research.

IMPACT OF THE FISCALÍA ON CIVIL SOCIETY

While the cabildo was busy representing subgroups and reconciling them with Spanish legal requirements for the altepetl, fiscalía members were charged with running a parish that only periodically was visited by an itinerant Spanish priest. Identifying the work of the fiscalía then begins to answer the question posed by John Chance and William Taylor: is the cabildo the core of the community?[90] It's the fiscalía members who worked mainly for their own local constituents, helping them establish devotional associations, secure financial resources, and networks with neighboring parishes. Their purview appears to transgress exclusive categories of secular and ecclesiastic. It is well known that parish organizations offered local banking services such as business loans and helped Nahua people keep control of estates by avoiding mortgages and debts to outsiders. While concrete evidence for these transactions is sparse in testament sources, Mariano de la Merced, an escribano of the fiscalía, was identified as a member of the *cofradía* (guild) of San José who let a testator borrow ten pesos to support an undescribed business simply called "my work."[91] Overall, the impression is one of a well-organized fiscalía that supported many aspects of their community's self-governance.

Revisiting the idea that fifty-four years earlier the total population in San Bartolomé included only eighty-nine households, we determine that the 194 different fiscalía positions filled in the span of three decades means that most men in San Bartolomé entered the ranks of the fiscalía.[92] In other words, serving one term was nearly universal, and this figure of 194 does not include the cabildo positions. Thus, San Bartolomé was not run by a cluster of powerful men that controlled all decision-making.[93]

This finding imparts a profound vision of the altepetl structure. Sharing the load of leadership does more than delegate tasks, it also corresponds to a Nahua social objective of shared leadership—the whole community benefits when public servants train and acquire new skill sets, and this also serves as a leveling mechanism for horizontal leadership. More than legitimizing itself by fulfilling colonial religious expectations, the fiscalía functioned in support of autonomous social formation.

A group of lead officers, fiscales, alguaciles, and topiles worked together concurrently in the fiscalía in a way that established its group identity.[94] The division of labor allowed don Juan Antonio, as lead officer/fiscal mayor, to work alongside his assistant don Rafael Angel, the fiscal menor. Vicente Ferrer, as alguacil mayor, also worked with his deputy, the alguacil menor. And Ponsiano Perfecto, the topile mayor, collaborated with his deputy, the topile menor. Thus, "division" of labor, implied by rank, belies the fact that officials counted on a cohort during their tenure. In other words, lead officers not only worked with their own deputy assistants but also generally operated alongside each other. Acting together in the same year, sharing many of the same challenges, they also witnessed together the last wishes of their families, friends, neighborhood groups, and altepetl members. They allocated land and resources according to the interests of citizens and groups. Having major and minor ranks, and alternating them all each year, allowed lead officers to exercise their training, through service in a deputy role or another sequence of "lower" positions. This allowed his peers to ascertain his leadership skill, a test of his training, before being elected to and serving in a higher position. Many officers in minor roles served in a way that required specific performances among their cohort. Lead officials and deputies interfaced by serving as witnesses on a variety of transactions, so community members outside their leadership cohort would also experience a given officer's effort, style, and form.

The existence of this type of cohort enabled me to identify officers not clearly identified by the escribano. For instance, situating "Felipe" within his cohort confirmed his identity. A couple of times his name was attested in this truncated form, leaving me wondering who this "Felipe" could be. Cross-referencing the year with the other officers at this time solved the dilemma. "Felipe" turned out to be don Felipe de la Cruz: same cohort + same period = same person. One's political cohort contained a predictable social context of leadership once I recognized this pattern. Public servants with the same career cycle trained and moved up or out of the ranked positions every year.[95]

Vibrant altepetl rituals, an active financial sector, yearly rites of passage: if the goal of a community is to bring everyone into participatory leadership, the fiscalía offered a broad training ground for effective decision makers. If so, this also would not be an innovation but rather recognition of a long-standing cultural expectation documented by archival scholarship across the Americas.[96] Evidence establishes San Bartolomé as an altepetl that trained community members to serve and deliberate on participatory councils, horizontal decision-making that presupposes and fosters an active community.

The colonial objective to homogenize people, specifically aimed to destroy Aztec intellectual culture, appeared with the onset of Iberian rule. Yet three hundred years later, conquest in this sense remained incomplete: parishes—in many places the ground zero of cultural genocide—can now also be understood as ritual spaces transformed by indigenous participants into institutions that protected their community's values and interests. Fiscales, alguaciles, topiles, and escribanos in San Bartolomé were not simply assistants to a priest. And their complex administrative body was comprised of a broad cross-section of ordinary people; calling them "fiscales" obscures the group's structure and local autonomy. Overall, the well-organized succession and rotation of parish fis-calía officials (and others of acquired status) describe a stable political organi-zation in which many men participated in addition to, and distinct from, the cabildo—a multifaceted cultural milieu supportive of their community's cul-ture of writing. Just as San Bartolomé was not governed singularly by one chief, indigenous notarial cultures were not dependent on one singularly literate per-son in town.[97] We meet the escribanos who wrote in Spanish next.

2

SPANISH-LANGUAGE TEXTS
BY NAHUA ESCRIBANOS

A COLLEAGUE FROM UCLA, now a professor in Berlin, stopped into the weekly flea market near the university. While signing a receipt, a German began lecturing him about how he was spelling his name incorrectly, that *Rezakhani* is pronounced *Retzakani* in German. She insisted that he should write it *Resachani*. My friend, Dr. Khodadad Rezakhani, gently said, "I understand, but really, my name is not spelled *Rezakhani* or *Resachani*, rather" and he wrote رضاخانی. Her face twisted in confusion.[1]

It is easiest to dismiss written strategies as nonstandard when you don't know the rules used to create them. After translating the Nahuatl-language wills crafted by San Bartolomé's escribanos, I came to an understanding about what was happening. Instead of dismissing these texts as a degraded Spanish, in this chapter I present their structure and word choice as thought-provoking examples of continuity from each altepetl; their documents make perfect sense to communities of Nahuatl-language speakers, even if they are at first puzzling to the reader.[2] Thus, I argue that the transition to Spanish happened in an intimate way, reflecting the nuances of local traditions hidden from and adding dimension to regional studies.[3] The careful work of the escribanos themselves, the way they apply their centuries-long Nahuatl traditions in each altepetl, allows a window into Nahua society—its unique character founded in indigenous concepts of space, time, and grammar.

With the object that one day it come to pass that the different idioms used in those same dominions may be extinguished and only Castilian be spoken—as has been ordered by repeated laws, Royal decrees, and orders issued in this matter. (Spanish royal edict in 1770, Edicto XV[4])

An irony of Mexican Independence is that despite adopting the Roman alphabet to retain Nahuatl-language writing through three centuries of close contact with colonizers, it is not until the struggle for nationhood, effectively overthrowing Spanish control, that Nahua escribanos finally feel the need to adopt Spanish. This chapter shows how the shift did not come from a whole-sale copying of Spanish writing. Rather, by comparing texts from four altepetl, we find a Spanish that emerged from translating their own long-standing and nearly unchanged Nahuatl-language formulas. Thus, after an entire colonial period of selectively tolerating or ignoring and defying the legal decrees aimed at eradicating indigenous languages, Nahua escribanos begin to adopt Spanish as a means of preserving their communities' interests.

Nahuatl-language texts, the seeds of this "new" way of writing in Spanish, I describe in more detail in chapter 4. Within this chapter I focus on the enigma of the Spanish-language texts as they evolve in this period: how escribanos used Nahuatl to shape Spanish, first in terms of general language use and then how each altepetl's individual escribanos use Spanish in ways that contribute to our understanding of his local society. This compartmentalization of chapters into Spanish- vs. Nahuatl-language texts is artifice; it simply aids the presentation of new texts written in different languages. The Spanish is most striking, awkward, nonstandard. It allows entry into the more standard philological approach to Nahuatl-language texts in chapter 4.

In figure 7 we see that preferences for written language vary from place to place, even among neighboring altepetl. Ocotitlan's escribanos mainly wrote in Spanish. In San Bartolomé Tlatelolco, 18 percent of people left wills in Spanish, mainly in the last decade found in the Independence archive.[5] In Yancuictlal-pan, escribanos wrote mostly in Nahuatl, and the transition to Spanish can be barely detected. Further, the evidence demonstrates clearly that several Nahua escribanos exhibit bilingualism, writing both in Nahuatl and in Spanish. At least one escribano in each of the three well-documented altepetl writes in both languages at Independence; I introduce each of them in this chapter.[6] Con-quest, if defined as language loss, had not reached completion, and escribanos'

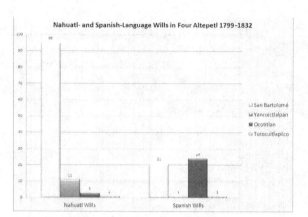

FIGURE 7. Nahuatl- and Spanish-language wills in four altepetl, 1799–1832.

adoption of Spanish shows complex responses based firmly in local Nahua cultural-linguistic knowledge.

THE NATURE OF NAHUA TESTAMENTS IN SPANISH

Figure 8 shows an excerpt of a testament written by Máximo Calistro, Nahua escribano of the parish ficalía (de la santa madre yglesia). Written at the same time that Mexico claims itself a free nation, 1821, the first thing one notices in this (and other Spanish-language testaments from the Independence archive) is that they challenge our expectations of standard Spanish.[7] The way words form in figure 8 gives a feeling of disorientation—words combine to form an aggregate of words: "amidifunta . . . selaboy de Jando . . . serre conpartira e nguales partes Cun plase mipalabra." To give the English reader an approximate sense of what this looks like, imagine a combination of both aggregated and dismembered word-phrases like, "*mydeceased* [aggregation] . . . *iamleav ingher* [the first three words lumped together, with division of leav-ing, the *ing* added to *her*] . . . *willbede vided i nequal* [note the *n* divorced from *in*] *parts Re spectedshallbe myword*."

Conversely, in figure 9, the escribano Juan Máximo Mexía separates almost everything into lonely syllables, essentially over-correcting by applying his

FIGURE 8. Spanish-language testament of Tiburcio Valentín, written in San Bartolomé by Máximo Calistro, December 7, 1821, SBT#82. Archive: Ex-Convento of San Juan Bautista, Metepec. Photo by Melton-Villanueva.

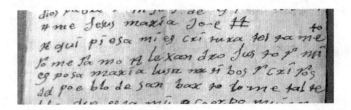

FIGURE 9. Spanish-language testament of Alejandro Justo, written in San Bartolomé by Juan Máximo Mexía, December 24, 1917, SBT#71. Archive: Ex-Convento of San Juan Bautista, Metepec. Photo by Melton-Villanueva.

understanding that Spanish does not aggregate. He separates syllables in a way that tells us how nonsensical dividing up ideas must seem to Nahuas: "A qui pi esa mi es critura" (read as, *Aqui empieza me escritura* or *Here begins my written document* [or more approximately, *H ere be gins my wri ting*]). Nahuatl can hold very large words, more precisely called word-phrases, a grouping of many syllables that together create a composite meaning.[8] Juan Máximo Mexía, understanding Spanish disaggregation, employs a strategy opposed to Nahuatl combinations. In this sense, disassociated syllables mean "Spanish."

I was trained to ignore this nonstandard spacing and reproduce each recognizable word unit, with spaces on each side of Spanish and Nahuatl words.[9] Thus, while the transcriptions I crafted for this study make the words clear for translation, they also obscure some escribanos' basic orthographic strategy: a Nahuatl understanding of word structure.[10] Working with the original manuscripts proves a different experience all together; the aggregate nature of orthographic strings in Nahuatl provides a baseline for understanding the "random" Spanish forming at this time and place.[11]

Samples from the escribano Mariano de la Merced follow, illustrating the way Nahuatl rules are expressed in Spanish:[12]

Huna tierra de a do reales que se nos fue Dexando Mi difunta Madre Se los boy dexando Mijo Juan fransisco.
(As to a piece of land "of two reales" that my deceased mother left us, I am leaving it to my son Juan Francisco.)[13]

Meaning to leave the land to his son, Mariano de la Merced misses an *a* before *mijo* (for *a mi hijo*). This might be summarily dismissed as bad grammar. But on closer inspection something else is going on. Classical Nahuatl lacked prepositions and particularly the *a* (to) used in Spanish to indicate human objects, whether direct or indirect (veo a mi padre [I see my father]; (le) doy la casa a mi hija [I give the house to my daughter]). Thus, it makes sense that in Spanish, Nahuatl speakers omit this *a* in their documents; this construction is understood and makes sense to Mariano and his fellow officers, escribanos, and community.

The reader will notice some more unorthodoxies in this passage, aside from the missing *a*. Prefixes get popped in or dropped off, as if decorative. Here the first *se* is applied (se nos fue Dexando) even though it would have been omitted in standard Spanish. Upon inspection, Spanish object prefixes *se, le, lo, la, los,* and *las* were without close parallels in Nahuatl. Instead of the *los* in "se los voy dexando," we'd expect *a la,* referring to *tierra.*

And what about his curious use of the verb *ir* (to go) in "se nos fue Dexando" and "se los voy dexando"? They are not used like this in customary Spanish to mean "that she left us" and "I am leaving it to," respectively. But the construction might feel recognizable to students of Nahuatl. They represent the auxiliary of going *-tiuh/-to,* so familiar in Nahuatl, in this case meaning to do upon dying.

Another hallmark of Nahuatl language continuity comes in the wide-ranging use of the *n* at the end of a word. Mariano de la Merced's text, like many others in Spanish, continues the tradition of Nahuatl texts by often omitting an expected syllable-final *n,* or putting one where it is not expected. This entire text has *berdaderon* for *verdadero, doblaran* for *doblará, declaron* for *declaro, aplicaran* for *aplicará, pagaran* for *pagará, cuiden* for *cuide, primeron* for *primero, estan* for *está.* The *n* appears unexpectedly only to the non-Nahuatl speaker.

Because of the aggregate structure of Nahuatl "words," they carry enough information to be called a phrase, or sometimes a whole sentence. That is how we can say that the syntax of this passage, preposing the object and not giving the verb that applies to it until much later, is clearly more Nahuatl than Spanish.

Let's look at another excerpt from Mariano de la Merced:

> Si ce acordare de mi A mi Redentor Jesu cristo se lo hencomiendo Mi alma a mi santisima Madre La limpia Concepsion.
>
> (If my redeemer Jesus Christ should remember me [bring about my death], I commend my soul to my most holy mother La Limpia Concepción.)

Since Nahuatl speakers' understanding of how to use the Spanish *a* was associated with persons (not noticing that it was used only with objects), through what some call hypercorrection they sometimes used this *a* for human subjects too. That's how we find *se acordaré de mi, A mi redentor*; we would omit the *a*, because the redeemer is the subject of the verb *to remember*.

Gendered use of *lo* and *de* further illustrates Nahuatl structure in escribano Mariano de la Merced's Spanish-language excerpt. Nahuatl does not mark gender for object prefixes (or for anything else for that matter). As one strategy to avoid the tricky minefield of gender agreement, Nahuatl speakers tend to prefer *lo* for all direct objects and even for indirect objects. The way *lo* is used in the passage it should agree with *alma* and be *la*. Actually, the wording should be "le encomiendo mi alma," not using either *se* or *lo/la*. In the beginning of the same text Mariano writes, "Fui Casada de Juan Anselmo" (I was married to Juan Anselmo), where standard Spanish would use *con* instead of *de*. Nahuatl speakers are often vague in their use of Spanish prepositions. It's not evasiveness or wrongheaded Spanish: gendering in the Spanish way made as little sense as the prepositions; Nahuatl solutions make perfect sense to the writer, the speaker, and the audience.

The question arises as to the timing of these unorthodoxies; they were not limited to just a few stressful years of transition represented by Mariano de la Merced during the epidemic of 1813. Overall, as the years passed, phrasing in San Bartolomé moved in the direction of a more standard Spanish. But this process does not represent a uniform experience. This passage from 1825 was written down by the escribano José María:[14]

od esta sePultado á Mi difuta Madresita

(where my deceased mother is buried)

The hypercorrect *a*, used where it is not needed with a subject (instead of an object), still occurs in 1825. Notably, gender agreement continues to be weak, the masculine *sepultado* referring to the female *Madresita*. This last word uses a Spanish diminutive, but the intention is reverential, and the diminutive is the equivalent of the Nahuatl reverential suffix *-tzin*. "Mi . . . Madresita" is a literal equivalent of the Nahuatl *nonantzin* (my beloved mother). The *-tzin* gives a phrase like "my mother" a formal devotional sense, and it is this operative sense that infuses the diminutive in Mexican Spanish to this day. Similarly, *diosito* as used today, if literally translated as "little god," misses the full sense of the reverential Nahuatl intention.

Broadly, the Nahuatl traits and expressions found in Spanish when written by indigenous escribanos cannot be said to be uncommon but are rather a representation of a particular stage of contact phenomena. The Nahua nature of Mexican Spanish can be seen outside the geographic and temporal limits of this study. "Nahuañol," a blend of Nahuatl and Español, is not unique to the corpus studied here nor to this time period; it was already identified regionally as coexisting with Nahuatl in the second half of the eighteenth century.[15] Further, this phenomenon can still be found in use today.[16] Predicted by Lockhart, this is the moment when escribanos adopted Spanish but still obeyed Nahuatl rules.[17]

In sum, adoption by Nahua escribanos does not equate to erasure of the mother tongue. General patterns of speech and grammar illustrated here testify to a living Nahuatl tongue in dialog with colonial and national pressures to adopt Spanish. That is true across the Independence archive. In the altepetl of San Bartolomé, Yancuictlalpan, Totocuitlapilco, and Ocotitlan, escribanos used a Spanish they adapted to Nahuatl rubrics, a Spanish crafted with Nahua expectations. Some escribanos express themselves with a more fluent and standard Spanish, some less, but Nahuatl foundations are seen in all the texts of all four communities.[18] Mexican Spanish, rich in Nahuatl context, thus represents the evolution of a national treasure: the intellectual patrimony of Nahua custodians.

ESCRIBANOS AND SPANISH-LANGUAGE TEXTS, BY ALTEPETL

Unique to the Independence archive is the quantity and period of Spanish-language texts found in context with their local Nahuatl prototypes. Taken as a whole, I generalized altepetl-level patterns to extrapolate a common notarial model. Thus, this section offers key elements from the Spanish-language texts for each community, which I compare to the Nahuatl. Each community's notarial scheme is considered in turn: San Bartolomé, Yancuictlalpan, Ocotitlan, and Totocuitlapilco. I present these local templates with the general reader in mind, focusing on what they tell us about indigenous society. The Nahuatl precedents then appear in detail in the next chapter, for a more in-depth view into the historical process as traced through word usage. Here, I focus on documenting the extent to which escribanos, when writing in Spanish, reproduce or diverge from their Nahuatl prototypes.

SPANISH PROTOTYPES IN THE ALTEPETL OF SAN BARTOLOMÉ

The small number of Spanish wills confirms the question of timing in terms of language transition in San Bartolomé. The collection contains twenty testaments in Spanish, written by a group of seven known escribanos and an additional one to three people writing anonymously for others.[19] Six of the documents issue from 1813 and 1817. Three more are from 1821 and another three are from 1823, the last year that Cipriano Gordiano worked as an escribano. Five are from 1824, two from 1825, and one from 1832. During Cipriano Gordiano's time, testaments in Spanish represent a small minority, though escribanos continued producing them for over a decade. It appears that after Cipriano, testaments here were written only in Spanish, coinciding with the 1821 ending of Spain's colonial rule and transition to a national government.

Mariano de la Merced left especially invaluable records because he wrote in both Spanish and Nahuatl. His writing serves as the archetype for Mexican Spanish with Nahuatl influence; he produced much of the text used above to illustrate the influence of Nahuatl in the Spanish manuscripts. And Mariano de la Merced also produced Nahuatl-language wills in the same year, a year significant for the 1813 epidemic.[20] Other escribanos worked with Spanish in San

Bartolomé, but in his case, we can compare his Spanish with his Nahuatl and take as a given the close parallel between his Spanish and Nahuatl (the Nahuatl formula detailed in the following chapter). By comparing his Spanish manuscript with the Nahuatl text he wrote under his own name, we will see that Mariano de la Merced did not adopt Spanish formulas of the time. Instead, he carefully reproduces every single item and element from the Nahuatl-language will as literally as possible.[21]

His literal use of Nahuatl concepts in Spanish may catch the reader's eye due to its unorthodoxy. The goal is to gain familiarity with the Spanish patterns in this chapter, as a way to train the eye to interpret the Nahuatl forms of the next chapter. By comparing the Nahuatl in the next chapter, indirectly and through comparison with the Spanish presented here, one recognizes that the information is the same, and it is clear that Mariano's underlying thoughts were the same in both cases.[22]

While the Spanish meanings can be more fully understood by the Nahuatl texts, the Spanish-language texts also clarify heretofore unexplained puzzles in the Nahuatl. Because Mariano de la Merced's Spanish and Nahuatl are so close, particularly interesting phrasings emerge that promote a fuller understanding of the Nahuatl meaning. For instance, people call themselves *criollos* in the Spanish, which goes against the way the word is used by Mexican historians. Mariano de la Merced says, "Somos crioyos y nasidos deste pueblo de San Bartolome Tlatelulco" (read as "criollos y nacidos"; we are native and born in this pueblo San Bartolomé Tlatelolco). For comparison, people in their Nahuatl-language wills refer to themselves by saying *nican tichaneque*, which I translated as "we are citizens here." But that translation obscures the fact that *chaneque* can also mean "residents," "householders," or "natives." The extent to which the Nahuatl carries the sense of "native" is of special interest because such formulations support the phrasing people used throughout the Independence archive in Spanish, not only in San Bartolomé. Often the word *criollos* is found paired with the word *nativos*. *Criollo* in this time and place did not mean a person claiming Spanish descent, but rather a person claiming to be native to a place.[23]

A tangential benefit of this comparison is having reinforced that *criollo* did not mean someone of Spanish descent, the ubiquitous meaning in Mexico for the Independence period. Nor was it used as an independent noun but rather in connection with a place, here *criollos de este pueblo de San Bartolomé*. It is possible that as in some other times and places it did not necessarily mean born in a place but growing up there, which would explain why a word meaning "native" so often accompanies it. *Chaneque* and *criollos* signify a local indigenous identity.[24]

Mariano de la Merced also solves a small question that arose while I was translating the number of bells used in death rites in San Bartolomé. People on their deathbed usually request for the bells to ring upon dying; it can be said to be a standard escribano pattern in this altepetl. But in the Spanish we learn something never made explicit in the Nahuatl-language manuscripts. In Nahuatl phrasing, the loanword *campana* always appears in the singular, which would be expected as inanimate nouns in Nahuatl do not pluralize. So I was persuaded by my inclination to translate *bell* using the English plural, but I could not be absolutely sure without evidence. Here in the Spanish we see the plural *campanas*, and the question is settled. The presence of more than one bell in the original tower is now established.[25]

A rhythmic orality visible in people's will-making is the repetition of Nahuatl catchphrases, oral formulas urging the listener/reader to take their appeals seriously. After each testator's command, Mariano de la Merced continues to insert exhortations in Spanish, just as in Nahuatl-language wills. This is a feature of Nahuatl orality ordinary Spanish-language wills would not include and thus acts as a marker of Nahuatl derivation. The formula, "cumplace mi palabra" (standard spelling, cúmplase mi palabra; let my word be fulfilled) sounds unfamiliar in Spanish, not a very idiomatic expression. In studying Nahuatl models, however, we soon realize that it is a literal translation of the ubiquitous *neltiz notlatol* (my statement is to be realized), an often-repeated appeal familiar to students of Nahuatl testaments.

Sometimes, the name of the Virgin we invoke may have greater meaning. Mariano de la Merced is one of the few escribanos in San Bartolomé who when mentioning the Virgin in the preamble always names Concepción instead of the more usual Asunción. It is the same in his Spanish wills: always Concepción.[26] This fact may hint at another possible trait among the different notarial schools detailed in the next chapter: alliance with a particular *cofradía*. As posited below, the pattern of naming Mary in the opening section of the notarial formula points to two different cofradías. If this holds true, because de la Merced always named Mary in her avocation as Concepción, his personal or notarial lineage may have been a significant factor in his choice of names. Another factor could be that his clients had barrio/cofradía alliances to Concepción, and both these factors could overlap. Whether he was a member or not, social and geographic alliance to a cofradía could have meant that he was called upon by members of the cofradía dedicated to Concepción, which is why he never mentions the more prevalent Virgin of Asunción.

Some other notarial unorthodoxies remain enigmatic. In both his Nahuatl and his Spanish wills, Mariano de la Merced situates a common declaration about the testator's soul. But the Spanish wording, "mi alma estan en buena y sana" (my soul are in good and healthy), is structured as if *soul* were plural, the meaning perhaps including the physical body. As written, the phrase needs some word like *state* or *condition* to be complete and make sense, perhaps reflecting the ubiquitous use of the *n* at the end of a word. Nevertheless, this is not just a slip, for it is repeated the same way in Mariano's other Spanish wills. This rendering foreshadows a point of confusion seen in the Cipriano school in the subsequent Nahuatl formulas.

Overall the Spanish-language texts, including the later ones, continue to follow the traits delineated above. This general model was followed by escribanos in San Bartolomé, sometimes more strictly and sometimes more freely. While escribanos did not adopt embellished formulas common in Spanish-language testaments, there are exceptions. This excerpt from a will written in 1823 gives much more in the way of a religious credo than is traditional in San Bartolomé:[27]

> Creo fiel y verdaderamente En el misterio de la Ŝ.ticima trinida y Creo En el misterio de la EnCarnacion del divino vervo y espero que E de yr a su Gloria.
> (I faithfully and truly believe in the mystery of the most holy Trinity, and I believe in the mystery of the incarnation of the divine word, and I expect that I am to go to his paradise.)

While eye-catching for the pronouncement of mystery, incarnation, and paradise, such a wholesale introduction into the San Bartolomé Spanish model is rarely found in the Independence archive, even in any other section of the formula. Thus, evidence suggests that the escribanos were still mainly consulting each other, instead of seeking inspiration from this kind of fashionable Spanish model. The traditional San Bartolomé model still figures at the root of the wills produced.

Another phrasing springs from an old Nahuatl concept. It can only be considered an undercurrent to the predominant local model but of special interest to those familiar with older phrasings for one's physical body. In 1824, Dominga

Bonifacia uses the phrase "mi cuerpo y lodo" (my body and mud), which reveals traces of the old phrase *notlallo noçoquiyo* (my earth and clay or mud) to designate the body.[28] The Nahuatl concept of one's body as earth and mud persisted in meaning with the transition to Spanish; it made sense to the speaker to say "body and mud" instead of just *cuerpo*.

What is clear in the testaments is that people describe their place of burial differently in the Spanish model and give less detail about the location. Whether this is a new tradition associated with the change in notarial languages or a general trend developing, what one notices is that escribanos in the Spanish wills begin to use the word *cemetery*, not seen in the Nahuatl texts. And the way people imagined their burials changed too. The Spanish wills describe fewer features about burial rites and gravesites than when the escribanos write in Nahuatl.

Statements of faith on the main look ordinary when compared to the Nahuatl. In matters of Christian doctrine, San Bartolomé's escribanos writing in Spanish also follow local Nahuatl forms, to the point that Spanish-language texts also contain occasional hints of the same unorthodoxies seen in the Nahuatl. Wrinkles in standard mysteries of the faith and the health of the soul will be traced next in the Nahuatl; here a Spanish will of 1825 by José María follows in exactly the same vein:[29]

> Mi curpo y Mi alma Se alla mui enfermo.
> (My body and my soul are very sick.)

Legal expectations require the person to assert their ability to give a last will, despite being sick. In this case, the soul is also called unfit, not just the body.

Another unorthodoxy is the predominance of the Virgin in San Bartolomé's local tradition, and this focus also transfers into the Spanish. San Bartolomé's notarial model says the soul is to belong to the Virgin; in most other Nahuatl testaments of all times and places, the statement is to give it to God.[30] It arouses the suspicion that Mary is seen as more than an intermediary, but nothing more definite on this point is ever said in the Nahuatl texts. One of the Spanish wills written in 1817 by Juan Máximo Mejía, however, goes a step further:[31]

> En el poder de mi madre SSma mi señora de Assup..no pogo mi alma que es su eChura.

(I place my soul in the custody of my most holy mother my lady of Asunción, for it is her creature.)

This is a version of the traditional phrase saying that the soul is to be returned to God because it was made by him. Here the soul's return, found applied to the Virgin as creator, has significant theological implications for this time and place—if taken at face value. Despite local religious understandings, it probably in fact cannot be taken quite straight in terms of escribano doctrine. This avocation of the Virgin may have a meaning connected to the activities of one of the two cofradías named after the Virgin. Further, it contains a strong element of the carelessness with formula seen in the Spanish; possibly there is some confusion too. By all evidence the Virgin takes universal precedence at this point in the notarial formula that usually is ascribed to God; arguably it carries intriguing implications for identifying emergent Mexican Catholicisms.[32]

SPANISH PROTOTYPES IN THE ALTEPETL OF YANCUICTLALPAN

Isidro de la Trinidad, the bilingual escribano who wrote the only Spanish will known for Yancuictlalpan, also wrote the largest number of the Nahuatl-language wills for his altepetl.[33] He and his notarial community still preferred Nahuatl as the primary language of record. Though Nahuatl was clearly preferred, he considered Spanish critical enough at this moment to feel the need to learn to write in Spanish as well. The pressure to include Spanish in daily records finally, after centuries, leaves an impression.

Because he did not commonly write in Spanish, when he wrote the one Spanish-language testament for his wife, Juliana Viviana, we may assume that writing in Spanish carried a special status for Isidrio de la Trinidad and his family. Dated 1823, he wrote his wife's will eleven years after he began making Nahuatl testaments for his community (the first text in the corpus attributed to him is dated 1812). Bilingualism, in Nahuatl and Spanish, was occurring at different moments in different places, but Yancuictlalpan does not even begin to use Spanish until 1823. All evidence shows that Yancuictlalpan did not shift to bilingualism quite as expected, much less to monolingual Spanish. Thus, unlike the other two major settlements represented in the Independence archive, the altepetl of Yancuictlalpan remains unique in that the trend toward writing in Spanish remains indistinct. After the one will he penned in Spanish, Isidro did not stop writing in Nahuatl. He continued to produce Nahuatl testaments in 1824 and 1825. It is clear that this reluctance does not spring from an inability to write in Spanish; retaining long-standing escribano traditions in Nahuatl was his conscious choice.

In fact, Isidro de la Trinidad uses a Spanish that is a bit more standard than that of Mariano de la Merced in San Bartolomé from a decade earlier. He uses prepositions correctly and makes no mistakes with the object prefixes, and indeed his Spanish could be taken simply for ordinary Mexican Spanish of the time. He writes *y* for *ll*, as in *yamados* for *llamados*, but he was not alone in that; some texts written by Spaniards did not yet standardize the *ll* in this period.[34] If we look closely, noticing his syntax, we also see Nahuatl influence, as in the following passage:

> Mi Cuerpo en donde Se a de sepultar dentro del seminterio.
> (My body is to be buried inside the cemetery.)

Literally this says, "My body, where it is to be buried, inside the cemetery," with an order and structure much more Nahuatl than Spanish. Or consider:

> Nos mas dejo apuntado.
> (That is all that I leave recorded.)

The *nos mas* appears in place for a more standard *no es más* (it is no more). In Nahuatl-speaker Spanish this phrase becomes contracted and fused into almost a single phrase *nosmas* (no more). In standard Spanish one might have said "no dejo más apuntado." And though this phrase is literally Spanish, it also falls into the general category of rhythmic, emotional Nahuatl exhortations.

As to the general structure and order of the will and the wording of the succeeding items in his formula, escribano Isidro de la Trinidad's Spanish does follow the Yancuictlalpan Nahuatl model in a general way, but with quite a bit of deviation. He too, like the San Bartolomé escribano quoted above, adopted a flowery Spanish-style doctrinal statement toward the beginning of his formula:[35]

> En presencia de la SSS.ma trenidad. angeles y santos de la corte selestial protesto y digo. que quiero vivir. y morir Cofesando todos mis pecados y Confio en

Vuestra bondad. y misericordia me as de perdonar. todo lo que yo me faltare en mis culpas.

(In the presence of the most holy Trinity and the angels and saints of the celestial court I say and protest that I want to live and die confessing all my sins, and I trust in your goodness and mercy; you will pardon me all that I should be lacking in my faults.)

This statement of faith, as we shall see in the next chapter, does not come from the local Nahuatl model. The phrasing also shows that Isidro de la Trinidad does not copy the statement; rather, he recounts language he previously read or heard in Spanish. After a very good start, in the second half of this passage he veers somewhat away from standard Spanish grammar and idiom; this is not a copy of the Spanish. Isidro de la Trinidad, even in this most non-Nahuatl section, adds his own local relish, giving the effect of improvising from memory.

SPANISH PROTOTYPES IN THE ALTEPETL OF OCOTITLAN

The epidemic year of 1813 marks a deep change in the notarial community of Ocotitlan, when only one escribano writes in Nahuatl. By the next year, all the escribanos shift to writing in Spanish. Of the three altepetl studied in depth here, the escribanos convert to Spanish first in Ocotitlan. For comparison, in the post-1800 corpus of Ocotitlan testaments, twenty-four are in Spanish and three in Nahuatl. As seen in the next chapter, those in Nahuatl are dated 1801, 1810, and 1813, while those in Spanish date from 1805 to 1820. In other words, escribanos in Ocotitlan moved to Spanish definitively by 1814. Nahuatl continued to be written until 1813, but even at this time escribanos writing in Nahuatl comprised a small minority in this altepetl.

Escribano Pablo Leonardo serves here as the outstanding example from the local notarial corps. Again we see the skill of bilingualism surfacing as a feature of a notarial career, this time in Ocotitlan. He not only wrote the largest number of Spanish wills, half of the sample, but also wrote one of the Nahuatl-language wills. Pablo Leonardo writes with the Nahuatl as a model, much like escribanos in the other communities studied. The following evidence concentrates on a Spanish-language testament he wrote in 1813.[36] Consider the following phrase:

mi esposa yamadose soverana Maria

(my wife named Soberana María)

Note the form *yamadose*. This structure can be said to be highly characteristic of the Nahuatl-influenced Spanish of the time. From *se llama* (he or she is named), Nahuatl speakers derived the past participle *llamádose*, the equivalent of standard Spanish *llamado*.[37] Notice also how the participle is masculine, even though it would in a standard Spanish agree with the feminine noun—another small example of Nahuatl-speaker gender ambiguity.

He used the following phrase as part of the exhortation placed after bequests:

noy quien diga mañana u otro dia

(there is not anyone who should say tomorrow or the next day)

[This literal translation loses its meaning without understanding the Nahuatl intention of "in the future," illustrated below.]

Just like Mariano de la Merced (San Bartolomé) and Isidro de la Trinidad (Yancuictlalpan), here Pablo Leonardo translates a common Nahuatl oral exhortation into Spanish. These common idea-phrases usually come attached to the end of a specific bequest and are frequently repeated, a rhetorical strategy used to great effect. As Nahuatl perorations (here phrases at end of a specific inheritance described by person leaving the will), they carry emotion and rhythmic emphasis. The testator (person leaving a will) might say, "I give this land to my son" and add "ayac tle quitoz moztla huiptla," straightforwardly meaning no one is to say anything in the future, ensuring that the bequest is not contradicted. Literally translated, it says, "There is not anyone who should say tomorrow or the next day." In these types of phrases, typically repeated after every bequest, repetition itself adds emotional weight and emphasis. A Nahuatl oral strategy that becomes written testimony, it stresses the speaker's precision. Such emphatic declarations, repeated, effectively anticipate criticisms or objections by dispelling any potential uncertainty about whom inherits what and about the accuracy of the speaker's intent.

Thus, the baffling "mañana u otro dia" only sounds awkward until one realizes that this Spanish phrasing is a translation of the Nahuatl *moztla huiptla*. Literally it means "tomorrow, the day after tomorrow," hence the puzzle. It's actually the most frequent Nahuatl expression for "in the future." The Spanish version used here stops sounding bizarre when understood to carry this very ordinary Nahuatl meaning in the giving of wills: "don't in the future contradict this legacy!" Thus, "unorthodoxies" in Spanish express what for the speaker and writer are equivalents of uniquely Nahuatl phrasing.

To reinforce how this process works, let's look at how the small contraction *noy* is sometimes seen among Nahuatl speakers for *no hay* (there is not). "There is no one to object [as in, speak against this] in the future," and a word for *something* or *nothing* is simply missing. To correctly translate the Nahuatl meaning, it must be understood that people are giving an oral warning, "do not contradict my will," by saying that no one should say anything (about their gift to inheritors) in the future.

Lest I give the impression that escribanos simply sit down with a copy of a previous text and "fill in the blanks," it must be emphasized that it's not a meticulous copy. As they write down people's last wishes, each escribano adds his preferences, while at the same time applying the method of adhering to tradition. They work from memory. Thus, the conservative Nahuatl training is evident as a foundation for the Spanish, but it is not absolute and does not negate an individual escribano frame of mind. The following passage might not be considered standard for Ocotitlan but gives an example of an escribano's restrained embellishment. The following testament from 1805 shows a modest attempt at an embellished statement of faith in the Spanish style.[38] This phrasing surrounds the usual dedication to the Trinity as Father, Son, and Holy Spirit:

> Creyndo el ynefable Misterio de la santicima, Trinidad . . . y creo la encarnacion del Berbo divino y creo haquello que Cré Nuestra Madre La Santa yglecia Catolica Apostolica.
>
> (Believing in the ineffable mystery of the most holy Trinity . . . and I believe in the incarnation of the divine word, and I believe that which our mother the holy apostolic Catholic Church believes.)

The quote looks a great deal like the phrase quoted above from the 1823 Spanish-language testament made in San Bartolomé, where the escribano adds more of a credo. As such, this evidence suggests that 1805 in Ocotitlan and 1823 in San Bartolomé may have been at similar points of language transition.[39]

In generalizing a basic Spanish model testament for Ocotitlan, comparison shows its structure and content follow the local Nahuatl model. The Spanish version created by Pablo Leonardo quite closely fits their Nahuatl model. All the key elements, such as the offering for Jerusalem, are present.[40] No showy Spanish-style religious credo is adopted directly from the outside, such as we have seen in the records from the other communities. Based on this more conservative form, plain like the Nahuatl scheme, Ocotitlan's Spanish corpus reflects a basic irony: the altepetl with the earliest and most complete adoption of Spanish also reflects the most conservative Nahuatl influence.

ALTEPETL OF TOTOCUITLAPILCO

Only two wills from Totocuitlapilco have yet been found for this period, one written in Spanish and one in Nahuatl. While details are useful for comparison, due to the scarcity of sources, data from this altepetl I generally omit from the overall statistics and avoid making generalizations about because of the relatively scanty data. In the absence of more examples, it is not possible yet to extrapolate a model reliably, but the evidence does allow me to offer provocative glimpses of the endurance of Nahuatl meanings. Two escribanos wrote down two citizens' last testaments, manuscripts that carry intrinsic value for what they say about who wrote them and their social networks. Here I treat the one will written in Spanish and describe how it corroborates the pattern in his own community from an earlier period as well as substantiates the patterns found in his contemporary neighboring communities.

Escribano Antonio Ambrosio in 1826 wrote the one available Spanish will made in Totocuitlapilco.[41] His Spanish writing confirms the now familiar Nahuatl-influenced style. His notarial structure and conventions fall in the same general range as the testaments of the other communities represented in the Independence archive. Here I compare Antonio Ambrosio's example with the much-earlier Nahuatl testaments that exist from his own community, especially the two issued in the eighteenth century.[42] Comparing his texts with wills from the previous century shows dissimilarity, though formulaic similarities do appear. The date is given in the same location in the local notarial blueprint, as are the names of the witnesses, also found in the same spot in the text. And bell ringing is specified in both time periods. Specific changes over time also surface. Antonio Ambrosio reverses the order of the testator's name with mention of the Trinity in the 1826 text. Although his 1826 testament gives the testator's name and affiliation in the expected place in the text, the earlier testaments only name the testator, taking the community for granted. Because they don't identify the altepetl name within the main text, this may imply that their escribanos were not based in their community.[43] In another change, the earlier Toluca testaments describe the Jerusalem offering (used to raise regional Spanish assets) as regionally common, but in the 1826 text the offering to Jerusalem disappears, which would be expected at Independence, with the destabilization of parish offices.

A particular way that Antonio Ambrosio's Spanish version reflects local meanings comes in the translation of Nahuatl concepts of land measure. Yancuictlalpan measured land in the early period in *quahuitl*, using the precolonial vigesimal, base-twenty number system. But in this 1826 Totocuitlapilco text, Antonio Ambrosio uses *palos* in the same way. On its face, it is a Spanish word and might not attract much attention. But the way he uses the word *palos* in this text represents a translation of the Nahuatl term. Evidence of its Nahuatl sense comes from how Antonio Ambrosio associates *palos* with vigesimal numbers, despite the fact that the vigesimal system appears supplanted in many other places. Antonio Ambrosio, however, is not alone in the continued use of a vigesimal system; in the next chapter Ocotitlan's escribanos in their native tongue also apply their ancient way of using base-twenty counts for marking time.

━━━━━━

These texts, unique to the way Spanish developed in Mexico, written by Nahua escribanos of the Independence archive, offer a way to think about the timing and transition to the colonial tongue that does not categorize their work as substandard. It sounds like a contradiction, but simply put, their Spanish manuscripts preserved Nahuatl. Their phrasing, which we decoded by tracing the Nahuatl rules they followed, shows how Nahua escribanos used their longstanding traditions as the framework for their "new" written language; the first few decades of Spanish-language texts remained nearly as indigenous as their Nahuatl predecessors. The resulting Spanish only looks awkward until understood as strict adherence to a different set of rules. Just like the mainly Nahuatl testaments that make up the Independence archive were not supposed to exist at this time, Nahua Spanish-language texts also reveal great cultural continuity. Nahuatl impelled the development of indigenous documents at Independence by aiding in the construction of Spanish-language texts, and local escribanos made them relevant to Nahua ideas, needs, and cultural expectations.

3

THE ESCRIBANOS WHO STILL
WROTE IN NAHUATL

B EFORE MARÍA FRANCISCA took her last breath in 1811, her son came to her bedside. This was not unusual, except that he, the escribano who sat down to write her last will, was her son. He worked as an official escribano in the fiscalía of San Bartolomé Tlatelolco and had once worked for the cabildo. She spoke not only of her illness but also of her membership in her cofradía, saying she belongs to her "precious mother Santa María Asunción, and bells are to ring for me." Witnesses to her final words included other fiscalía officers who worked alongside her son, the parish fiscales (mayor and menor) and alguacil.

In her only deathbed instructions about three different saints, she leaves them to her son Cipriano Gordiano, the very escribano writing down her will. In her bequest, we glimpse the unstated religious apprenticeship duties he inherits from his mother, detailed in chapter 6, "Household Ritual." In this chapter we trace a different lineage, the apprenticeship with his father—also an escribano—within a broad culture of writing. This part of the story begins with the hands who wrote for their altepetl, the escribanos who left us the Nahuatl portion of the Independence archive.

In contradiction to the near-invisibility of indigenous communities in Spaniards' records, a notarial culture of writing continued in force beyond the colonial period—in Nahuatl. Strictly adhered-to norms continued to be passed on not just within one family or lineage (in itself startling for its continuity with ancient practice) but also among a corps of Nahua men who collaborated with each other and had wider knowledge of practices not contained in their local standards.

This tradition of writing in Nahuatl using Roman script, so important to the American colonial experience, survived within the bureaucratic workings of the various Latin language crowns: a highly trained class of people called *escribanos* wrote down people's agreements with each other. Languages used to create these notarial archives included Spanish, French, Portuguese, and many indigenous tongues. These written contracts could prove that someone owed you money for a specific piece of land or that your child was to return from training as an apprentice within a certain amount of years . . . everything from rents to dowries, loans to wills were set upon paper for a fee and kept by the notary, who was obliged to keep every record.[1]

Nahua escribanos worked in that interstitial space between distinct cultures and languages, laws, and devotions. They wrote down phrases that communicated evolving ideas, and when compared, their words reflect local alliances and ways of life. These men's stories intertwine with the story of their literacy—Nahuatl precedents that reflect their training and skill in support of a complex social environment. Chapter 1 identified the fiscalía, examining internal Nahua structures, as well as the career patterns of these officials that helped shape the altepetl. Chapter 2 described how the Spanish-language escribanos developed their practice based on Nahuatl precedents. We now turn to the escribanos who wrote the Nahuatl corpus: their names, their stories, their alliances. Just as striking as Nahuas' Spanish writings in this period is that significant numbers of manuscripts continue to be written in Nahuatl.[2]

NAHUA APPRENTICESHIP: FATHER TO SON IN SAN BARTOLOMÉ

Cipriano Gordiano wrote most of the known testaments for San Bartolomé, but he learned his trade from neither a Spaniard nor an outsider. His notarial tradition does not closely reflect the conventions of Spanish notaries at this time or their cursive script. He wrote in Nahuatl, using script that evokes the block-straight Gothic strokes of medieval print—not the cursive handwriting current in the Spanish-language circles of his era. How did he learn to write in this older, conservative way? Cipriano's conventions do not reflect contemporary trends in his external world. Cipriano's training reflects an inside job and expresses an intact tradition, internal to his community.

He studied the craft of escribano at his father's knee. It takes the closest examination to detect slight differences between father and son. From the number and timing of wills, it becomes clear that his father, active as a notary in the same community, stopped practicing his profession in 1809, around the time Cipriano began. Cipriano took over the mantle of his father's work, a legacy that infers apprenticeship to his own father. This interpretation of apprenticeship finds substantiation in Cipriano's own hand, a near mirror image of his father's. At a glance, their handwriting looks identical and the styles of writing almost equally so.

This family connection did not readily appear to me, despite the stacks of wills he wrote. The lists of names I generated did not reveal any clues; indigenous naming patterns can obscure kinship grouping. The pairing of two religious-themed "first" names, a naming style common in the early colonial period, continued nearly universally in the Independence archive.[3] The link emerged from a key bit of evidence. In a steady, precisely legible hand, Cipriano wrote 82 of the 115 wills in his community, including the one for his own mother, quoted above. When Francisca María referred directly to Cipriano Gordiano as her son, as well as to Francisco Nicolás as her husband, the connection materialized.[4] Because she named both of them in her will, I grasped that Francisco was Cipriano's father.

Comparing the work of father and son, we glimpse the family's long learning arc. I cannot say how many hours Cipriano spent every day copying his father's writing, but I can describe a carefully duplicated and nearly identical script, evoking a writing culture that venerated conservative tradition over innovation. At the beginning of his career, Cipriano Gordiano followed his father in serving as escribano in the secular government (San Bartolomé's indigenous cabildo) for two years, in 1803 and 1808, before becoming the notary of the fiscalía in 1810.[5] Similarly, his father Francisco Nicolás served twice as the elected notary of their secular government, decades earlier, in 1776 and 1791.[6] The wills Cipriano wrote down for his community members as escribano appear almost indistinguishable from those written by his father. The shared conventions include the structure of the preamble and even the near-identical phrasing within his general formula. We can observe the transmission of knowledge from one generation to the next by analyzing the timing and their particular handing of techniques, from calligraphy to vocabulary and conventions.[7]

Given all the similarities with his father, Cipriano's little idiosyncrasies stand out, delineating the limits of apprenticeship. Cipriano stopped using the line over *q* to mean *qui*, which his father used, an antiquated form no longer common, incrementally changing what can be considered a remarkable conservation.[8] While his father used a standard colonial period abbreviated style for Jesus Christ, Cipriano wrote out *Jesu Christo* in the more contemporary way. Cipriano took up the verb *cahua* for delivering the soul and universally used *nehuatli*, with an *i* at the end. Also of note is Cipriano's use of the term *amatlacuilolli*, for testament, early in his career; later he switches to the Spanish loanword *notestamento*. With the former word, Cipriano's usage seems more conservative than his father's, evidence that implies the use of even older Nahuatl models. Small departures like these may have seemed like significant deviations to each writer, given the formulaic unity ascribed to by the notarial corps, detailed in the next section.

In 1816 Cipriano fashions a more elaborate style, adding several extra elements to his father's formula. With the Mass or responsory prayer, he added that it was for the help of the testator's spirit and soul. Sometimes he now doubled the peroration, adding "my will is to be done" to the usual "my statement is to be carried out." Even a few years before, he used exalting language in a fashion used more frequently by the other notaries, calling San Bartolomé holy. While his father could also call San Bartolomé holy, his father's style tended, with exceptions, to be plainer when referring to their community. In addition, he now structured the testator's preamble to invoke the patron saint as "my precious revered father" and make him possessor of their altepetl. At this time he also added to the mere listing of the members of the Trinity the classic statement, "three persons but just one very true God," though he stumbled a time or two before he got it right. In comparison to his father, Cipriano's language seems to aim to elevate not only his community but also his own work as notary. The remarkable thing is that, though occurring in the second and third decades of the nineteenth century, his innovations in no way reflect the times but instead are all elements that had been included in relatively elaborate wills for generations and were new only for the notary and the community at that time.

In a prominent elaboration, Cipriano expands his signature. Contrary to local practice, he adopted one of his father's names. He at one point styled himself as Cipriano Gordiano *Romero*, openly taking the high-sounding Spanish surname that his father had used. Locally, this may have sounded affected, as if Cipriano arbitrarily raised his own status, or indicated that he indeed attained a more prominent status in his community. It remains possible that his father also appropriated the name *Romero* later in his career to mark a life event, for don Francisco's name on the early election lists do not carry *Romero* added on at the end. But Cipriano himself never adopted the *don* that his father always assumed, though his stand-ins did—adding the title *don* to Cipriano's name in two nominal wills.[9]

Cipriano's precise, almost printed hand follows his father's characters and form. In the transmission of orthography and styles from father to son, one finds a rarely documented example of the family succession of Nahua escribanos in the colonial period. In joining his own father's lineage, Cipriano adopted not only the general formula, analyzed in depth below, but also the personal style and handwriting that one could easily imagine to have been formed by a distant great-grandfather, centuries earlier.

Both worked within eighteenth- and nineteenth-century standards for escribanos of the Toluca Valley. In terms of reflecting his father's standards, Cipriano's only significant irregularity relates to the portion of the will about the body and soul. This section of the formula corresponded to Spanish legal expectations, where the testators are supposed to say they are of sound mind. In other words, they affirm that despite nearing death or being ill of body, they

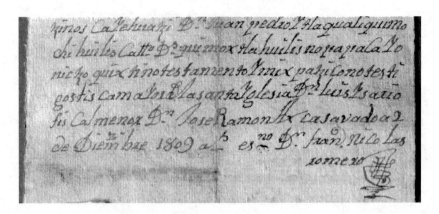

FIGURE 10. Nahuatl-language testament of Tiburcia Valenciana, written by Cipriano's father, don Francisco Nicolás, 1809, SBT#6. Archive: Ex-Convento of San Juan Bautista, Metepec. Photo by Melton-Villanueva.

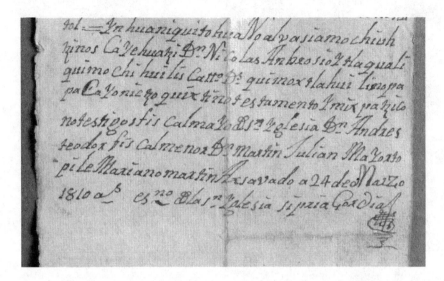

FIGURE 11. Nahuatl-language testament of Manuela Lugarda, written by Cipriano Gordiano, son of don Francisco Nicolás, 1819, SBT#10. Archive: Ex-Convento of San Juan Bautista, Metepec. Photo by Melton-Villanueva.

are capable of creating a legally binding will. From early in his career to the last documents we know by him, he sometimes gave this formula in the standard fashion but more often reversed it, making the soul sick and the body sound, or both sick, or omitting one, or producing ambiguous phrases.

To illustrate for comparison, let's first look at how Cipriano's father don Francisco Nicolás wrote it. Don Francisco used *cuerpo* instead of the traditional Nahuatl approximations to *body*. For soul he used *anima*, already widespread for generations. Both terms are loaned from Spanish, adopted into the Nahuatl phrasing. He never made out-and-out errors in this department, but some of his formulations display ambiguity and may have led to what happened with Cipriano. This is Cipriano's father's wording:

Ca hue [sic] seCa teCuitiCa noCuerpo yhua noAnimatzi que q̅monequiltzinos y tto Jesūxp̅o
(My body is very greatly hurting [literally throbbing], and my soul is as our lord Jesus Christ would wish it.)[10]

Notice the word for *and* here is *ihuan*, which most often connects nouns, rather than the usual *auh* (*and* or *but*), which most often connects whole clauses. Small changes can influence meaning. Thus the passage could very well be understood as "my body and soul are very greatly hurting, as our lord Jesus Christ would wish it." Is he saying that Jesus wishes our soul to suffer? The legal expectation is that the soul should be declared sound.

In his first extant testament of 1810, Cipriano reproduces his father's wording on body and soul in literally the same way.[11] He was capable, however, of a fully unambiguous traditional legal rendering, declaring that despite a sick body, one's soul is sound:

> Ca huel teCuitiCa noCuerpon y noAnimatzi sa pactiCa que quimonequiltis y tto Jesu~xpo~
> (My body is greatly hurting; my soul is sound, as our lord Jesus Christ would want it.)[12]

But as early as 1811 Cipriano began making highly unorthodox statements. All he had to say on the body/soul matter in one will of that year was "huel seCa mococotiCA noanimatzi," (my soul is very greatly sick).[13] Yes—the soul was declared sick not sound. And there is no mention of the body's illness. This reversal conflicts with Spanish legal expectations of one's mind being clear and able to create a will, despite the body's illness.

In a startling turn, for another will from 1811 Cipriano declares both body and soul sick:[14]

> Huel cenca tecuintica nocuerpo ihuan noanimatzin tecuintica quen quimo-nequiltitzinoz in tto
> (My body is very greatly hurting, and my soul is hurting, as our lord would want it.)

Cipriano also completely reversed the conventional phrases, proclaiming the body healthy and the soul sick:[15]

> Huel cenca tecuintica noanimatzin ihuan nocuerpo quen quimonequiltis in tto Ds
> (My soul is very greatly hurting, and my body is as our lord God would want it.)

Over the years Cipriano continued to produce versions that were occasionally standard, often ambiguous, and often fully unorthodox. Here are examples of both standard and unorthodox formulations from 1823, the last year he was active. A fully orthodox version:[16]

Ca cenca nechcocotica centetl nocuerpotzin inhuan noanimatzin çan pactica quen nechmotlanequilis in tto
(My whole body is greatly hurting me, and my soul is sound as our lord would want it.)

And a fully unorthodox version:[17]

Huel cenca nechcocoticatqui noanimatzin nocuerpotzin san pactica quen nech-motlanequilis in tto
(My soul is greatly hurting me; my body is sound, as our lord would want it.)

His one great eccentricity, surrounding the body/soul dichotomy, represents Cipriano's only truly striking deviation from his father's formula. It is hard to know just how to interpret this phenomenon. Cipriano's Nahuatl in general seems little different from what is seen in Toluca Valley Nahuatl-language documents of a century earlier, or even further back, demonstrating a very strict, conservative apprenticeship lineage. Some slippage with ecclesiastical concepts is seen here and there in the older corpus too, such as an impression that the Trinity is a fourth entity in addition to Father, Son, and Holy Spirit.[18] Even in early colonial Culhuacan, the members of the Trinity are once said to have been just one person.[19] Moreover, in the Nahuatl-language testament corpus overall, slips of all kinds are most frequent precisely in the formulaic portions and above all in the religious matter of the preamble. Imagine writing the same theological assertions every time; it's the section that requires the least focus and causes the writer to lose concentration. Yet soul and body had been handled in the standard manner for centuries without anything comparable to Cipriano's versions. If a discrete dichotomous soul and body had been a strange new classification in the sixteenth century, they were no longer. Either the soul/body slot was a matter of great indifference or refutation to Cipriano, or he was really confused about it during his whole career, or both.[20]

As the last Nahuatl-language notary in a settlement with a long tradition, Cipriano's nonconformity on this point surfaces perhaps as an indication that the end of the written tradition in Nahuatl was approaching. In a will penned during the 1813 epidemic, when so many in his community were sick and issuing wills, he shows an extreme example of absentmindedness, or indifference in form. The entire contents of the soul/body slot says, "Quen nechmotlanequilis in tto Jesuxpo" (As our lord Jesus Christ would want it for me), with neither body nor soul mentioned at all.[21]

When escribanos altered formulaic religious ideas, like the subject of body and soul, and then repeated the alteration of these long-established phrases, the local Nahuatl-language formula resisted change. These archetypal formulas are presented in chapter 4. But the various discrepant or standard phrasings are by no means attributed to the testators; they depend entirely on the particular escribano's conventions and his momentary state of mind. As traditional phrases become obsolete outside of notarial formulas, they function for escribanos more as isolated segments, simply fulfilling a legal requirement. These examples show how over time, like the small print in a contract, the words lost individual meaning—even to the escribano who was writing them. This phrasing is in contrast to the portions of wills that reflect the grammatical first person, testator's oral emphasis, or personal bequests, analyzed in remaining chapters.

Here we are, in the nineteenth century—a time when indigenous writing was no longer supposed to have been practiced—with a remarkable example of transmission by father to son, evoking a past when tlacuilos represented noble lineage.[22] Their apprenticeship shows us an intimately detailed and intact process heretofore only obliquely seen for the colonial period, but they were not alone. Cipriano Gordiano was only one of many other escribanos who clearly considered it an advantage to reproduce faithfully the style and conventions of one's lineage. This conservative approach to reproduction retains styles long eschewed by Spanish writers of previous centuries. Their preservation of conventions allows us next to distinguish groups of escribanos into discrete notarial lineages.

NETWORKS OF WRITING WITHIN SAN BARTOLOMÉ

As the last Nahuatl-language escribano, Cipriano's work on its own might be considered a dying tradition—but taken in context with his local colleagues, a more complete picture of escribano culture develops. San Bartolomé housed a diverse group of notaries for centuries, and they continued their work in the National period not only by practicing in Nahuatl but also, as detailed in the previous chapter, by using their long-standing culture of writing to transition to Spanish. Escribanos do not alternate in the same regular rotation of other fiscalía officers, so it can be assumed their influence was relied on and helped shape their institution.[23] Whether or not father and son had great influence on their peers who practiced in San Bartolomé in this time cannot be answered definitively; other escribanos' phrases and conventions diverge from their standard. Conventions in the matter of body and soul—and beyond—show that even though Cipriano wrote the vast majority of wills in this period, the influence of the father and son (below also called the Romero school, after Cipriano's father) did not determine the whole scene. To get a better idea of the situation, let us look briefly at the other writers in their small Nahua community.

At this point the entire corps of escribanos in Cipriano's altepetl is introduced and compared. The diversity of their written conventions—even when they develop into an object of some confusion within the ranks of escribanos—are considered below for what they say about the evolution of two notarial schools within San Bartolomé. Small phrasings denote different customary rubrics, which identify distinct alliances among them: distinct ranks *within* one altepetl, all following the same conservative local model. Recognizing these small "lost" changes in the formulaic portions of the local notarial standard aids inquiry, serving as tokens of difference between local escribano lineages. Even though they left fewer samples than Cipriano's extensive production, these other Nahua writers describe something happening at a community level: a different, perhaps competing, lineage. In the contrast, alliances emerge.

PEDRO AGUSTÍN

Pedro Agustín's career pattern exemplifies the porous division between secular and ecclesiastical offices, between the cabildo and fiscalía. He was elected as San Bartolomé's *escribano de republica* (notary of the indigenous cabildo) for at least three years before he appears as the parish escribano in the Independence corpus. Pedro Agustín only left two wills in the Independence corpus, because the collection of sources begins at the very end of his tenure.[24] But we can see he worked as a main notary, not just as an assistant, because of his earlier appearance in the secular record. And he served as more than escribano. In local elections called *elecciones de republica* Pedro Agustín served as alguacil mayor in 1766 and later was elected to escribano with the cofradía in 1790, 1795, and 1798, as escribano de república.[25] His tenure as escribano in the fiscalía came later, before that of Cipriano's father and Cipriano himself.

Pedro Agustín emerges in the testament corpus as counterpoint to Cipriano and his father don Francisco Romero, representing another authority within the San Bartolomé standard. In his earliest surviving Nahuatl-language will, which he wrote in 1803, he not only still uses the full traditional body and soul phrasing in orthodox form but also retains the older indigenous -*tlalnacayo* instead of *cuerpo* for body.[26] He continued to use the Nahuatl term even though the loanword *cuerpo*, issuing from the Spanish, had been common—outside San Bartolomé—for generations. By 1806, however, he joins the local "new wave" in San Bartolomé by going over to *cuerpo*.[27] Except for that limited shift into newer vocabulary, he remains squarely in strict continuity with orthodox legal phrasing. Without mixup, Pedro Agustín treats body and soul in a more standard, or customary way, than Cipriano and his father.

Within overall traditional expressions, Pedro Agustín uses only slight variations. He once used *choca* with the bells and the other time he used *tzilini*, perhaps merely shifting individual preference among his broad repertoire. In one case he speaks of praising the Trinity in the heading. That formula, common from the eighteenth-century Toluca Valley, veers from the San Bartolomé norm of taking the Trinity as one's sign. This departure speaks to his personal knowledge of conventions beyond his altepetl. However, in the other testament, he uses the San Bartolomé standard; otherwise, he embodies the general San Bartolomé model entirely. Thus, for his chronological position in the corpus, his status as secular official, and his devotion to general San Bartolomé conventions, I named the notarial school that diverges with Cipriano and his father after Pedro Agustín. Taken in sum and especially recognizing his early tenure, Pedro Agustín represents escribanos who engaged a distinct force within San Bartolomé.

RUFINO FAUSTINO

That Pedro Agustín (and Mariano de la Merced, below) represents a counter example (to Cipriano and his father's relative unconventionality) only begins to tell the whole story. It turns out that the Romero lineage (Cipriano and father) was not alone in unorthodoxy with soul and body. In a testament of 1815, Rufino Faustino wrote:[28]

> Ca huel chicahuac tecuitica noanimatzin quen nechmotlanequililis in totecolle Dios.
> (My soul is very strongly hurting, as our lord God would want it for me.) [The body remains unmentioned.]

A bit of mystery surrounds Rufino. In the testament cited above, the testator called herself and her husband citizens of Totocuitlapilco not of San Bartolomé, the only testator to cite citizenship in another altepetl. The question arises whether Rufino worked in Totocuitlapilco too. Or perhaps the sister altepetl shared notaries? A few clues, like the organization of this will, and virtually all the vocabulary and conventions, are in the San Bartolomé style. One departure, marked by the verb *choca* instead of *tzilini* with *ringing the bells*, represents a preference in Totocuitlapilco. But a few instances of *choca* appear in some well-authenticated San Bartolomé wills, presented below when describing the writing forms of Juan Domingo de la Cruz and Basilio Martín. Like some other locals, Rufino does not abbreviate "our lord God" (though his spelling, "totecolle Dios," is different from Mariano Merced's "toteco de Dios").[29] The greatest evidence for Rufino belonging to San Bartolomé stems from the witness don Juan Crisóstomo, who is part of San Bartolomé's fiscalía. Don Juan Crisóstomo, listed here as fiscal menor in the subsequent will done the following year, turns up as San Bartolomé's fiscal mayor. This is a typical promotion within the fiscalía; the evidence shows that Rufino is writing in San Bartolomé throughout, even when writing a will for a woman from Totocuitlapilco.[30]

Otherwise, Rufino Faustino relies entirely on the San Bartolomé model, outlined in detail below. He does not say "here in San Bartolomé" because the testator is from elsewhere (though probably living in San Bartolomé). But a lingering question emerges in that instead of saying "before my witnesses" Rufino writes, "I say or declare my witnesses" (*niquitoa notestigos*).[31] Because *naming* the witnesses dodges the more common assertion that testaments are said *before* (in the presence of) witnesses, the mystery about place cannot be completely settled and leaves open the possibility that the will was made with witnesses in absentia.

RUFINO FAUSTINO #2

Two other wills also bear Rufino Faustino's name, but that cannot be taken for face value.[32] Two demonstrably different people wrote testaments in San Bartolomé under that name. Everything about them shows that the authors are not one and the same as the Rufino with ties to Totocuitlapilco.

The first Rufino's particularly distinctive hand separates each succeeding syllable from the rest.[33] Bartolomé de Las Casas in the sixteenth century described not being able to distinguish Nahua manuscript from printing: "They write skillfully and quite elegantly, so that most often we are at a loss to know whether the characters are handwritten or printed."[34] Rufino #1 writes in this block

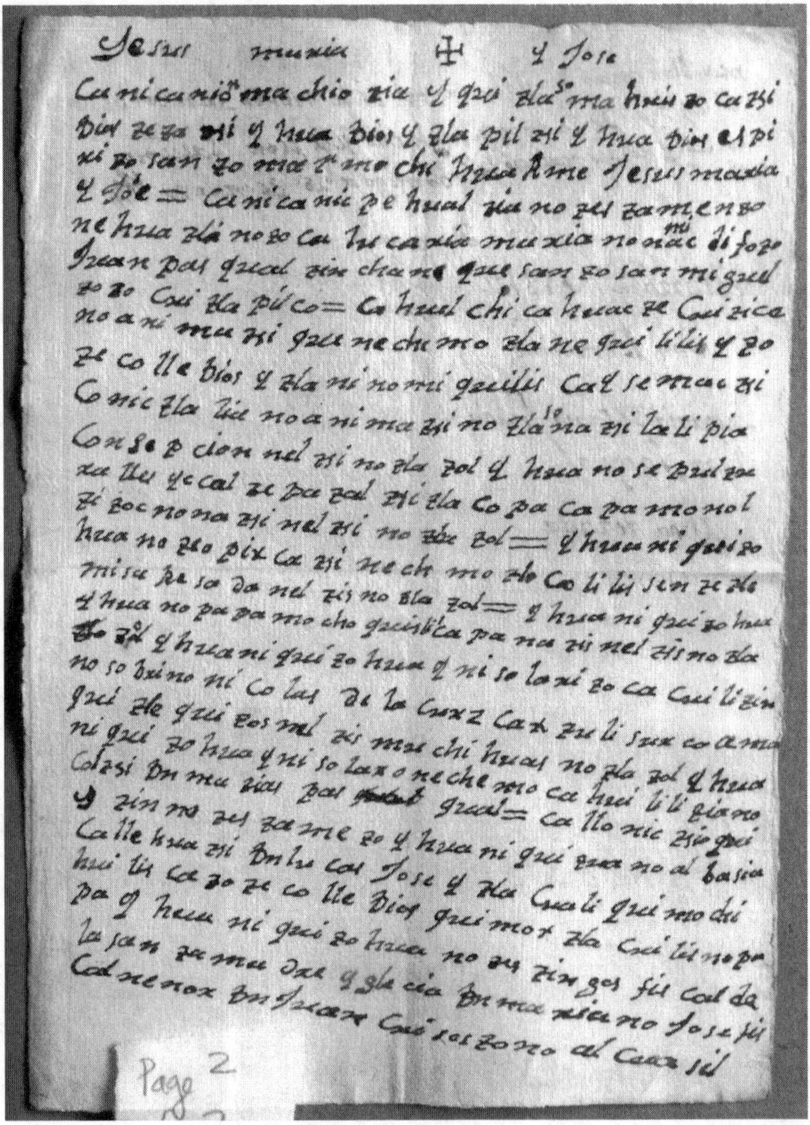
Jesus maria ✠ y Jose
Page 2

FIGURE 12. Example from the hand of Rufino Faustino #1. Archive: Ex-Convento of San Juan Bautista, Metepec. Photo by Melton-Villanueva.

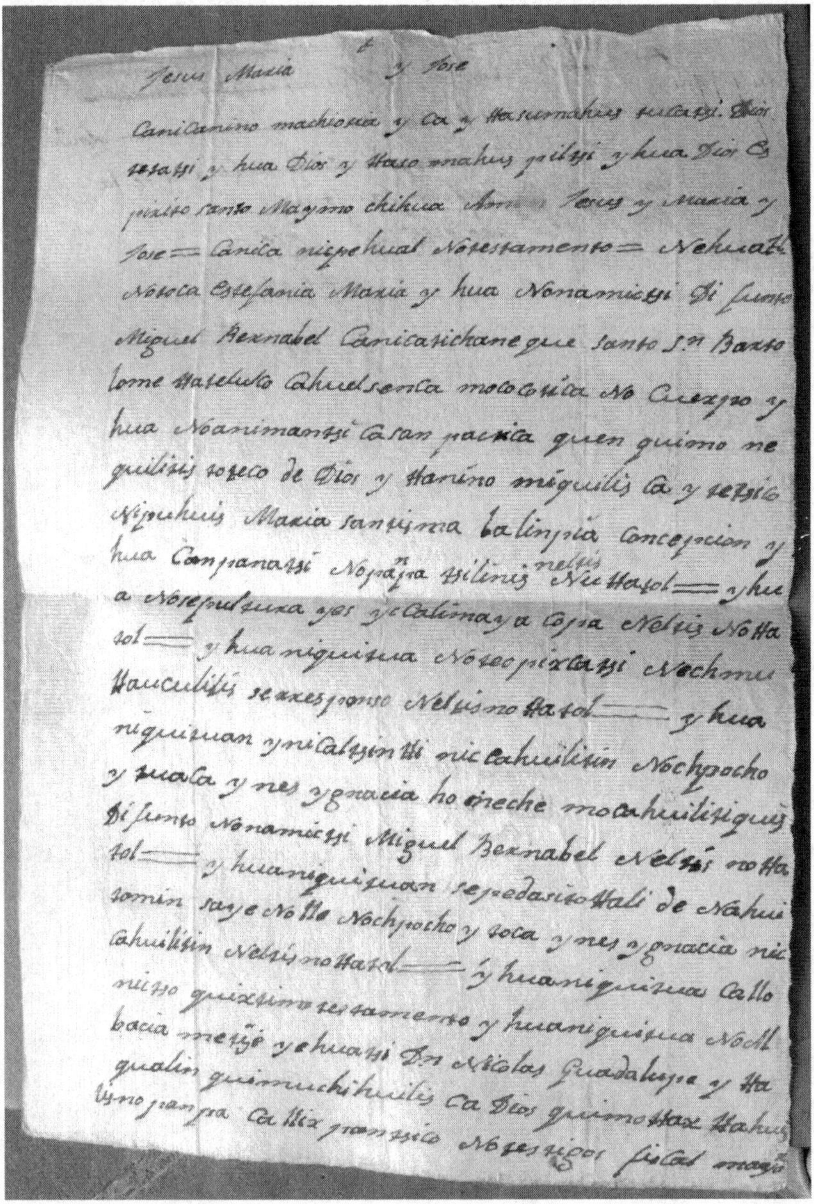

FIGURE 13. Example of the hand of Rufino Faustino #2. Archive: Ex-Convento of
San Juan Bautista, Metepec. Photo by Melton-Villanueva.

"print" hand associated with traditional Nahua escribanos, perhaps derived of the Carolingian miniscule originally taught by friars. This blocky Gothic calligraphy contrasts with the two nominal wills written in a more cursive *encadenada* (connected) hand, reflecting Rufino Faustino #2's relatively more contemporary lineage.[35]

For the purposes of clarity, the Rufino not connected to Totocuitlapilco is called Rufino #2, and he actually wrote more wills. Whether Rufino Faustino #2 used the name of another notary (like Mariano for Cipriano) or they both actually bore the name remains a matter for speculation. Either another notarial clerk with the same name worked in the same place at the same time, or more common to this corpus, a different person wrote a testament in Rufino Faustino's name. Unlike Mariano de la Merced, who assisted Cipriano, this helper remains unnamed, for they do not leave a testament in their own name in this period (unless they by chance bear the same name). This Rufino Faustino, #2, wrote a will for Cipriano Gordiano in 1819 and two under Rufino Faustino's name in 1820.[36] His style overall, indistinguishable from the usual manner in San Bartolomé, helped to confirm the local template presented below. He does once use *choca* with the bells (though also *tzilini*), and once for body he uses the old Nahuatl *-tlalnacayo* instead of the Spanish *cuerpo*. At one point he uses exactly the same unusual form, "toteco de Dios," for "our lord God" as Mariano Merced, offering a compelling connection between assistants—if not a temporary labor pool, a ready supply of notaries trained in the local model.

Unlike Cipriano, Rufino #2's statements on soul and body all follow orthodox form. This can be contrasted with the original Rufino Faustino, as already mentioned, who followed Cipriano Gordiano's manner of reversing soul and body. Further, because Rufino Faustino #2 uses the soul/body statement in an orthodox fashion, he clearly inserts his own content, so it can be inferred that the form was not simply dictated by Rufino Faustino #1 but written independently. For a closer discussion see below; further hints of unorthodoxy appear in the region when testaments in Spanish are examined.

JUAN DOMINGO DE LA CRUZ

Juan Domingo de la Cruz in 1799 wrote the first testament of the Independence collection—earlier than the first wills by Pedro Agustín and don Francisco Nicolás Romero preserved in San Bartolomé.[37] Yet from election lists we know the latter two, elected as official escribanos of the community before the start of the Independence corpus, both worked before this time.[38] Thus, Juan Domingo de la Cruz happens to log in as the first notary of this period, but he worked alongside others in his community and represents continuity between those before and after him. The temporal limitations of the corpus might deprive him of this rich context and culture of writing; the fact that his 1799 will ranks first chronologically should not be taken as much more than a function of record keeping; many writers came before and after him. Overall, Juan Domingo de la Cruz conforms to the general San Bartolomé pattern.

That said, he also uses a particular opening phrase, distinctive for initial statements in San Bartolomé. But even Juan Domingo de la Cruz's personal phrasing, found in his picturesque opening, also appears occasionally in the general eighteenth-century Toluca Valley corpus:

> toteCuiYoye Diose Ma YPaPa Yn imachio Cruz+ ma xitehmomaQuixtilitziNo Yn ihuiCPa toYahua.
>
> (O our lord, o God, for the sake of the sign of the cross deliver us from our enemies.)

Thus, even his "unique" phrasing was only unique to San Bartolomé. The fact that in his local context no one else used this phrasing indicates he had outside contact because such phrasing appeared earlier in the Toluca region. Though he worked within the San Bartolomé model, his context included a wider but unknown circle of writers.

Compared with the Cipriano Gordiano "Romero" model, Juan Domingo de la Cruz also diverges in a few other ways. All mention of the state of body and soul is omitted—though this could be explained as carelessness in a profession that requires exacting attention, it remains another case of no longer using this legal wording in the standard way. The phrase about finishing the testament is missing, and the executor is introduced much earlier than usual. The bells he observes as usual, but they are to sound (literally "cry," *choca*) instead of being rung (*tzilini*).

BASILIO MARTÍN

Writing a testament in 1803,[39] Basilio Martín sticks a bit closer to the Romero model than Juan Domingo de la Cruz, putting in the part about finishing the testament. However, Basilio Martín follows Juan Domingo de la Cruz's preference for using *choca* instead of *tzilini* for ringing the bells. The part about the body and the soul starts out standard enough but is truncated, so we cannot be sure what the intention was; at any rate, he uses the old Nahuatl wording *-tlalnacayo* instead of the Spanish loanword *cuerpo*. He uses the very old *amat-lacuilolli* (document [writing on paper]) in addition to *testamento*, but then Cipriano himself did so too, on occasion.

MARIANO DE LA MERCED

Mariano de la Merced worked in San Bartolomé during the 1813 epidemic that killed Cipriano's mother. Compared to Cipriano's Romero lineage, Mariano de la Merced kept things traditional in the Nahuatl, yet he also wrote in Spanish, a departure detailed in the previous chapter.[40]

By this time, he had adopted the Spanish *cuerpo* into the Nahuatl form. Keep in mind that this loanword would not be considered an innovation outside San Bartolomé, in comparison with writing from other Nahuatl-speaking communities. In other words, *cuerpo*, while rather new in San Bartolomé, would regionally have been understood as orthodox usage.[41]

Perhaps due to the tragic demands of an epidemic year, Mariano de la Merced worked as an assistant for Cipriano, using Cipriano's name.[42] This fact almost remained hidden within the mass of data for this study because he not only wrote for Cipriano but also signed Cipriano's name, obscuring Mariano's presence. Three different times in 1813 Mariano wrote wills for Cipriano, but in translating from my original photographs, I discerned a different hand; these three were clearly not written by Cipriano. Since Mariano also wrote in his own name, Mariano's style can be confirmed and matched to his hand. While the wills nominally say they were written by Cipriano Gordiano, after comparing those three not-Cipriano wills to Mariano's attested work, the style leaves no doubt that Mariano de la Merced did them. And the nominal wills handle body and soul much like the will signed by Mariano.[43]

We can deduce his authorship in those cases from special characteristics of his spelling. For example, Cipriano and his father almost always wrote the independent form of the pronoun *I* as *nehuatli*, with an *i* at the end that was not standard for central Mexican Nahuatl but was often used in the Toluca Valley. Mariano Merced, however, wrote the standard *nehuatl*, and he did so whether he was writing under his own name or under Cipriano's. Overall there is almost nothing other than the orthography to distinguish his style. He does have a particular way of writing "our lord God."[44] It was generally rendered as *tto Dios*, in San Bartolomé as elsewhere, but Mariano had a special form, *toteco de Dios*, which apparently incorporates Spanish *de*, though there is no related Spanish phrase that would use the word. Of course in a sense this feature too is merely orthography.

Mariano's case shows the cultural resources for writing available in San Bartolomé. His unique orthography does not exactly reflect the close apprenticeship of the Romero lineage of Cipriano's family. Even though the two very much belong to a common local tradition, and they worked closely together on the same jobs (Mariano signing for Cipriano), Mariano's characteristics express independent training. Apparently he worked as a stand-in when Cipriano was not available, even though he was not from the Romero school. In other words, Mariano reflects a separate notarial school coexisting within San Bartolomé that was drawn upon by Cipriano at a time of crisis. Even Santiago Cristóbal came to help out as a Spanish-language notary in San Bartolomé, after working for years in neighboring Ocotitlan. Thus, in a place as small as San Bartolomé, separate streams of escribanos not only passed on skills and conventions to successors but also supported each other in need.

DISTINCT LINEAGES IN SAN BARTOLOMÉ

As represented in table 3, one discerns two lines of escribanos who wrote in Nahuatl at this time. One main lineage represented by Cipriano Gordiano's family, the Romero school, includes Rufino Faustino #1.

The second lineage, represented by Pedro Agustín, holds a much smaller percentage of authorships but holds a larger group of writers, by a ratio of 3:5. The earliest writers of the Pedro Agustín line include Juan Domingo de la Cruz, Basilio Martín, and in later years Mariano Merced and Rufino Faustino #2. The Pedro Agustín school generally tended to share the characteristic of not confusing the Spanish distinction between soul and body, as well as some smaller features such as preferring *choca* instead of *tzilini* in speaking of the bells ringing or using a written-out and unusual form of "our Lord." In all, the Nahuatl-language escribanos outside the Romero school seem to have belonged to the Pedro Agustín tradition, apparently passing their manner of doing testaments from one to the next without any close intervention by the Romero school.

TABLE 3. Fiscalía Notaries "Escribanos de la Santa Iglesia" in San Bartolomé, 1799–1832

NAME OF ESCRIBANO	YEARS*	LANGUAGE	NOTARIAL SCHOOL AND NOTES
1. Juan Domingo de la Cruz	1799	Nahuatl	Pedro Agustín school
2. Basilio Martín**	1803	Nahuatl	Pedro Agustín school
3. Pedro Agustín**	1803–1806	Nahuatl	Pedro Agustín school
4. don Francisco Nicolás Romero**	1809	Nahuatl	Romero school
5. Cipriano Gordiano**	1810–1823	Nahuatl	Romero school
6. Mariano de la Merced**	1813	Nahuatl and Spanish	Pedro Agustín school
7. Rufino Faustino #1	1815	Nahuatl	Romero school (one testator from Totocuitlapilco)
8. Rufino Faustino #2	1819–1820	Nahuatl	Pedro Agustín school
9. Juan Máximo Mejía	1817	Spanish	
10. Máximo Calisto	1821	Spanish	
11. José María	1824–1825	Spanish	
12. Félix Nabor [Mulia?]	1824	Spanish	
13. Santiago Cristóbal	1824	Spanish	also active in Ocotitlan, 1809–1812
14. José Guadalupe Camacho	1832	Spanish	

NOTE Shaded rows refer to the Romero school.
* Years refer to attested wills in the Independence archive; careers are known to exceed time frame. List arranged according to chronological appearance in the Independence corpus.
** Also confirmed to have served in cabildo as escribano de la republica; since cabildo election records stop at 1810, overlapping membership expected to be greater than attested in this sample.

In sum, an impressive culture of writing continued in force beyond the colonial period. Texts in San Bartolomé tell us about the evolution of Nahua notarial schools, escribanos that according to the Spanish record did not exist. At first glance, and based on sheer numbers, it would be tempting to classify the San Bartolomé canon as simply that of don Francisco and Cipriano personally, but the local standard reaches beyond their "Romero" lineage and encompasses another stream, identified as the "Pedro Agustín school." No other escribanos in San Bartolomé had the impact of the father and son team of the Romero school in this period, and no one produced anywhere near as many testaments as Cipriano, himself responsible for more than four-fifths of all those in Nahuatl. Yet precisely because the remaining writers follow the general format closely (a form presented in the following chapter in comparison to the nearly identical form in San Bartolomé a century earlier), it confirms a blueprint specific to the altepetl of San Bartolomé Tlatelolco. It is from comparison with this general local model that different writers' small discrepancies emerged, which in turn linked them to their associates.

In contrast to the invisibility of the Nahua fiscalía in Spanish records, numbers of escribanos, as official ficalía notaries, continued to construct altepetl autonomy, as they had for centuries. Strictly adhered-to norms continued to be passed on not just within one family or notarial lineage (in itself startling for its continuity with ancient practice) but also among a whole corps of Nahua men who assisted and collaborated with each other, drawing from a wider knowledge of practices not found in their local standards.

4

NAHUATL FORMULAS OVER TIME
AND IN OTHER ALTEPETL

ONE BARE LIGHT BULB hangs in the archive of the Ex-Convento of San Juan Bautista Metepec.[1] I snuggled my tripod against the French doors to encourage weak light from a north-facing balcony. Thick walls speak of the local people who built the adobe back in the mid-sixteenth century when Spanish was only the language of a handful of immigrants. The floor, worn smooth, leads from the reception area into a large courtyard. A wide staircase ushered me upstairs into a hallway with a south-facing, fading, fresco mural. The door to the archive, a dark smooth wood, forms a small portal with large cast iron latches and locks, the kind that knock and groan across the courtyard; not a place you could enter in secret. Inside, the ceilings are high, the red unglazed tile floor smooth and warm in the winter and cool in the summer. Life-sized saints stored against the wall protect this space and stare beyond you, gesturing to another time and place.

These thick walls have seen devoted archivists' fingertips conserve paper manuscripts for six hundred years. In Metepec, before the Spanish arrived, the Nahuatl-speaking calpixque kept records for the Mexica of Tenochtitlan for about a century.[2] Iberian colonizers found the calpixques useful and hired them to keep track of the same tribute payments.[3] Thus, the same administrative bureaucracies that kept track of colonial transactions when the Aztecs held power continued their work under the new Iberian bosses, then speaking Castilian as well as Nahuatl. The shift from pictorial-based writing to Roman script happened during this change of management.[4] The altepetl of Metepec exists beyond memory as a place where people treasured writing for its power.

I found the Independence archive between two pieces of wood. An unknown artisan cut the edges of thick planks by hand, made them smooth to the touch, and then tied them together with a rough, twisted *mecate* (a sisal string). I hesitated before untying it, studying the slipknot. The wood protected two stacks of papers with uneven edges, each sheet made individually, not cut down or trimmed. Most testaments used two sides of a small sheet. If the will needed three or four pages, the escribano used a longer sheet and folded it in half, like a book. The black ink varies in color from black to a reddish-brown, without a hint of precolonial palette, though even this variation suggests pathways of research forged by Diana Magaloni Kerpel.[5] The paper's density and texture contrast favorably to thinner, larger, more standard paper manuscripts with which I had been working in the State of Mexico notarial archive; there, most of those

FIGURE 14. Opening the Independence archive. Archive: San Juan Bautista, Metepec. Photo by Melton-Villanueva.

FIGURE 15. Two-page testament style. On one sheet of paper, both front and back were used. Archive: Ex-Convento of San Juan Bautista, Metepec. Photo by Melton-Villanueva.

FIGURE 16. Four-page testament style written on one larger sheet that is folded to make four pages. Archive: Ex-Convento of San Juan Bautista, Metepec. Photo by Melton-Villanueva.

standard papers carried the colonial seal. This handmade bond feels thicker and shows negligible sign of decay, as if made yesterday, not two hundred years ago.[6]

Because these documents were not stamped, these sheets were made outside the colonial system that controlled and taxed paper. Made to order, each sheet fit the needs of individual projects; in this case escribanos assessed the size of paper they needed based on the amount of property people had to distribute, as that part of the written formula varied most. My challenge was to record every

FIGURE 17. Official seal not found on local paper used for testaments. This sample is from the secular notarial archive, with the official seal in top left corner of paper. Archive: State of Mexico State notarial archive. Photo by Melton-Villanueva.

detail on this paper, given the low light. Rainy season brings a volatile sun—bright one moment, veiled the next—but even on her overcast days, she offered enough light to photograph these manuscripts from San Bartolomé, Yancuictlalpan, Ocotitlan, and Totocuitlapilco, with a tripod for long exposures.

Escribanos exercise a long view when it comes to their craft, as if Spanish *cedulas* (laws) explicitly outlawing their language did not exist. This chapter shows how they adhered closely to a testament form and traditional Nahuatl vocabulary very near to what it had been in San Bartolomé a hundred years before. When escribanos use the original Nahuatl *-tlalnacayo* instead of the regionally common Spanish *cuerpo* or *amatlacuilolli* (document [writing on paper]) paired with *testamento*, it catches the eye. These phrasings would have been considered old forms—even a century before. Thus, these old Nahuatl forms show the extraordinary connection escribanos kept to their ancestral instructors, unexpected for the contact stage of Nahuatl at this time.[7] Over time, Nahuas replaced common nouns with corollaries in the Spanish-language system (loanwords) early in the colonial period. Yet the Independence archive houses traces of the original Nahuatl words.

We have seen in previous chapters how escribanos revered, expanded, and challenged ancient formulas; a process reinforced by altepetl groups such as the fiscalía that valued, and were in turn manifested in, their written craft. From this insight follows the need to grasp the parameters of standard local formulas. In detecting escribanos' strict notarial conformity despite the passage of time, the previously described eccentric deviations of the Romano lineage can be truly appreciated. Before comparing escribano formulas from different altepetl, I begin with continuity and change over time within San Bartolomé itself. Earlier norms here derived from several eighteenth-century documents—also from San Bartolomé—are found in Pizzigoni's published testament collection. Thus, the following compares local standards in the altepetl with its own escribanos' norms from the previous century.

COMPARING STANDARD WILLS OVER TIME IN SAN BARTOLOMÉ

To allow quick comparison, I present two schematic models of formulas, generalized for the eighteenth and nineteenth century:[8]

San Bartolomé, 1715–1731
Jesus, Mary, and Joseph
I take as my sign God the father, God the son, and God the Holy Spirit.

Here I begin my testament, I named _____; my wife or husband is _____; we are citizens here in holy San Bartolomé Tlatelolco. I belong to my precious revered mother Santa María de la Asunción [or la Limpia Concepción].

My earthly body (notlalnacayo, etc.) is very sick, but my soul is sound as our lord God would wish it. If I die, the bells (using campana) are to ring for me. My statement is to be carried out. And I say that my grave is to be (location). (same peroration), [or abbreviated to it is to be carried out.] And my precious priest is to perform for me [or favor me with] (a Mass) [or a low Mass].
  Bequests to inheritors.
  And my intercessor, my executor [more often two], is to be _____; if he does it well, God will reward him. I have concluded my testament before my witnesses the fiscal _____, the deputy fiscal _____, and the church tepisque _____.
  Today, (day) the __th day of the month of _____ in the year of 17__.
  Notary [of the holy church] _____.

San Bartolomé, 1799–1823
Jesus, Mary, and Joseph

I take as my sign God the father, God his precious revered son, and God the Holy Spirit. Jesus, Mary, and Joseph.

Here I begin my testament, I named _____; my wife or husband is _____; we are citizens here in holy San Bartolomé Tlatelolco. I am to belong to my precious revered mother Santa María de la Asunción [or la Limpia Concepción].

[The part about body and soul comes here, often a bit different; body is *cuerpo*.] If I die, the bells (using *campana*) are to ring for me. My statement is to be carried out. And I say that my grave is to be (location). (same peroration), [or abbreviated to it is to be carried out.] And my precious priest is to favor me with (a responso or a low Mass).

Bequests to inheritors.

And my intercessor, my executor, is to be _____; if he does it well, God will reward him for me. I have concluded my testament[9] before my witnesses the fiscal mayor _____, the deputy fiscal _____, and the alguacil [or topile, or mayor topile] _____.

Today, (day) the __th of (month) of the year 18__.

Notary [of the holy church] _____.

As the two testament formulas show, notarial conventions peculiar to San Bartolomé in the eighteenth century carry on into the Independence period. Notice the way the escribano corps of both periods designate the bells by the same loanword, *campana*, not by the Nahuatl term; this "novelty" happened a century before. The declarative statement saying that the testator belongs to the Virgin (Asunción or Limpia Concepción) contradicts the more general formulation in the Toluca Valley of entrusting the soul to God and remains a distinctive feature of the local model within San Bartolomé a century later. Also of note is the way people appeal to their local priest in connection with a Mass or responsory prayer—one would assume that the individual priests would change over time, yet the relationship of the notary, the testator, and the priest remain codified in a way particular to San Bartolomé. A testimony to the precise local training within the lineages of Nahua escribanos, the overall structure remains exactly the same.

People begin each testament with crossing themselves. This kind of detail, because it is particular to San Bartolomé, traced back to the eighteenth century, distinguishes their escribano corps from the influence of more regional conventions. While many notaries of the Toluca Valley in the eighteenth century (and most in the areas of Toluca proper and Calimaya/Tepemaxalco) began each testament by speaking of the praise of the Trinity, in San Bartolomé they began testaments with the early colonial Nahuatl phrase, "I take as my sign," by which they mean "to genuflect."[10] Also note that the oral-style peroration of San Bartolomé wills vary slightly from the main convention of the orbit of Toluca proper (*neltiz notlatol* [my statement is to be carried out]). Finally, three or four fiscalía officials appear in the same sequence in both periods as witnesses to the declaration of the will, starting with the fiscal mayor. No one else from outside the fiscalía serves as witness in San Bartolomé.

Carryovers of traditional practices appear where least expected. Because the wills are written on relatively small pieces of paper, one might assume simplification or diminution compared to an earlier period. But one of the three eighteenth-century wills was also written on a small piece,[11] so it seems that even the local choice of small, good-quality paper carried forward from the previous century.

Imagine the remarkable way the Nahua escribano corps, with so many different people, learned and transmitted the sequence of formulas so strongly, writing each will by hand. This persistence of a specific San Bartolomé testamentary style speaks to an even broader cultural continuity, to other forms of culture-making (like Nahuatl influencing Spanish, active self-government discussed in previous chapters, and religious rites discussed in the following chapter) whose success allowed individuals to work, move, and play within tightly held traditions. Escribanos demonstrate that the altepetl of San Bartolomé resolutely advanced their own testamentary culture into this late period, below the radar of Spanish recordkeepers, for approximately eighty years after the last known document from San Bartolomé.

INNOVATION AND STABILITY

Against this background of embraced conventions, escribanos also contributed changes. To appreciate escribanos' local creativity, a larger context proves valuable: Barry Sell and Louise Burkhart offer a discussion of how two early friars, a Franciscan named Fray Alonso de Molina (in 1565) and a Dominican named Fray Martín de León (in 1611), dialogued with Nahuatl-language escribanos to publish wills used as models in a way that "familiarized Nahuas with Catholic practices and discourse related to death . . . even the most formulaic wills indicate that people were conversant with the concepts [of faith]." The purpose of such models was to standardize Nahua escribanos' forms into a procedure that included an *encommendation* (statement of faith that imposed a dualism of body and soul) and an opportunity to bequeath property and arrange for Church rituals like Masses and funerals.[12] Wills can be seen as derived from these early colonial standards and influenced by Nahua notarial expectations throughout Mexico. Local examples, or "diversifications of Catholicism," can also be seen among Maya escribanos, where analysis and comparisons with Nahua preambles reveal "differences within polities . . . that can be ascribed to notarial preferences."[13] Thus, as presented below, many innovations that may seem insignificant and involve only slight variations on eighteenth-century wording can show how individual escribanos interpreted their local form over time in nonstandard ways that influenced their local standard.

One primary example of variation from the previous century appears in how "belonging to the Virgin" is now put in the future tense. This slight innovation hints at what "belonging" meant, beyond individual devotion to the Virgin. Though it is never specifically mentioned in the Nahuatl-language sources, Mauricio Mateo's words in Spanish reveal in 1825 that the Virgin also represents a cofradía dedicated to her.[14] Or more specifically, the Virgin represents two cofradías dedicated to Asunción or to Limpia Concepción, two different aspects of her. A possible implication of the use of the future tense is that the testator expects to enter the cofradía at death, perhaps via a membership ritual to which people only now allude. Other interpretations are also possible, in a more general sense, as if the testator expected to belong to, or to be dedicated to, the Virgin in the afterlife, as if duties normally performed for one's cofradía group extended beyond death.

Other changes in style appear in the Independence archive. The eighteenth-century Nahuatl office name *tepixqui*, rendered in Spanish as *tepisque*, has been dropped by the fiscalía; in the nineteenth century the Nahuatl term completely disappears. At the end of the invoked names for the Trinity now comes a repeated Jesus, Mary, and Joseph that was not there earlier. In the part about God rewarding the executor, the phrase "for me" is added. In the colonial period varying phrases identified the role of the priest, while now it is standardized to always say "he is to favor me with" (*tlaocolia*; always in the nonstandard form *tlocolia*). Perhaps not strictly a style change, the variation from asking for two executors to asking for one executor is discussed in chapter 1 in depth—the one executor now fuses the two different terms previously meant for two types of executors.

The largest change has been in the phrase speaking of the state of body and soul. The early wills use the well-known Nahuatl expressions for the body, notably *notlalnacayo* (my earth-body, my earthly body). This and the other traditional phrase *notlallo noçoquiyo* (my earth and clay, my earthly body) are seen, but only exceptionally in the Independence corpus. The standard word is now the Spanish loanword *cuerpo*. Moreover, although the full expression about the sick body and sound soul as God would want it is seen occasionally in the late texts, it is usually streamlined in a way that leads to ambiguity. As we have seen, Cipriano, the main notary of early nineteenth-century San Bartolomé, repeatedly confuses it, changing its logic.

Overall, circumscribed changes identify underlying stability. The importance of identifying this notarial conformity over time comes in establishing that the transmission of technique and knowledge is happening in the context of adversity: internal groups responded by adhering to and adapting the conventions of

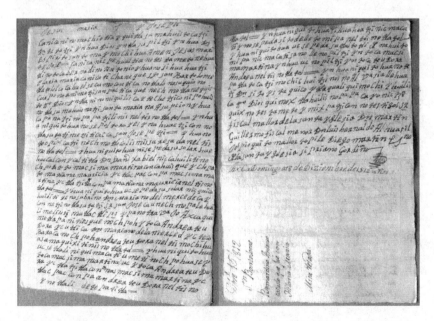

FIGURE 18. Front and back view of Bernardino Antonio's 1812 Nahuatl-language testament. Archive: Ex-Convento of San Juan Bautista, Metepec. Photo by Melton-Villanueva.

their ancestors. As we saw in chapter 3, lineage could still be preserved by blood, from father to son. Epidemics created demand for new labor, perhaps brought more people into the escribano corps. Yet comparing the entire corpus, different and perhaps competing streams worked within the larger altepetl model. Writing practices, shared and diffused by many, were not just the purview of a lone knowledgeable individual in this small altepetl of San Bartolomé. On the contrary, one is left with the long-term impact of a vibrant, cohesive culture of writing that incorporated diverse lineages working together to support their friends, neighbors, and altepetl.

YANCUICTLALPAN'S STANDARD WILL

Yancuictlalpan, the community that left nearly all their records in Nahuatl, left only one known will to us in Spanish. Twelve people in Yancuictlalpan left testaments dated from 1809 to 1825. By comparing these Nahuatl-language texts, I generalize the similarities to construct a model will formula. Then, to test the degree of uniformity or variety of escribano practices, I compare this Yancuictlalpan model to San Bartolomé's prototype.[15] A standardized formula looks like this:

Jesus, Mary, and Joseph.

Today, (day of the week) on the __th day of the month of _____
and the year count of _____.

I take as my sign the precious revered name of God the father, God his precious son, and God the Holy Spirit. May it be done, Amen. Jesus [, Mary, Joseph].

Know all who see this my memorandum of testament that my name is _____; my (husband or wife) is named _____; we are citizens (*chaneque*) here in the altepetl of my [or our] consummate mother Santa María de la Rosa [Nativitas], Yancuictlalpan. I say that my body (*-tlallo -çoquiyo*) is very sick; my soul is healthy. If in the future our lord God summons me [and I repay the death or mortal passion] of our lord Jesus Christ, [I place it entirely in his hands, and] first of all I say that I offer half a *real* for the holy places of Jerusalem; it is to be given. [My command is to be carried out and executed.] And I say that God will provide what my body is to be wrapped in (using a word related to native *quimiloa*). And I say that as to where my body will lie buried, they are to favor me with a place in the churchyard (*teopan ithualco*).

[The help of my soul is to be that] a low Mass is to be said for me within (one month, two months, etc.).

Bequests to inheritors.

And I say that this is all that I have recorded before [my deity and ruler] God and those who are being made my executors who are to speak for me; if they do it well, God will give them their reward; they are _____ and _____. I say that I have made my memorandum of testament before all my witnesses, my lord alcalde current alcalde _____, my lord the fiscal of the holy church _____, and _____. Municipal notary _____.

While the nonbequest portion of wills in Yancuictlalpan illustrates a cohesive formula, the heart of each will tells of the different things people leave to their loved ones: the bequest section. Because these legacies vary with each person, they are too assorted to generalize. What can be said in a general sense about bequests is that the rich listing of household objects is no longer found by the time escribanos wrote the Independence corpus.[16] As with San Bartolomé, the bequest section of wills mainly offers directions about how to endow their land.

On first inspection, one finds a general similarity in form to San Bartolomé's escribanos; subtle variations in this scheme used by Yancuictlalpan's escribanos follow. Many differences fall into the realm of insignificance, if taken by themselves. Patience with the minute details rewards the reader with an intimate appreciation of escribano traditions internal to each community: what emerges is the sense of allied yet distinct identities. Demonstrating patterns of difference between escribanos in two adjacent altepetl highlights a surprisingly high degree of internal consistency in each.[17]

Both standard wills begin with the Stage 3 formula "Jesus, Mary, and Joseph," but they specify the date in different ways.[18] This apparently inconsequential difference reveals a difference in logistics. In Yancuictlalpan, escribanos put the date at the beginning; in San Bartolomé escribanos write the date in at the end. In Yancuictlalpan, escribanos specify the date as they begin to write the testament, which means it cannot be changed after writing it out.[19] Clues like differences in ink color amplify the story: escribanos in San Bartolomé often add the date somewhat later, probably when the testator actually died or when the testament was materially sent in to Metepec to be registered. The implication is that escribanos in San Bartolomé have a unique flexibility, essentially leaving the date unwritten until registered with a date favorable to unrevealed interests.

Because these fiscalía documents don't enter the colonial bureaucracy unless they are pulled into litigation, paired with the fact that land is rarely ever sold at this time, potential conflicts of interest on this topic are specific to San Bartolomé and implicate the fiscalía's escribanos.[20] The phrasing for the exact date in both traditions is very similar in each case, but in Yancuictlalpan escribanos keep more Nahuatl vocabulary, using the Nahuatl *metztli* (month) omitted in San Bartolomé. Escribanos in Yancuictlalpan go as far as using the precolonial calendrical language alongside the specific name of the Spanish month, still saying *xihuitl tlapohualli* (year count)—breathtaking.

The Trinity, featured in the heading proper of wills, is the same in every detail in both altepetl. This section is how escribanos launch into the body of the will, appearing in Yancuictlalpan after the date and ushering in the preamble. While San Bartolomé's escribanos at this point write, "I begin my testament," escribanos in Yancuictlalpan retain the old formula, "Know all who see." Further, in a wording widely distributed in the Toluca Valley, Yancuictlalpan's escribanos add *memorandum* to *testament*, perhaps alluding to a dual metaphoric structure identified in classical Nahuatl.[21]

In the next standard will formula testators identify who they are. They name their spouse and affirm their relationship to their community. Escribanos use basically the same form in both places. However, notaries in San Bartolomé used the term *altepetl* somewhat later and less consistently: more evidence of the hypothesized political shift; self-identification as an independent altepetl came after originally self-identifying as a tlaxilacalli subunit of a full altepetl.

Escribanos next use the legal formula of the body and soul. In Yancuictlalpan, they retain an older Nahuatl expression, as opposed to the loanword *cuerpo* that became dominant in San Bartolomé. Also, escribanos in Yancuictlalpan never show any sign of confusion about whether the soul or the body is sick, like the Romero school in San Bartolomé.

Ideas about death, found in the subsequent section of formulas in the standard model, tell us how differently adjacent pueblos practiced and/or emphasized particular rites. Death-toll bell ringing and belonging to the Virgin, both important invariable elements of the standard formula in San Bartolomé, are completely missing in Yancuictlalpan. Instead we see an embellished reference to the testator's death, another elaboration found commonly in Nahuatl-language wills. Escribanos in the valley as documented by Pizzigoni are known to place the soul directly in the hands of God or Christ, also a local preference in Yancuictlalpan. Specifically, they invoke the hands of Christ. For contrast, the reader may remember San Bartolomé's escribanos instead name the Virgin (meaning the Virgin's cofradía). Other burial rights also differ. In Yancuictlalpan the offering of half a *real* for the holy places of Jerusalem is a standard form for the valley; in San Bartolomé it is entirely missing. And in San Bartolomé escribanos do not mention a shroud, while in Yancuictlalpan they use a modest formula, saying that God will provide the shroud, using traditional Nahuatl phrases having to do with wrapping.[22]

Other comparisons of note relate to the churchyard, prayers, and priests. Escribanos in Yancuictlalpan use the verb *tlaocolia* (to favor with) in association with the burial place, always in the churchyard (using native vocabulary), whereas escribanos in San Bartolomé give much more exact locations and rarely if ever mention the churchyard. In San Bartolomé the priest always "favors" the testator with a Mass or responsory prayer, while in Yancuictlalpan the priest is not mentioned.[23] Further, in Yancuictlalpan, the rite requested is always a low Mass. People in Yancuictlalpan also direct priests to say their funeral Mass within a given time after their death, which people in San Bartolomé do not.

The last part of standard formulas can impart significant information. While escribanos in San Bartolomé end the body portion of the standard model with a statement, "I have finished [using *tzonquixtia*] my testament," the equivalent in Yancuictlalpan is, "This is all that I have recorded [using *machiotia*]." Ending formulas reveal distinct roles for secular and Church officials between altepetl. Names of witnesses present at the telling of the will are officials of the community and given in a descending rank order. In San Bartolomé the officers are always fiscalía officials, whereas in Yancuictlalpan secular cabildo officials are included and even emphasized. Even the notary's position in Yancuictlalpan is clearly defined as escribano of the república (the cabildo), not the fiscalía.[24]

A mother might leave property to a nephew and then warn, "My command is to be carried out and executed." The oral quality of the texts reveals the adherence to Nahuatl form. Repeating oral appeals, called exhortations, appear somewhat less consistently than in San Bartolomé, and they vary a bit more in Yancuictlalpan. But in general, exhortations after commands and bequests in Yancuictlalpan are similar to those in San Bartolomé.

Overall, comparing how two communities reflect local escribano customs, we see distinct practices, despite belonging to a common tradition. Many points of departure concern small but invariant differences in a community's notarial style. In terms of actual practice, whether mentioned or not, or mentioned in a special local way by escribanos, there may not be strong differences in the way people celebrated their beloved dead. On the other hand, differences in exist-ing social spheres can be involved as well, such as the mention of two specific cofradías or evidence of a stronger fiscalía.

In both cases, we see each escribano community's concern for keeping its own practices and asserting its own identity through the meticulous reproduction of a local form. Comparing San Bartolomé and Yancuictlalpan, we see that the lat-ter uses much more indigenous vocabulary and older, traditional formulations. Based on this evidence, the Yancuictlalpan style is even more conservative and more like that of the traditional Nahuatl-language testament style in general. Even by the mid-eighteenth century, their standard form would have seemed rather archaic in the context of the Toluca Valley as a whole. Since samples from the early eighteenth-century local style are available for San Bartolomé but not yet found for Yancuictlalpan, it cannot be absolutely asserted that the style of the latter rests as firmly on earlier precedent as it does in San Bartolomé. Given the date and the way Yancuictlalpan's escribanos use a scheme that repeats even older Nahuatl vocabulary and structure than San Bartolomé, I fully expect that it rests on precedent as yet undocumented.

Given the relatively smaller number of testaments preserved, the notarial corps represents only two escribanos who wrote the eleven extant Nahuatl-language wills of Yancuictlalpan. Marcos Antonio wrote the first three, from 1809 and 1810. Isidro de la Trinidad, apparent successor to the office, wrote the remaining wills from 1812 to 1825. Isidro clearly succeeded Marcos, perhaps on his death, as escribano offices lasted much longer than others. Their career patterns as cabildo officers appear to differ from escribanos in the fiscalía, but without more data, I leave that an open question. Virtually no differences be-tween Marcos's and Isidro's manuscripts appear beyond the smallest details of orthography and the fact that Isidro was especially prone to leaving slots entirely unfilled (imagine the blanks on a form). Both escribanos were rather unpredictable with word-final -tl. Sometimes they use the standard -tl, some-times the -tli also seen in San Bartolomé, and sometimes even the strange -lt. The very close style and form tells us that Marcos trained Isidro in this small community; a family connection has not yet been established.

To Isidro de la Trinidad fell the task of writing a will for the woman of his household. When Juliana Viviana died in 1823, Isidro wrote her testament, and she tells us she is his wife.[25] In terms of social data her will doesn't connect kin-ship networks like the will of Cipriano Gordiano's mother in San Bartolomé. But her testament does reinforce the important classification of escribanos as members of a middle class or typical, not outstandingly wealthy members of their communities.

The most notable aspect of Isidro de la Trinidad is that he could also write in Spanish.[26] In fact, he wrote his wife's will in Spanish. His precision and skill in both languages astounds. Thus, it can be said that Yancuictlalpan's known wills illustrate a notarial lineage that shifts over to Spanish with a Nahua escribano who writes fluently in Nahuatl.

OCOTITLAN'S STANDARD WILL

Escribanos in Ocotitlan mainly shifted into working in Spanish by this time. I only recovered three post-1800 wills in Nahuatl from Ocotitlan. Because Spanish dominates in this altepetl, this small grouping of samples, from 1801, 1810, and 1813, proves most useful for purposes of triangulation to generalize a model.[27] Ocotitlan's Spanish-language manuscripts are discussed in detail in chapter 2, showing how the Nahuatl language formed the structure of the escribanos' Spanish. In terms of the Nahuatl tradition presented here, after the typhoid epidemic of 1813, no more Nahuatl-language texts appear. The following template illustrates a standardized Nahuatl format for Ocotitlan:

Jesus, Mary, and Joseph.

Today, (day) the __th of (month) of [the year] 18__.

I take as my sign the precious revered name of God the father, God his precious [revered] son, and God the Holy Spirit. May it be done, amen. Jesus [, Mary, and Joseph.]

    Here I named _____ begin [or issue] my testament; the name of my spouse is _____; we are citizens here in Santa María Magdalena Ocotitlan; Although my body (using *-tlallo -çoquiyo*) is sick, my soul [is sound and] is just awaiting death, [from which no one can flee]. When [my precious revered father] God has passed sentence on me, I place my soul entirely in his hands, for I am his creation [or he created me], and I say first of all that half a *real* is to be given for Holy Jerusalem. [My statement is to be carried out.] And I say that God will provide my shroud (using a word related to *quimiloa*). My statement is to be carried out. And I say that they are to designate my grave for me in the churchyard (*teopan ithualco*) [or just it is to be in the churchyard]. My statement is to be carried out. And I say that the help of my soul will be a low Mass [or responsory prayer] to be said for me [within twenty days]. My statement is to be carried out.

Bequests to inheritors.

[And I say that] this is all that I have recorded [before God. I have nothing; I am very poor]. And I say that [I greatly implore] those who are to be my executors to speak for me; they are _____ and _____. If they do it God will reward them. [The witnesses are:] Fiscal of the holy church, _____; fiscal teniente _____. [topile mayor, ____.] Notary, _____

By comparison, it will be seen that the Ocotitlan model shares a great deal with that of Yancuictlalpan and by the same token differs greatly from that of San Bartolomé (granted overall commonalities for all three). Escribanos write with more Nahuatl vocabulary and more conservative conventions in Yancuictlalpan and Ocotitlan than in San Bartolomé—aside from certain features the first two share as opposed to the third, such as putting the date first instead of last. The first two altepetl in a meaningful way represent a unit of contrast against San Bartolomé. That said, some differences between Yancuictlalpan and Ocotitlan surface too.

To begin, let's look at a quick summary of the escribanos' traits as shared in Yancuictlalpan and Ocotitlan, as opposed to San Bartolomé. Both put the date at the beginning. Both use a Nahuatl phrase instead of *cuerpo* for body and have an orthodox version of the statement about body and soul. Both traditions put the soul directly in the hands of the deity. Both omit bells for death rites. Both have a Jerusalem offering of half a *real*.[28] Both notarial corps mention the shroud and use preexisting indigenous vocabulary for it. Both call specifically for burial in the churchyard, using Nahuatl vocabulary. Both traditions specify a time period within which the rites are to be performed. And both end the substance of the will with the same formula.

Despite strong similarities, a local form in Ocotitlan can also be distinguished from the Yancuictlalpan model. Escribanos give the date using less Nahuatl vocabulary; in this Ocotitlan and San Bartolomé traditions converge. Yancuictlalpan's phrase "know all who see" is lacking; instead one finds, as in San Bartolomé, "I begin my testament" (or sometimes "I issue it"). The formula for describing death also differs. Both written traditions in Ocotitlan and Yancuictlalpan require a specific time within which their requested rites are to be performed by the priest, but the time frame itself differs. In Ocotitlan escribanos ask for fulfillment of requests in the indigenous intervals of twenty days (a typical vigesimal period, based on the Nahua base 20 system of calculation), while in Yancuictlalpan escribanos require a less stringent time frame: a month or two. Local officials serve as the witnesses in both cases. But in Yancuictlalpan, mainly secular cabildo officials serve as witnesses; in Ocotitlan Church fiscalía officials serve as witnesses, as in San Bartolomé. Evidence of an active fiscalía shows complex cellular bodies of internal self-governance in Ocotitlan, an altepetl transitioning into Spanish for recordkeeping. Thus, even escribanos who can be said to follow similar formulas can be distinguished by differing practices and altepetl-level distinctions.

Three different escribanos wrote the Nahuatl-language testaments in Ocotitlan; they each created one of the three Nahuatl-language wills in this corpus. Santos Alberto, Sebastián Fabián López, and Pablo Leonardo continued to write in Nahuatl, even though, as we shall see in the standard model, Ocotitlan's notarial tradition had largely already moved to writing in Spanish. All three notaries followed the general local model very closely. Occasionally, they leave a word unsaid or a slot vacant. Sebastián and Pablo use the full traditional phrase *noyolia nanimatzin* (my spirit [from the Nahuatl] and soul [from the Spanish]), whereas Santos Alberto uses the Spanish loanword alone.[29] Thus, at first glance, notarial models in Yancuictlalpan and Ocotitlan look alike; on close inspection local differences emerge. Overall, in terms of divergences in local notarial form, in Ocotitlan most notarial phrasings appear in instances both more conservative than Yancuic Halpan, and like San Bartolomé, less conservative.[30]

Taken in sum, local cultures of Nahua writing were not imposed but instead nurtured, changed, and reproduced from within, a sheltered place from where they made norms new. Culture-making in the realm of escribanos (and other fiscalía leaders hidden from imperial legal structures) was performed by durable altepetl-based institutions that supported local needs. These cultural practices relied on enactment by men; anchored by necessity to known written records, many historical studies stop here. But the richness of the Independence corpus allows us to shift to the next chapter, in which we discuss how women not only participated fully in terms of religious practices but also often predominated.

5

DEATH RITES, LOCAL RELIGION, AND WOMEN ON CHURCH GROUNDS

S AN BARTOLOMÉ'S main *square* forms a semicircle, which somehow explains everything. An arched stone doorway leads onto church grounds. After visiting other parishes in the west, north, and east of the central volcano, I expected to see similar grounds, paved over with pink brick, bare, open to the sky. But even from a distance you see large trees; up close, the canopy feels tall, though the shaggy-bark redwoods appear less than a hundred years old. I was surprised to see plants at all, much less trees. But this was the altepetl where at Mexican Independence people asked for copal, date palm, cypress, and *pirul* pepper trees at burial. If any community from that period would hug their trees, would resist deforestation over time, it would be San Bartolomé.

The hands that tend these grounds form a little Eden. Pears grow plump. A fruit that looked like nectarine grew among the yellow *nisperos*, various types of *calabacitas* (squash), roses, lilies, giant yellow dahlias, and narrow-leafed eucalyptus. All found a home under the canopy of trees. Ferns grow from the mossy bark; their yellows, greens, and browns contrasted with the silver lichen on the north side of trunks. One groundskeeper called the trees *cedros, truenos,* and *gigantes.* I didn't see copal, so I asked the municipal historian if he could introduce me to their copal trees. Don Pedro said they don't grow there, that they only grow in more tropical climates. When I pursued the question, he felt sure the copal never grew there.

FIGURE 19. San Bartolomé's canopy of trees, as seen contemporaneously from sanctuary entrance. Photo by Melton-Villanueva.

This statement contradicts the Independence archive, when the copal grew in groves. By looking at ritual, we find trees. The chart in figure 22 shows evidence of copal. When examined closely, the numbers link women most strongly to copal trees in the Independence era. We will find that this change in the environment impacted women most, in terms of their personal choices in death, for burial rites were allied with trees. Sometimes we have to turn over leaves to find treasure, and so we begin to see the contribution of women.

Before presenting the ways in which Nahua women intersected with Church rites, I begin with a larger context that emerges from the Independence-era archive: indigenous women as culture makers. Women in the previous chapters have been largely invisible to my description of Nahua society. But turning to look at the trees, the prayers, the testament issuers, we meet the other half of the population. This chapter describes ceremonial traditions that continued on church grounds in dynamic, local, living ways: burial trees, time calculations, the function of indoor vs. outdoor space, changing Masses, bells, and local cofradías. The proportion of who participated in these rites has changed along gender lines, allowing a new perspective on the contribution of Nahua women in the forging of local cultural traditions. Women worked alongside men, participating in their long-standing rituals and actively forming new ones.

WOMEN'S WILL MAKING

As surprising as the persistence of men's deep culture of writing is that women issued the most testaments in this period. Figure 20 shows the rate at which women and men left instructions via formal testaments, written down by their altepetl's escribanos. Women represent the majority of testators in all altepetl of the Independence archive, not only in San Bartolomé, as previously reported.[1] Since typhoid does not discriminate by gender, the fact that women become the majority of testators in this period cannot be attributed to the concurrent epidemic cycle described in chapter 1. Further, table 3 includes the number of wills written in both Nahuatl and Spanish; thus women's predominance in the traditions cannot be attributed to the changes involved in the transition to Spanish. How the crisis of Independence affected Nahua men's presence, or absence, in their communities deserves further research, for the details remain as yet unclear. What can be said, taking the Nahuatl-language wills of San Bartolomé alone, is that sixty-three of the ninety-five wills were made by women.

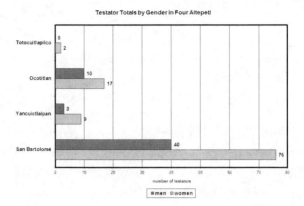

FIGURE 20. Graph of the gender of people who left wills, broken down by altepetl.

This nearly two-to-one majority of 66 percent women holds true across the testator group of all four altepetl.[2]

Nahua women, faced with death, issued testaments throughout the colonial period; taking the long view, women's predominance at Independence falls above the average but appears to not actually be out of character. Women's testamentary production is acknowledged as large but generally not considered a majority, which occludes the total proportion. Women's wills are nearly 40 percent and men's wills are 60 percent in the total range of known wills from indigenous communities of the colonial period; let's examine those numbers. In the earliest collection of testaments, the late sixteenth-century Testaments of Culhuacan, women represent nearly 38 percent of testators. In a large sample of eighteenth-century testaments of Toluca, the wills by women made up about 37 percent of the total wills made near Toluca proper and 39 percent in the combined Calimaya/Tepemaxalco double altepetl.[3] Various parts of the Rojas Rabiela collection, which includes a greater geographic and temporal sample, shows women acting as from 27 percent to 41 percent of testators.[4] Being more regional, the numbers for the last two collections average out the places where women *take a leading role* in testament making. For example, in Pizzigoni's Toluca collection, women in central Calimaya outnumber men as testators, at 56 percent.[5] In other words, Nahua women throughout the colonial period participated widely in the legal strategy to pass on their resources, at times outnumbering men's contribution.

Thus, the Independence archive helps put women's overall participation into perspective. We can now clearly see that indigenous women participated at near-full potential in the testamentary tradition, in most places and most times known. To quote Lisa Sousa, women's sources are "not extraordinary."[6] Variations, such as women's predominance, can now be understood to represent local patterns hidden within the regional sampling, as in the groundbreaking work by Pizzigoni, for example.[7] Geographic variations, or differences between neighboring altepetl, highlight the strength of the Independence numbers: these data sets represent whole communities. Another influence on the data comes in patterns of archiving, as many collections rely on testaments found within litigation. This means that wills were plucked out of their place of origin (parish archives) and placed into court proceedings as evidence. These legal tactics could have somewhat favored men's wills in the later colony, chosen for the audience of a Spanish court. Regional collections may not necessarily describe the norms of their individual communities.

As a legal vehicle, the testament can be said to have two main purposes: to request and pay for a Mass for the soul of the person issuing the will and to formally register the inheritors of their property. Testament making was a common practice, including even those with no property to bequeath. When someone died with no property, a testament could be issued just to give instructions for a Mass in their name. This means that testaments, as sources, tend to include all economic sectors of Nahua society.

Nahua women commonly issued wills, a trend that remained widespread throughout the colonial period. Women were always a significant proportion and usually a numerical minority; in other times and places, compared to men, women did predominate. Against this background, it can be said that women's participation in the Independence archive may reflect altepetl and tlaxilacalli traditions also seen elsewhere in the colonial period: not a sea change but an expression of existing patterns. Local variation, as in this case the predominance of women making wills, has until now been obscured by not just gendered assumption but also the lack of sizable data from altepetl, which this work corrects.

However, precisely because people could die without leaving property, it should be noted that predominance in testament making on its own does not necessarily correlate with predominance in land ownership. To disambiguate actual land tenure, figure 21 shows the ownership of land by people actually leaving property to heirs.

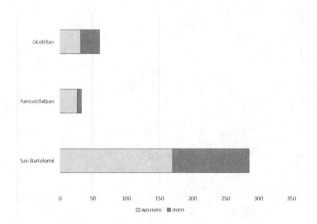

FIGURE 21. Ownership across altepetl of all land types, 1799–1832. I count a property as one parcel, even when subdivided and left to multiple heirs.

Thus, based on the number of properties that people described in their wills, women owned the majority of land. The largest and therefore most reliable sample, from San Bartolomé, in which women made 66 percent of the wills, documents that women owned 59 percent of the properties. In Ocotitlan, where women left 63 percent of the testaments, women owned 53 percent of all land bequeathed in this period. In the altepetl of Yancuictlalpan, where women left 75 percent of the testaments, women owned 82 percent of the land. Thus, Nahua women in this time and place not only represented a majority of people leaving wills but also owned the most land.

WOMEN'S STATUS AS CULTURE MAKER

Nahua women's contribution to Mexican society and culture can no longer be sidestepped. The data are clear. Women participated fully as landowners and testament makers, which leaves us with an understanding that women also moved within the vibrant civic cultures described in the previous chapters. This was hinted at when I only found the connection between father and son escribanos through the testament of their wife and mother.

Yet if we were to form our idea of Nahua society based entirely on the Nahua cabildo or fiscalía presented in previous chapters, the assumption would be that women played no significant role in the creation and maintenance of indigenous society. As we move into the world of prayer and devotion, women become visible as we glimpse the way people make meaning of their lives. The difference lies in the sector of society: the more local the records, the more women are documented. In the cabildo or fiscalía, gender plays a significant factor—only men serve in those official positions at Independence. This is not a change that happened with the National period—cabildo officials of the colonial period were men. Just as I have shown that the Spanish monarchy (despite its laws to the contrary) actually fostered indigenous cultural institutions in a way the National period did not, I follow this line of thinking to show how the colonial Church, in its decentralized practices, continued to offer indigenous communities a venue for local organizing and acquisition of status that included (and still includes) the work of women.

Women never stopped working; their "official" work just became less visible to Spanish bureaucrats outside their altepetl subunits. To understand this trajectory inward, it is important to know that official power became gendered male in the early colonial period, to the point that women's official Nahua titles, such as *cihuatepixque* (female civil officials), disappear with the growing influence of Spanish colonial institutions.[8] Sarah Cline attests that Juana Tiacapan served as the ward elder, *tlaxilacalleh*, for Coatlan in the sixteenth century.[9] Susan Schroeder finds that Chimalpahin mentions *heuhetque* who were women elders.[10] Susan Kellogg shows that this phenomenon extended to women who worked as administrators in the marketplace of Tenochtitlan; as Spanish men took control of lucrative production and distribution networks, administrative posts converted to the exclusive prerogative of men.[11] Rebecca Horn shows that women frequently served as witnesses in early colonial period Coyoacan land sales.[12] Edward Osowski finds gender-parallelism at work in the eighteenth century: women and men paired together as traveling offering-collectors for saints.[13] Women in the early colonial period appear commonly as witnesses in testaments. This changes over time to the point that women are never listed as official witnesses: the Independence archive lists not one woman as witness.

These examples show that indigenous women in many places continued to hold local status within their communities early in the colonial period, but everywhere power intersected with Spanish legal expectations—whether as legal witnesses, executors for a will, or as a local official—women eventually lost the opportunity to perform formal positions.[14] To find women's work requires a large number of sources, records made inside local communities by their own escribanos. Active subunits like the fiscalía of chapter 1, as cellular strategy, may prove to be a factor that fostered women's leadership, integrating their political labor into the altepetl and documenting their lives.

BURIAL TREES

Despite its disappearance, copal did once exist here, in a special relationship with San Bartolomé (figure 22). Since don Pedro's memories barely reached back one hundred years to the Mexican Revolution, the historian's link to a social memory of trees—two hundred years past—ended before his time. Today they no longer grow on church grounds, even though most people who asked to be buried by trees at the turn of the nineteenth century chose the parish's copal trees as their resting place.

Women enter the record here in an interesting way. Nahua women participated in the tradition of choosing their burial trees in an even greater proportion than their overall predominance in the record.[15] Of the thirty-eight requests recorded, women make up 68 percent of the people asking for specific trees. In addition, women are much more strongly associated with the copal

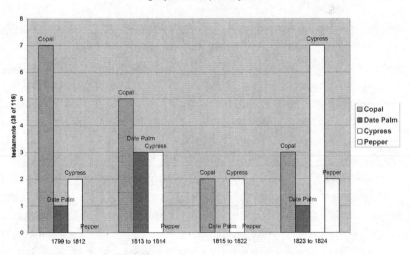

FIGURE 22. Graph demonstrating the species of trees used in burial rites over time.

trees. Thirteen of the seventeen people who asked for copal were women, so the decline of this species impacted women more than men. This association shows women responsible for over 76 percent of the burial rites by copal, linking them with an overall conservative impulse not unlike that of the escribanos.

A rough timeline emerges for copal's disappearance. By the time of the typhoid epidemic in 1813, date palm and cypress trees increased their presence in people's wills, without *yet* supplanting the copal. A few years pass and the copal and cypress become evenly represented in people's Church burials. By 1823 the cypress overtakes copal to become the most preferred tree for burial rites. Over time, the copal declines to the point that cypress predominates. The copal trees could already be showing signs of environmental stress, which could be why a new tree, the pepper, was introduced into this tradition. While new trees appear in burial rites, the reasons for these particular species' appearance remains yet unclear and could be related to ritual restrictions and demands of colonial trade. What I can say conclusively is how people at this time change their requests; I cannot yet make linkages to likely environmental factors such as growing aridity that would have limited the range of copal, but new research points in this direction.[16]

San Bartolomé's custom of burial "by the copal trees" originates at least a century earlier. Early in the previous century, a father and son both left testaments, asking to be buried at the same site near a copal tree, *copalquahuitl*.[17] Sacred trees and copal's special significance to Nahuas can also be traced to an even earlier time, before Spanish colonialism.[18] The tree's resin-blood and the tree itself, as depicted in codices such as shown in figure 23, held strong influence on the ordering of space from the earliest times.

So many people in San Bartolomé asked for burial near the copal trees that they must have ended up with a grove of them, just to accommodate everyone.[19] Not only did burial trees endure through the Independence period but also a new tree entered the pantheon. Overall, copal was the most favored, but the illustrated chronology in figure 22 allows us to see how copal use drops off over time. This is not to say that the tradition itself was waning. On the contrary, other trees took the place of the copal, gaining more precedence, expanding in quantity the variety of species: the *tlatzcan* cypress, the *icçotl* date palm. And a species new to the church grounds, called by the loanword *pirul*, is known to have been introduced as seedling plantings throughout the Pacific Rim to compete with the Dutch East Indian production of black pepper.[20] *Pirul* could have been adopted at this time as an alternative source for "white fragrant resin,"

FIGURE 23. A page from the precolonial Codex Féjervary-Mayer showing trees
associated with the cardinal directions. (Illustration by John Pohl.)

which, like copal, had many uses.[21] The reference to specific species of trees paints
a carefully defined landscape that (with a change in species) can also be said
to describe the grounds today. Different species of trees correspond to unique
places on church grounds, not to an undefined wooded area.

Burials outdoors appear nearly universal in neighboring altepetl too, but
only the people of San Bartolomé included trees in their burial rites.[22] Even
this type of burial, in the churchyard—irrespective of the rites with trees—
could be seen as something new, for in the eighteenth century there is evidence
that the majority of burials occurred inside the church.[23] Further, a simulta-
neous change in language occurred; the word *cemetery* was introduced late in the

Independence period and found in Spanish-language testaments but not in the ones written in Nahuatl. Of the twenty-one people that left Spanish wills, four use the word *cemetery*. The first incidence was in 1817, and then the word appears three more times in 1824 to designate the cemetery portal and the cemetery proper in the phrase "dentro del sementerio."[24] The term *patio* (churchyard) was not used in this altepetl. The introduction of the word *cemetery* into the Spanish at this time appears due to external factors such as the Campos Santos ordinances.[25] However, nearly all these burials took place outdoors even before the term *sementerio* gained currency. At no point does the Spanish loanword for *cemetery* get mentioned in Nahuatl. One's sense is that the shift comes from internal forces—by the time of the 1820 Campos Santos reforms, which restrict indoor Church burials in response to growing awareness of disease transmission, the outdoor tradition had already been long established. Despite the new near-universality of outdoor burial, whether called *churchyard* or *cemetery*, only in San Bartolomé do people reveal their affinity with specific species of trees for burial.

WOMEN'S RITES

At Independence women's participation in other Church rituals changed also, in that now women paid for the most sumptuous types of Masses. Following the greater participation in testament making, women in this period reverse earlier proportions by asking for more elaborate rites in the Church setting than men. In the previous century, men asked for proportionately more elaborate and expensive services than women.[26]

Specifically, the types of Masses women request change over time, a change that illustrates how at this time women participated significantly in the ritual life of the Church. In the communities covered by this study, men and women still ask for a virtually obligatory Mass. But in the best-documented altepetl of San Bartolomé Tlatelolco, people begin to use a two-level system in which the numbers of people requesting Masses and those requesting only responsory prayers are almost equal.

This switch in the type of rites, identified in the Independence archive, contrasts to the previous eighteenth-century Toluca Valley. In the previous century, when a Mass remained nearly universal, overall only a few people requested the cheaper responsory prayer, *responso*, instead of a Mass. And a small fraction

asked for no such service. By Independence, people begin to ask for the responsory prayer just as much as the Mass, with women preferring the more extra-
vagant Mass.

Not all altepetl trended toward responsory prayers. Women in Yancuictlalpan represent a clear numerical case of majority in requesting Masses in
church. All twelve testators ask for a Mass: nine women, three men. They all
ask for Masses, so not much has changed over time in terms of the type of rites.
What has changed in Yancuictlalpan is the proportion of women that ask for
customary Masses to be performed in their name.

What women do in San Bartolomé presents a much more complex picture. Of the one hundred and fifteen people who left testaments,[27] fifty-eight
requests came for responsos in San Bartolomé. Most people ask for this sim-
plest rite, at a rate of 59 percent women and 41 percent men.[28] The other fifty-
six testators in San Bartolomé chose the more elaborate Masses (as opposed
to responsos). Within this group, 70 percent of the women and 30 percent of
the men choose Masses.[29] That women predominated in respect to ordering
Masses in church reflects two dimensions. In some localities it is the result of
the increase in women leaving testaments.[30] In the largest case study of San
Bartolomé, however, women prevail not only in absolute numbers of Masses
but also in the proportion of people asking for Masses as opposed to responsory prayers. In the case of rites in San Bartolomé, the change is qualitative as
well as quantitative.

Both responsory prayers and Masses were becoming an option in other places
as well. In the altepetl of Ocotitlan, twenty-five people—seventeen women and
eight men—requested rites of some kind.[31] For comparison, seven people asked
for responsory prayers, at a gender breakdown of about 57 percent women and
38 percent men.[32] In the remaining eighteen requests for rites, 72 percent women
and 28 percent men requested the more elaborate Masses.[33]

The significance of these numbers is that in both San Bartolomé and Ocotitlan a far higher percentage of women than men ordered Masses as opposed to
responsory prayers. This surpasses a numerical predominance in overall participation by describing the type of rite each person chooses. Further, it is notable
that the only person in the whole archive to request a high Mass was Margarita
Feliciana of San Bartolomé, a woman. To reiterate, women were not only issuing
more wills at Independence but also participating in more elaborate rites than
men, overturning previous patterns. These data invite us to reframe our assumptions about women's participation in both testament making and ritual.

FIGURE 24. The new sanctuary in San Bartolomé dates from the
late nineteenth century. Photo by Melton-Villanueva.

Overall more than twice as many women as men chose Masses, implying
that at this time women either had more resources than men or were more
involved in the ritual life of the Church, or both. This prominence does not
bring Nahua women back into the ranks as witnesses nor are they given official
honorary titles aside from *doña*. But in the matter of death rites we see women
both retaining and expanding local custom.

RITUAL TIMETABLES

When María Antonia gave each of her two sons a piece of land that yields an
almud of maize, she asked them to split the costs for her low Mass to be said
in her parish, "Declaro q.e han de Pagar una Misa resada en esta Paroquia De
metepeque entre ambos dos hermanos" (I declare that they are to pay, split between both brothers, for a low Mass in this parish of Metepec).[34] In a gesture

common for her community in Ocotitlan, she also set a specific timetable during which this was all supposed to happen.

People leaving wills at Independence calculate time in specific ways, establishing ritual timetables for their personal funereal Masses, and in Ocotitlan gender appears to be a factor. The altepetl of Ocotitlan and Yancuictlalpan can be distinguished from San Bartolomé on this topic of timetables. People in the former two altepetl give definite time frames, a specified time after they die, in which the priest is supposed to celebrate the Masses they request. In Yancuictlalpan, every person making a will, with only one exception, specifies a time limit for their Mass to be performed. Most say within one month; a few say within two months. In Ocotitlan, people are even more particular in their measure of time and choose varied schedules. In this altepetl, most people gave a time limit of twenty days, though a few set the time at fifteen days or one or two months. And women in Ocotitlan are much more concerned about setting a time frame than men, by a ratio well over 2:1.[35]

These clear boundaries may spring from a real concern about their payments and requests not being honored in a timely manner. Someone made a notation on Ana María's will: "se aplicó misa resada dec 22 'or" (a low Mass was applied dec 22 'or).[36] Given that her testament was issued in January 1801, it took a full year before the priest showed up, was paid, performed his duty, and applied the payment. It could be that the priest only came around once a year, but complaints had arisen in Mexico City in earlier times about clergy not doing their duty after being paid.[37] Annotated by priests, eighteenth-century Toluca Valley testaments imply that Masses regionally were performed promptly on payment. Either way, the payment could often be delayed for months or years after the testator's death, which delays the Mass. I cannot yet be sure that the time limits tell us anything definitive about the relationship between the community, its payments, and its itinerant priest. The specific phrasing implies these kinds of stipulations were a long-established feature of the tradition of Yancuictlalpan and Ocotitlan, though it was something not often seen in other Toluca Valley texts of earlier times. What I can say for certain is that these time frames existed in some communities and not in others, and it deserves further inquiry.

What this temporal caveat discloses are local concepts of time-counting in Ocotitlan. People most commonly set a time frame of twenty days, an apparent vestige of precolonial systems of calculating and marking time. The time frame cannot be correlated to individual preferences of the escribano, as Pablo Leonardo, the escribano who wrote most of the wills that do not set a time frame at all, also wrote wills for people who asked for twenty-day, one-month, and two-month periods. Women preferred not only time frames in general but also the twenty-day period by a ratio of 2:1.[38] This proportion represents their predominance in the record as well as their full participation in and understanding of vigesimal methods of calculation.

Feliciana Petrona's will says, "Se de me dira huna miSa Rresada dentro de veinte dias" (A low Mass will be said for me within twenty days).[39] A vigesimal system, with twenty as the base number, appeared in many aspects of precolonial calendars, especially in the twenty-day "month" featured on the Aztec calendar, or sun stone. Particularly striking is that these twenty-day schedules were also used in most of the Spanish-language wills in Ocotitlan; people continued using Nahuatl concepts to determine time in Spanish. This feature of Ocotitlan wills implies a local survival of a precolonial vigesimal system. Today, vigesimal mathematical/temporal cycles like "veintenas" continue to overlap with the dominant, fully Spanish/Christian calendrical reckoning.

Other concepts also influence the day counts. In Alejandro Marcos's will issued in San Bartolomé in 1824, he asked for a responsory prayer to be said in fifteen days, "p.a el SuFragio de mi alma Sera un rEsponso dentro de quince dias." This pattern also turns up in Ocotitlan, in the testaments of three women. To this day, in Spanish-speaking countries you say *ocho días* (8 days) for a week and *quince días* (15 days) for two weeks or a fortnight because the present day is counted as well as the same day at the other end (for example, this Monday as well as next Monday). Thus, the use of *quince días* clearly shows Spanish influence. This stands alongside, and is affirmed by, the base 5 calculations that many mathematicians consider to be at the heart of the indigenous vigesimal twenty-day term. Indeed, without more specific evidence, the concurrent use of a local indigenous ritual-agricultural calendar at Independence for broader purposes cannot be completely ruled out.

CHURCH RITES EVOLVE

As late as the 1820s, people used their testaments as the forum in which to request their personal death rites—Masses or prayers for the dead to be celebrated in the community of the church—but the resilient bond that ties last Masses to last wills at this time shows signs of decline. In this process, the escribano's relationship to the dying, as the one documenting the requests, may also be changing. Religious services of some kind remain important to nearly everyone in the Independence archive, but the Mass for the dead is no longer standard in every altepetl. In San Bartolomé, everyone, with one exception, requests Masses or responsos, as all but two do in Ocotitlan. In Yancuictlalpan, everyone asks for a low Mass, as did the small sample of testators of Totocuitlapilco. Thus the connection between testaments and religious services was still strong, but the services were changing.

Overall, the perceptible shift away from wanting Masses in the eighteenth century to wanting more responsory prayers at Independence shows strong geographic variation among altepetl and appears to correlate with disease cycles. During epidemics, responsory prayers increase, reinforcing the notion that this change is ushered in as an emergency measure or an attempt to reduce expenditures during times of stress. Though people in Ocotitlan generally continued to request low Masses, a significant shift to responsory prayers happened during the epidemic of 1813.[40] People in San Bartolomé showed the strongest shift toward requesting responsory prayers, a trend even more pronounced during the epidemics of 1813 and from 1823 to 1824. To keep things in San Bartolomé in proportion: responsory prayers outnumbered Masses by only two requests, a nearly even split of fifty-eight to fifty-six. But this count for Masses includes only one high Mass. Thus, high Masses, the most elaborate public rites which once had been frequent in some parts of the Toluca Valley, became rare in the Independence altepetl. Yet in some communities, such as Yancuictlalpan and Totocuitlapilco, everyone continues to request a low Mass. When Juliana Viviana of Yancuictlalpan asked for an uncategorized Mass, "la misa Se me a de aplicar" (the Mass should be dedicated to me), we learn from the priest calendaring her testament that by "la misa" she meant a low Mass: a *misa rezada* had become the standard.[41] Even in places where Masses were still chosen as prayers for the dead, these were low Masses, not high Masses.

At some point the purpose of the testament, and by extension the escribano, changed. When I interviewed the municipal historian, he showed me a handwritten will dated 1933.[42] The testament's yellowed paper seemed a little longer than what I'd consider legal size, and the paper felt as thin as a sheet of blue-lined college bond. The will's testator reveals his father's name, Pablo de Jesús; this name reflects the last generation to use indigenous naming patterns.[43] Pablo de Jesús's children shift to Spanish-style naming patterns in San

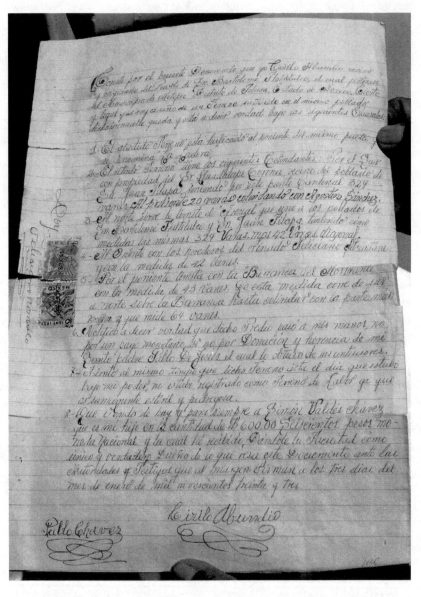

FIGURE 25. Don Pedro's family testament, San Bartolomé, 1933.
Photo by Melton-Villanueva.

Bartolomé. Thus, as late as the turn of the twentieth century, this testator's generation begins to adopt Spanish surnames, instead of the pair of saint names still used by their parents.

This will (figure 25), in the personal family collection of the late don Pedro Valdez Martínez, no longer requests religious rites or other services. The will functions mainly to document the legal categories and disposition of land in don Pedro's family.[44] I cannot yet say if the traditions of requesting prayers for the dead and leaving land for the purpose of funding rituals (described in the next chapter) were broken after the twentieth-century Revolution, or earlier. But a strong movement in the direction of responsory prayers instead of Masses could have been a first step. The research challenge remains to locate local testaments through all the intervening decades.

LESS EXPENSIVE HYBRID RITES IN CHURCH

As Nahua women and men choose fewer Masses as prayers for the dead, responsory prayers in some cases expand. As if compensating, responsos become more elaborate, taking on some aspects of the Mass, as in a "sung" or "high" responsory prayer. The language people use for these rites indicates a real or perceived recategorization of services. Lázaro Martín requested "Vn rresponso Cantada" [sic] (without gender agreement) in 1823, and Martina Bonifacia requested a "responso grande" in 1824. I cannot tell yet if these two responsos were practiced identically or if the "large" responsory prayer was actually sung, but the language points to some type of hybridization of form.

There could have been a real need for more frugal equivalents of "greater" rites at a time of economic and social crisis. It is also possible that the Church's ability to perform elaborate services may have been curtailed by the upheaval of Independence. Indigenous communities may have had trouble getting the priest to visit on a regular schedule. The question arises as to whether Church liturgy itself was changing to accommodate local needs.

One century earlier, we already see a hint that the Church responded to local preferences. At that time indigenous people in the immediate Toluca City region often requested high Masses, and never responsory prayers. But in the Calimaya/Tepemaxalco region to the south, people did ask for Masses as responsory prayers; three wills from San Antonio de Padua (a Calimaya tlaxilacalli in that period) requested responsory prayers only. Though the eighteenth-century data pool is too small to say that the practice was universal there, they do catch the eye, perhaps foreshadowing what is to come, for responsory prayers do not appear elsewhere in the Toluca corpus at that time as an important substitute for Masses.[45] Thus it can be said with certainty that by Independence, people significantly increase their choices for Church ritual with the responsory prayer. The greatest factor in this change, in the ratio of Masses to responsory prayers, hinges on locality, according to demand in different altepetl.

DEATH TOLLS

When I interviewed the municipal historian of San Bartolomé, don Pedro, he used many metaphors about bells. He said, "La campana es el alma de todo" (The bell holds everything's soul) while we were talking about trees in his community—at which point I asked him about the bell ringing playing a large role in the Independence archive. This is how I learned of a gendered ringing pattern he remembered from his childhood. They used the bells to communicate the news of a death in San Bartolomé. What caught my attention is that he said bells pealed differently depending on whether the deceased was a male or a female citizen; the ringing communicated gender. Specifically, the number of bells described the gender of the ill person. At the moment just before someone died, the church bells would ring for them, as if ushering them melodically from one world into the next. If the dying person was a woman, "tocan la consagrada campana," they played a sequence of seven bells; if the dying person was a man, "tocan las agonías," they played a sequence of five bells. As this point he confirmed the story the fiscal told me about the storm, saying they ring the bells "tambien cuando viene un tormentón" (when a storm comes). The historian, in true Mexican form, is also a poet. His nom de plume is Valdemar: "The bells of my countryside / voices of heart / reverberate to circumscribe / quivers of hope."[46]

At Independence, ringing bells represent another discrete detail about the ritual life of altepetl, but nothing has yet surfaced to identify a gendered pattern.[47] Tolling church bells to mark the passing of a community member became a well-established practice among the Mexican population as early as the sixteenth century, but in both the Valley of Mexico and the Toluca Valley, not all pueblos document it. Perhaps the practice was universal, but from an early time only some altepetl mention the bells, while others do not.[48] San Bartolomé is one of the few communities in which ringing the bells for the dead remains important enough to document consistently. The three eighteenth-century testaments from San Bartolomé all mention ringing the bells.[49] A century before Independence, escribanos verify the ringing of bells for the dead in the surroundings of the city of Toluca, in Atengo, and in a few other places—but not in most of the valley.

In the records of Ocotitlan and Yancuictlalpan, with mainly Spanish-language and mainly Nahuatl-language texts, respectively, escribanos never mention bells at all. Comparable records from the eighteenth century or earlier are not available, but it is reasonable to assume that bell ringing also went unmentioned in wills of many altepetl in earlier times, leaving this avenue of research open to more questions than answers about who chose bells to toll and how they sounded.

"COFRADÍAS" AS SUBUNITS, NEIGHBORHOOD GROUPS

Cofradía membership was open to women and men, yet history has generally ignored the contribution of indigenous women in these guilds organized within the church, frequently called lay church associations or "brotherhoods."[50] This was not a conscious choice by most researchers but rather the lure of more easily analyzed documents. The difficulty of finding and transcribing indigenous cofradía records factors in, as does the difficulty in interpreting social meaning from lists of names in account books. And because cofradía officers were men, their names appear more frequently in the record books. The sources directly influence the outcome; if we only look at officer lists, then women are excluded from the discourse. It is well understood that throughout the colonial period women play a significant role as members, organizers, and sponsors of their neighborhood groups.

At Independence both women and men in San Bartolomé say they are in the hands of Santa María de la Asunción (a large majority) or of La Limpia Concepción (translated to English as Saint Mary of the Assumption, or The Immaculate Conception, respectively), but they do not use the word *cofradía*, so a question surfaced early in my transcriptions regarding their status as church guilds. Then I transcribed a Spanish-language text that clearly states, "Soy

Confradia [*sic*, for cofrade] de Mi madre Santisima La lipian comsepcion" (I am cofradía member of my holy mother Immaculate Conception), in exactly the same place where the mention of the Virgin appears in the Nahuatl formula, adjacent to the request for bells to be rung.[51] This confirms that the two aspects of the Virgins universally mentioned in San Bartolomé were perceived as similar organizations to cofradías, even if the Spanish word cofradía does not appear in the Nahuatl-language texts. Further, the lack of adoption of the Spanish word cofradía implies that a local understanding of these types of cellular groups, altepetl subunits populated equally by women and men, predated its colonial introduction and deserves closer inspection.

A few clues point out that cofradías continue to support their communities with financial services. Bernardino Antonio said he left a piece of *solar* to his nephew because his nephew, a member of the cofradía Señor San José, had lent Bernardino Antonio ten pesos.[52] Gerónima Antonia's nephew loaned her money; when she died she left him family land adjacent to the cofradía Señor Santiago.[53] Cofradías also still hold land in common at Independence; the word *tequimilli* still is used to designate a special corporate tribute field of the community.[54]

Perhaps they were not cofradías in the strict Spanish sense. If they had the resources, women and men in colonial Mexico joined cofradías by paying membership fees and/or contributing labor. It has been shown in other times and places in the Americas that wealthy people joined many different cofradías. In such church guilds, you could participate in community building, acquire status, and develop financial networks. In contrast, people in San Bartolomé do not appear to overlap their membership in cofradías; no one belongs to both Asunción and Concepción. Everyone belonged to and allied with one of the organizations (but not both). Yet membership at this time is universal, even among those without property; thus it appears that belonging was not necessarily contingent on monetary payment.

At Independence, these cofradía-style groups appear defined by geography, implying that their church guilds may have actually served the functions of small tlaxilacalli, which also were defined in discrete physical space. This could explain why the word cofradía was not adopted into Nahuatl to identify people's own group; this subunit meant something quite different than a Spanish cofradia.

Of interest, escribanos of the fiscalía keep allegiance to one or the other "cofradía" at Independence. With rare exceptions, they only work for women and men of the cofradía with which they associate. Gerónima Antonia mentions the cofradía of Señor Santiago, and Bernardino Antonio's nephew, mentioned above, belonged to a cofradía called San José.[55] The cofradía of San José is not mentioned elsewhere. These other cofradías appear only tangentially in San Bartolomé's parish records. These diverse groups might have been under the jurisdiction of one fiscalía. It is also possible that these "other" cofradías, which were belonged to by others (not testators), belonged to another neighborhood church, meaning another fiscalía. In the latter case, the records would have been kept separately and therefore barely mentioned in the Independence archive. If members did not have to pay to belong to cofradías in the monetary sense, and membership was universal among both women and men, and escribanos seem divided by cofradía district, then a membership defined by neighborhood "barrio" boundaries seems likely.[56]

In the preceding chapter, describing a new use of the future tense for "belonging to the cofradías," I noted possible interpretations that open questions about their role in people's lives;[57] one possible sense is that, at death, people fully enter or belong, as if a special death rite is observed. Or, in a more general sense, the dying member shows they expected to belong to, or to be dedicated to, the Virgin of Asunción or the Virgin of Concepción in the afterlife, as if duties normally performed for one's cofradía group extended beyond death. Further, there is some association between types of Church services requested for the dead and the different cofradías. Of those who said they were in the hands of La Limpia Concepción, the majority (62 percent) chose Masses instead of responsory prayers.[58] Members of the much larger Santa María de la Asunción were more evenly divided between choosing Masses and responsory prayers, with a small majority (52 percent) asking for responsos.[59] The tentative implication is that the cofradía de La Limpia Concepción, though smaller, was associated with somewhat greater resources. If this proves true, horizontal and cellular social groups did not erase the reality of women's and men's relatively uneven, or exclusive, economic status.

In sum, this chapter describes the Nahua world of local devotion, where women enter the historical record as primary actors, contributing as significant culture makers. At the level of Church rituals—recorded in a local strata of documents removed from direct Spanish colonial influence—ceremonies persisted and adapted to people's needs within greater contexts of disease, altepetl tradition, and political change. In the Mexican Catholicisms of devotion to specific trees, the issuing of testaments to distribute their property (which women owned in the majority), the choice of bells at death, the gendered distribution of Mass arrangements, the use of vigesimal ritual timetables, the hybridizing of Masses, and the membership in or capital arrangements associated with a cofradía, women not only fully participate but can also predominate. Nahua women's contributions to the structure and content of Mexican culture deserve to find their way into our historical memory.

I'd like to shift the lens wider and leave you with a story as a transition to chapter 6. With the artificial dissection of ritual into "church" and "household" chapters, I inadvertently leave the impression that these spheres were separate. I do separate them, but only for the sake of analysis. Because I'm unfolding Nahua social life from two hundred years ago in this awkward way, Monica's story brings to light the natural way these spheres might actually flow into each other. Her story, a contemporary one, shows the weaving of domains; active roles ordinary women continue to play as leaders based in the parish, simultaneously intertwined with household inheritance, teaching the next generation of cofradía leaders. She inspired me to understand how a Church-based governance in provincial pueblos could be neither relegated to colonial history nor confined to men. It illustrates how women's unacknowledged work happens in life outside city centers, within the shelter of the local parish. My hope is for more research that connects the Church's significant if unofficial leadership of women to ritual production, beyond linguistic boundaries.

<hr />

When her mother died this year, Monica left everything related to a successful career in Los Angeles to travel back home to Peru.[60] Inside her neighborhood parish, in a small foothill town between Lima and Cuzco, Monica and her sister were taken into the arms of her mother's *hermandad*,[61] because they both inherited their mother's saints. Their whole lives they trained for this moment: she remembers participating in Masses and festivals, holding on to her mother's skirts.

The way Monica describes it, each neighborhood self-organizes its own hermandad. Members wake up at 6 a.m., a full hour before everyone else in town stirs. They walk down to the neighborhood's parish to take care of business. Members share and gather to learn the news and find out what happened overnight, who's in need, who's in triumph. Like tending a community garden, they make a point to know everyone and keep up on the latest-breaking neighborhood news to respond to people's needs. Before dawn, they produce a measurable social outcome in the Christian work of ritual: sun invoked by song, a new day whispered into being with prayers at Mass. News spreads with each greeting, eyes ready, hearts open, trained in holding hands.

When her mother first fell ill, Monica had to find help. She knew exactly what to do. She woke at 6:00 am and took the path down to church. There, within the prayer and song, she found immediate aid, a reference to someone *de confianza* (to trust). And one short hour later, she was back home at her mother's bedside with everything they needed, just as everyone else was waking up to start their day.

In this way, their neighborhood guild produces the celebrations of their lives, forging the bonds of belonging. Monica contrasted this arrangement to Church administration in a large city like Lima "where you go to church and the priest plans the service, collects the money, and sends everyone off with announcements, and no one really knows each other." In her mother's town, they do this work together to help each other out, with personal and corporate needs. Each neighborhood has a church, and in classic cellular organizing principles, each member in turn organizes everything for a particular saint—the Masses, the processions, the celebrations—and pays the priest. Members thus take turns producing and paying for various Masses and celebrations around saints' days, as their ancestors have done for as long as there is memory. Today, Easter has the largest processions, with giant community altars and uncountable candles, but every week there is a procession of something. Both Monica and her sister inherited saints from their mother; one of these saints has been served through her mother's lineage, from her maternal grandmother. They were trained to do this their whole lives, alongside their mother's heartbeat. They were also trained and welcomed by the hermandad, "They make sure you know the rules." Upon her mother's death she received the responsibility to carry on her family's tradition of serving a household saint. This doesn't just mean a Mass on the saint's day. It means organizing a full month of events *around* the saint's day: producing a Mass, financing it, organizing a procession, and throwing a celebration following it all. The final fête includes hiring musicians, giving gifts to participants (like flowers), and serving drinks similar to Mexican *champurrado*.[62]

In the next chapter, we move into the home; I propose that in quantifying the inheritance of saints, we can begin to grasp the diversity of Nahua household rituals.

6

HOUSEHOLD RITUAL

NAHUAS DIDN'T LIKE TO DECLARE their ancestor rituals in writing. Sometimes only secrecy could save a relic from destruction; ancestor veneration could be singled out as heresy. Yet Dominga Bonifacia, Diega Gertrudis, José Anastasio, Francisca Petrona, and Bernabela Antonia spoke words on their deathbeds that others did not or could not say. They either felt freedom or the obligation to write down instructions for heirs at this moment of great upheaval and change, directions that named the human objects of their devotions. Their words, as recorded by Nahua escribanos, describe the nominally Christian saints who inhabited household altars, affording a safe place within which to remember each soul connected to a specific piece of land.

Despite their scarcity, their words give insight into the steadfastness of rituals that honored saints *and* ancestors, in turn reinforcing society from within a home's outer walls, within the community's fields. Celebrating the beloved dead perhaps incorporated some unnamed practices in tension with Christian doctrine, yet the rites as described—thoroughly enveloped within the Mexican Catholicisms of "serving saints"—remained nourished in the shelter of the household. In the way ancestor rites were recorded, we know they were still considered part of the saints complex: Day of the Dead appears as All Saints' Day. Land use, in its greater civic and agricultural contexts, is presented as a way to understand ritual obligations inherited at the death of a loved one. In this way, we come full circle; household rites join altepetl institutions to forge cultural flexibility.

The story begins with a look at the numbers: a breakdown of the saints people venerate shows discrete jurisdictions—unseen without the large collection of testaments from three altepetl made during a compressed period of time.[1] In the previous chapter I presented the devotional life of Nahuas in terms of rituals and offices performed on church grounds, in an effort to glimpse social organization at the most local level: people's neighborhood groups, women issuing testaments, planning burial rites. However, a significant aspect of religious practices remains unaccounted for: rites practiced inside the household by both women and men. While these traditions are not well documented for this period, short phrases prove they do continue, and in the sheer diversity of saints, we can appreciate the uniqueness of household devotions.

HOUSEHOLD SAINTS

What researchers call the household cult, or the household complex, entered the written record in the Toluca Valley in the late seventeenth century.[2] Christensen identifies this moment an essential part of Phase 3, when communities openly bequeath household images.[3] In the eighteenth century the practice became firmly established; everyone who could afford it acquired a nominally Catholic saint at home. Wealthy Nahuas had whole collections of them. It is as if they had been there all along, waiting to surface with a Christian name. For the saints represented more than the martyr or hero of the historical Church. Saints symbolized the physical household, and they were considered its patrons and senior residents. By extension, the most usual way to express one's *residence* in a home was to speak of serving the saints there, a metaphor for life at home. The standard Nahuatl concept for a home still appeared at this time in the traditional phrasing; literally translated it means "house, lot, and saints."[4] To quote Margarita María:

And I say that as to this *house* together with the *lot* and the *images* of God, the male and female saints, they are to stay there in the house compound; I leave it to my son Francisco Joaquín and his wife named María Casimira to serve [the saints]. (Yan#2, 1810, emphasis added)[5]

Using this social metaphor of the home, the function of saints can be found within the composite nature of household identity: the inextricable ritual work to feed the people, the land, and the ancestors.

The numbers of saints in the Nahua pantheon epitomize a recurring theme: diversity. Embedded within a conservative Nahua society that values ancestral tradition, one also finds striking variety between altepetl. In contrast to the term *indio* that imagines all indigenous societies as an undifferentiated group, Nahua communities value distinct identities. These differences, as we have seen in previous chapters, take the form of competing escribano formulas, unique burial rites, and different political organizations. To quote Pizzigoni, "The discovery of variation within an area of the Nahua world usually studied as a unit has important social and cultural implications, showing the attachment to local reality to be even greater than had been realized before."[6] In the case of saints themselves, striking geographic variation shows how Independence-era households show very little overlap in the recipients of their ritual devotion: people served different patron saints. This pattern is found both within individual altepetl and as a way to contrast between altepetl communities.

This dispersal of roles implies that neighbors could attend each other's celebrations. Nahuas took turns, alternated festivities, and while employing the Catholic calendar, produced the celebrations of distinct saints' days. With three exceptions, specific Marian saints lived individually, one per altepetl. In the category of Jesus saints the differentiation is even more pronounced: Jesus saints were not even shared between different altepetl (not just a lack of overlap within each community's households), which means that even neighboring altepetl served distinct cults. This type of framework would have allowed for much ritual interaction between altepetl: a reliance on neighboring communities to produce festivities or at the very least to provide the saint on loan.

The same holds true with other female (non-Marian) and male (non-Jesus) saints. With the one exception of Mary Magdalene, non-Marian female saints were not shared among altepetl; they lived housed singly (with only one family) in the region. Similarly, in only two instances do people overlap in service to other male (non-Jesus) saints. In the first instance, San Marcos was found in two households in San Bartolomé. In the second exception, San Antonio, ubiquitous in Franciscan parishes, was found in one household in each of the three altepetl.

Glancing at the monotonous graphs, it becomes clear how rare it is to have more than one of the same saint in one altepetl, or even in the same area.

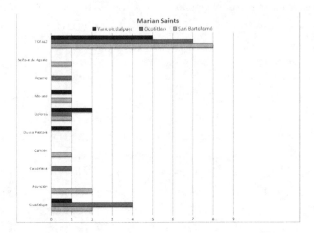

FIGURE 26. Graph demonstrating the number of Marian saints in households, coded for the altepetl in which the household resides.

Figures 26 through 29 illustrate the great variety of saints, as well as the differentiation of cults within altepetl, data visible because of the local nature of the Independence archive. As each altepetl is compared in terms of the saints represented within households, note the variety of saints supported by inheritors charged with serving them. Down to the household level, in these Nahua communities, people ordinarily served unique saints.

Peoples' strong preference for Mary cults can be traced from the previous century, when Wood found Mary the most popular saint in households.[7] At Independence, the variation of Mary saints grows considerably.[8] Comparing the nine different names for Mary, we see that the seven different representations of Jesus saints finds Mary still the favorite among Nahua communities. Versions of Mary account for twenty of the fifty-six total saints named, essentially the same ones popular in the valley through the previous century.

In figure 26, only cults to the beloved Guadalupe and Dolores are found in all three altepetl, out of a total of nine different Marian saints. These numbers support research suggesting that Guadalupe did not begin to gain traction in indigenous communities until this period and, further, that the growth of Guadalupe's popularity was rooted in the Marian devotions.[9] Of Marian saints, most are found only once in each locality.[10] The pattern of keeping different devotions is strong with Marian saints, yet compared to other favored saints, the Marian saints show the most overlap between altepetl households.

Figure 27 shows that in Ocotitlan people duplicated devotions to serve the same saint in the case of Mary Magdalene. This overlap is the one exception found among the non-Marian household saints. Aside from the three Mary Magdalene served in Ocotitlan, the pattern of serving distinct, varied icons holds generally true for non-Marian saints.

Figure 28, illustrating the distribution of Jesus saints, shows no overlap. Service to each saint fell to distinct jurisdictions, not even duplicated among the different altepetl communities. Various and differing images of Christ and Mary support what ethnohistorians call indigenous micropatriotism, with each corporate entity maintaining its own image of a saint.[11] Looking more closely at the social meaning of these numbers creates an image of only one household per community serving/feasting a given Jesus saint; the leadership alternated among hosts. Unless the cult was one of the most popular (and thus needing a larger celebration), only one household in each altepetl hosted a saint's feast days—rituals that vary regionally and even today can include procession to the church. In this arrangement, the work that produced celebrations was distributed horizontally, with many people taking part as producers of these events.

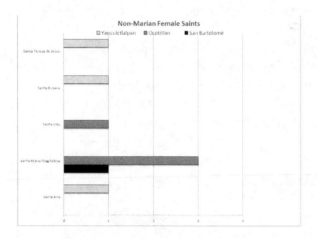

FIGURE 27. Graph demonstrating the number of non-Marian female saints in households, coded for the altepetl in which the household resides.

FIGURE 28. Graph demonstrating the number of Jesus saints in households, coded for the altepetl in which the household resides.

Osowski describes eighteenth-century Bourbon reforms aimed at controlling popular Mexican Catholicisms at a time when processions expressed "indigenous political values."[12] Even processions in medieval Spain are understood as performances of political authority, and they had an element of reciprocity.[13] In Mexico today, processions also carry associations with power, and indigenous influence abounds, even when not acknowledged. I had the honor to witness and participate in processions of icons in both the rural indigenous pueblo of Tepecxitla (Chicontepec, Veracruz, during Chicomexochitl) and in the large urban city of Guanajuato, Guanajuato (in its colonial downtown, during Candelaria). In Guanajuato I saw no indication that the procession was consciously considered an indigenous tradition, yet weeks in advance finding appropriate clothes for the household icon seemed a widespread concern in the marketplace. In Veracruz, older Nahuatl terms and ritual predominated. In each case, the icons and ritual objects were elaborately prepared in the household and processed outside, ending in a public ritual. In Guanajuato, the public service took place in church; in Tepecxitla, the final ritual of the day culminated around the community well.

It sounds contradictory to say it: in terms of households' rituals the differentiation is so uniform that it appears coordinated. Figures 26, 27, 28, and 29 give the impression that individual households hosted celebrations that their communities and neighboring communities attended; just as Diega Gertrudis

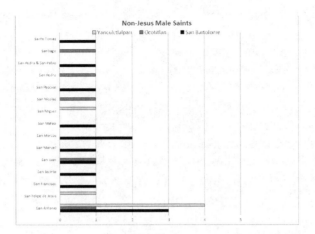

FIGURE 29. Graph demonstrating the number of non-Jesus male saints in households, coded for the altepetl in which the household resides.

of Ocotitlan left the large sum of six pesos for a celebration "para que se aga mi padre Señor Antonio" (so that it will be made [for] my father Señor Antonio), meaning Saint Anthony.[14] Evidence points to social opportunities: they took turns making parties. This corroborates John Chance and William Taylor's hypothesis about the nature of new cargo systems developing at the end of the colonial period, with "greater numbers of individuals . . . compelled to finance village fiestas"; clearly, this household data shows that "families . . . share in the economic burdens of fiestas sponsorship."[15] I cannot yet say exactly how individuals produced events within or for cofradías (or neighborhood subgroups), but this quantitative household record opens up new ways to think about this local strata of devotion, in terms of not only the saints honored but also the individuals charged with the work.[16]

Further, three shared feast days created opportunity for mutual support, celebration, feasting, and procession coordination among communities; Saints Anthony, Guadalupe, and Dolores were served by households in all three altepetl. Those three feast days were celebrated across the political boundaries that separated the other sacred icons, pointing to a few larger, more regional events. If so, this corroborates another dimension of Osowski's identification of indigenous participation in "provincial economies and religious devotions external to their communities."[17]

The total number of individual saints in the record remains steady at Independence, even when compared to the larger collection of sources from the previous century.[18] The number of saints named individually shows an increase (not counting collective terms such as *santas* and *santos*), representing fifty-nine cases. For comparison, the eighteenth-century corpus records fifteen total cases of saints named singly; if one adds that in that period people record thirty-three bequests of saint groups, one would imagine the total to be a larger number than fifty-nine but perhaps proportional.[19] The steady numbers in the inheritance of saints certainly show continuity with previous times; what appears to be increasing is the proportion named individually. This growth appears in juxtaposition with the expansion of phrasing regarding "service"—people, as described in the next section of this chapter, begin explicitly asking for ongoing ritual production for themselves. People continue to name their saints at this time in which the saints complex is changing and varying from the Nahuatl standard, and this may actually represent both an innovative and a conservative response fostering individual representation.

The diversity of saints points to the existence of active subunits in the altepetl. Not a single saint called San Bartolomé appears in the collections of saints recorded in the settlement of that name. The same appears to be true in Yancuictlalpan, though it is conceivable that some of the Marys there were thought of as being associated with the patron, like Santa María de la Rosa or Nativitas. Three people housed their patron saint in their homes; even so, it accounts for only a small percentage of the settlement's total of twenty-two. Where few patron saints of the altepetl are found on home altars, one might infer that these two social sectors, polity and household, existed independently as ritual spheres; I offer these charts in the hope of generating further research on the local intersections of people and polity in relationship to the sponsors of saints.

Gender distribution of the saints also varies by altepetl. In Yancuictlalpan people served saints of both gender equally: eight female and eight male saints. In Ocotitlan, a small majority of people served female saints, for a female to male ratio of 11:9. In San Bartolomé most people served male saints, for a female to male ratio of 9:14. Thus, even in the gender of saints granted devotion, altepetl show distinct preferences.

One small detail about the gender of saints should be noted: male and female saints are still thought of as separate classes—not subsumed under the masculine *santos* as expected in Spanish. In essence, people continue to regard the feminine gender of their saints as noteworthy, a clear continuity with Na-

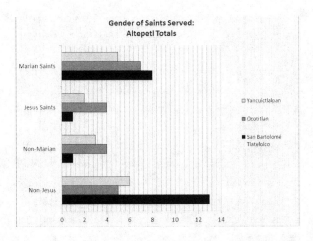

FIGURE 30. Graph showing altepetl totals of household saints, grouped by gender.

huatl thought. *Santo* and *santa* came into Nahuatl much earlier as separate loanwords, explaining how Nahuas retained the feminine form independent from the male, despite the influence of male-normative Spanish usage. It is significant that at this late date, Nahuatl speakers continue to use this Nahuatl form of naming both genders, even with Spanish loanwords. Thus, people still use the feminine paired with the masculine, *santos* and *santas*, when they speak of saints collectively, which has implications for interpreting Nahua gendered social status at this time.[20] This expression is detected not only in Nahuatl-language testaments but also in the Spanish-language testaments derived from them, even though it went against normal Spanish usage.

HOUSEHOLD RITES

Feliciana Petrona's bequests of land to her daughter typify what people expect of their inheritors. Before she died in 1816, she left a series of saints and properties to her daughter in ways that illustrate the complexity of meanings associated with her bequests. One parcel of land she leaves to her daughter, and even though it is agricultural land, she gives it to her with a mandate to support household rituals.[21] She does not explicitly mention the saints in this particular bequest:

Ahora Se la dexo mi hija Simona Cristina y Su marido polonio Basilio para que
dia Sacara p las belas y flores que Se cumpla lo que mando." (Oco#24, 1816, third
bequest)
(Now I leave it to my daughter Simona Cristina and her husband Apolonio Basilio so that from there she will extract the candles and flowers; may my order be
carried out.)

Without naming specific saints or ancestors, she describes the rites to be performed. She asks inheritors to use the land to fund rarely documented household ritual practices involving candles and flowers, devotional forms known for
at least two centuries in the Toluca Valley. We know this piece of land is to be
used by her daughter (and her daughter's husband alongside her) to support
rituals for the household saints because Feliciana Petrona describes the saints
in a separate bequest:

Que ellos Se queda en la casa para que le Sirba ha Mi madre Nuestra Señora de
Guadalupe y S.or San Nicolas y Santo Niño y todos lo himagenes No les falta
belar Saumexio los pasquar Grandes [for velas sahumerio los pascuas grandes].
(Oco#24, 1816, first bequest)
(That they may remain in the house to serve my mother our lady of Guadalupe
and lord San Nicolás and the Santo Niño and all the images. They are not to lack
candles, incense, on the High Holidays.)

In this separate gift, Feliciana Petrona gives her household to her daughter and
son-in-law. The saints, the house structure itself, and half of the house's lot,
called a *solar*, together make up the household she describes. It is in the language of this gift that we learn the names of the saints that are to be served
within the household complex. Thus her previous bequest of agricultural land,
meant to support the household rituals involving candles and incense, refer
to these saints: Guadalupe, Nicolás, Santo Niño, and more images not named
individually.

Feliciana Petrona shows us that her gifts of land are not to be sold and spent;
these bequests of land, to serve saints, come with strings attached. As inheritors, the daughter and son-in-law are obligated to work the land to provision
rituals for the household saints. And *service* does not mean just songs or prayers
but also rites that require capital outlay, significant resources. Candles burn and

need replacement. Flowers wither. Holidays return. All elements are still necessary for household rituals in this time and place, but the key is that they involve managing land to derive the required resources.

Nahua saints, surrounded by flowers and candles, required incense rising onto the household walls. Though altars are not described, because Feliciana Petrona tells her daughter to serve the saints in the home with candles, flowers, and incense, we infer the existence of altars there, in the space to nestle candles near the paintings or figurines, the places where these rites were performed in honor of their many names. It is this ritual work that codifies the plaited nature of land, house, and saints. Thus, while testaments are rightly considered a successful colonial legal strategy to hold on to land, there is more going on. Land devoted to saints brings a network of obligations that promote a daily weaving of culture.

ANCESTOR RITES, "QUE SE ACUERDE DE MI"

Tracing the saints featured in Feliciana Petrona's deathbed bequests illustrates the work involved in receiving land attached to household saints. In her sixth and last bequest of land, Feliciana Petrona expands the pattern. She asks her daughter to remember her (Feliciana herself) on those same high holidays:

> Se la dexo a mi hija Simona Crisanto y Su marido polonio Basilio los que se nombraro arriba *para que Se acuerde de mi* los dias porquas Grandes [for pasquas grandes] que Se cumpla lo que mando." (Oco#24, 1816, sixth bequest, emphasis added)
>
> (I leave it to my abovementioned daughter Simona Cristina [*sic*] and her husband Apolonio Basilio *so that she will remember me* on the High Holidays. May my order be carried out.)

The daughter is directed to remember her mother in the way saints are remembered. Feliciana Petrona asks her to produce rituals so that she will not forget her; this is her stated purpose for the inheritance of agricultural land issuing from her own father's family. These are to be ongoing rituals in her own memory, and they fall on the same timetable as the household saints. Feliciana Petrona names the major religious holidays with the same language she used for serving the saints, "los dias pasquas Grandes." Thus we see written evidence of Nahuas creating ritual networks of ancestor veneration and evidence that they make it part and parcel of the larger saints complex.

José Anastasio, dying in the epidemic of 1813, also uses this language.[22] He bequeaths two pieces of land. The smaller piece he dedicates in service to a saint, Santa María Magdalena. But the larger piece he dedicates to his own memory saying,

> Y digo que un tierra que de trese cuartillos ora me lo Fue degando deFunto mi padre ora le dego mi muger yamadose Juana estasia *para que se acuerde de mi* y no y quien diga mañana u otro dia que se cunpla mi palabra." (Oco#12, 1813, emphasis added)
>
> (And I say that one property of thirteen cuartillos left to me by my late father, now I leave it to my wife named Juana Estasia, *so that she will remember me* and no one is to say anything [against this] in the future [using Nahuatl metaphor for future in Spanish]. May my word be carried out.)

Note that José Anastasio bequeathed his largest parcel of land in service to his own memory, with explicit allocation of duties for that land: "so that she will remember me." The exact rites and agricultural labor involved in creating this service to his memory remain implicit.

Diega Gertrudis also asked to be personally remembered with household land.[23] In the epidemic of 1813, she left a lot/*solar*, inherited from her father, to her sister. With this household lot, she asks her sister to remember her, saying, "Paraque se acuerde de mi." While it was common to leave agricultural land to serve the saints, Diega Gertrudis's testament shows us that household land, lots/*solares*, could also be managed in one's own memory. Thus, it can be said with confidence that people considered household land compatible for ritual service to one's ancestors, not just reserved to serve the household saints.

The above cases all issue from Ocotitlan; in San Bartolomé one person also uses that exact phrasing about remembering the testator.[24] In 1824, Dominga Bonifacia made her son, Marcelino Antonio, her principal heir. In this request, serving the saints and service to the testator appear in the same sentence, indicating she associated rituals in her own memory with the saints cult. Just as Francisca Petrona asked to be remembered on high holidays, or "los dias porquas [pasquas] Grandes," here Dominga Bonificia in San Bartolomé gives similar instructions:

Y Digo y declaro que esta casa con un pedaso de solar . . . se lo dejo lo mismo mi jijo marselino Antonio para que le sirba Señor San Antonio y Señor San francisco no Faltara belas saumerio *y se acordara de mi* los dias pasquas y dia de todo santos compla lo que mando." (SBT#115, 1824, emphasis added)

(And I say and declare that this house with one lot . . . I leave it to the same, my son Marselino Antonio, that he might serve the Señor San Antonio and Señor San Francisco. Candles and incense shall not be wanting *and he will remember me* on the High Holidays and All Saints' Day. May my order be carried out.)

Dominga Bonifacia offers key evidence and documents it in writing. She spells out for her son that he is to use the land she is giving him to create ongoing devotional rituals on All Saints' Day, not just the generic "high holidays" to which other people refer. People say "high holidays" to refer to rituals celebrated cyclically within the Christian calendar. Here we have rare documentary evidence of a Nahua woman explicitly making sure she would be served with ongoing rites on All Saints' Day, earlier also known as *miccailhuitl* in Nahuatl, or today called Day of the Dead: active ancestor rituals.

Kin groups converge in the transmission of this land. The *pedaso de solar*, or lot, issued from the son's father, her husband, yet Dominga Bonifacia asks for *herself* to be "remembered" with this land, not her husband, though it is possible that the latter was implied. Either way, Dominga Bonifacia was participating in a tradition that spans generations and bloodlines, sharing a glimpse of ancestor devotions that most people seem reluctant to record. Returning to Feliciana Petrona, she bequeaths land from different lineages, her husband's family, her own father's family . . . multiple family groups converge to take on the work of inheriting land with saints. Just as Nahuatl-language research of the colonial period recognizes that saints were patrons in the Nahua home, David Tavarez's Zapotec criminal record sources describe how icons were considered people's parents and grandparents in their homes.[25] Nahua obligations to produce ritual span kin networks that include icons as patrons of the home: ancestors were served in the same way as the icons.

One other clue appears, with unique phrasing. This time in the Nahuatl language we hear about ritual service to individual ancestors.[26] In 1810, Bernabela Antonia dictated her last will, leaving one of her two properties to her nephew. She bequeathed him irrigated land with which "he is to help me along the way with something." She asks for service without using the Nahuatl word *tequipanoa*. Instead she asks her sibling's child to use the land after her death to help her on her journey "along the path/way." Her personal concept of the afterlife is only obliquely referenced, but she is saying she considered her nephew's future work in memory-crafting a benefit to herself. In this way, she fleshes out the above idea expressed in Spanish, asking to be remembered, "Para que se acuerde de me." Thus we learn that she considered serving ancestors with land a help to herself, beyond death—in her Nahuatl phrasing of things. Upon inheriting the land, her nephew was to work the land to support unspecified rites, in her name.

If not for this "new" direction, of people explicitly asking heirs to produce personal ritual services, we might not know about these rites inside people's homes, in the name of ancestors. These comprise a very small proportion of the total bequests. Five people leave enough details written down to confirm that ancestor rites were practiced in association with the veneration of saints. People directed their heirs to serve their memory—this is the purpose of the land they leave. On their deathbeds, Francisca Petrona, Dominga Bonifacia, Diega Gertrudis, José Anastasio, and Bernabela Antonia all considered their own ancestor rites important enough to support with bequests of land. And they used the legal tool of the testament to document their instructions; it was certainly a weighty proposition for them to ensure that these rites were carried on, just like obligations to household saints.

Further, because the ideas of "remembering the testator" and the Day of the Dead are also found in the sixteenth-century Nahuatl-language wills from Culhuacan, there is every reason to believe that the practices, recorded again in wills at Independence, existed all along in provincial Nahua communities.[27] In the nineteenth century the terminology becomes "día de los santos" instead of *miccailhuitl*, but people are still asking to be remembered in the same way, on the same day. This answers the question by cultural critics about how far back these rites that exist today can be traced in written sources.[28] Certainly many symbols we today associate with the Day of the Dead are regional and contemporary,[29] but the long-lasting scent of flowers and incense has mingled with candlelight on altars at least since the sixteenth century. And perhaps most importantly, in the nineteenth century people still inherit land to supply those altars, as tribute, expressly in memory of the beloved dead.

HOUSEHOLD, ALTEPETL, KING

Service to saints happened in the cradle of land, giving household-level rites a direct effect on the larger community. In this sense, Nahua women and men can be considered what Osowski calls informal *tlatoque*, or "guardians of local religion, which was inseparable from their work as managers of community resources."[30]

We have seen the way obligations are inherited to serve the saints and to serve the ancestors. Here I show how land was also bequeathed with obligations to serve the political community. Taken together, a triptych of household saints, ancestors, and altepetl emerges as a lens into the scope of land-use ritual. Reaching both inward and outward from the household, beyond physical and temporal boundaries, people express these three interlocking ideas as reasons to maintain and work their land. Following this line of thought, we come full circle, to consider how devotions at home joined with altepetl institutions to forge cultural syntax: a responsive vernacular that served those who most used it.

Deborah Kanter, who works extensively with litigation from the Toluca Valley, confirms what testaments from the Independence archive say: documents from 1810 to 1821 show little sign of the Independence movement.[31] In fact, her research shows that testaments from this period describe a conservative cultural impulse, a finding my research supports. In the case of the altepetl of Yancuictlalpan, conservatism extends to monarchal yearnings—a seeming contradiction found throughout Latin American Independence movements well documented by Eric Van Young.[32] In Yancuictlalpan, community members overtly caution their inheritors to use the land they give them to serve not just God but also the king. In 1810 Juana Nepomucena left a piece of land to her son, saying, "To serve on it God our lord and our great ruler the king, whom God keep where he is."[33] Alongside the service to household saints, in Yancuictlalpan people also inherit land with obligatory service to the altepetl or king. If the language can be said to express anxiety about shifting political boundaries, Juana Nepomucena plugs into monarchist thought, in support of the king, at the boiling point of Independence.

Margarita María in the same year left a piece of non-household agricultural land to her son and daughter-in-law, admonishing them, "To serve in the altepetl of our consummate mother [Santa María Magdalena, the patron] and to serve our ruler the king, whom God keep where he now is."[34] This new twist in phrasing indicates that people considered support of the king as a benefit to the community itself, couched in the traditional form of community service to their altepetl. People can bequeath land with obligatory service to the altepetl, along with the king.

Even though in said bequest the saints are unmentioned, Margarita María also left her household to heirs in service of saints. Note that her nominally personal, non-household agricultural land is (like land for saints) inherited with obligations to the community. The king, like the saints, remains an object of devotion. Further, in the year when the national struggle formally declares its aim of independence, Margarita María hails the king of Spain.

Eleven years later, Mariano Domingo still uses similar language, asking for service to the king and the altepetl. The reference to the altepetl asserts specific directions to serve the past and present officers of the local municipality, *norepublica*. He gave a piece of land to his wife and son, describing their obligations to work on it: "to serve; they are to serve our ruler the king and my lords the past officials and my municipal officers."[35]

Since earlier manuscripts from Yancuictlalpan have not yet been found, it is impossible to know whether these stipulations had long been traditional in the community and notarial practice—perhaps going back centuries—or whether, especially in reference to the king, they were inspired by complex alliances in the Independence movement. Either way, it is compelling to see people linking their service obligations to the altepetl with the king as late as 1821. It does suggest concern about how changes will affect local control.

As we saw in the first chapter, Nahua altepetl adapted and thrived within the jurisdiction of the Church and, by extension, the monarch. Land use for communal obligations that extended beyond the household is well known for the colonial period; at this time communal obligations are treated in the same way as obligations to household saints. Like other aspects of microlocal phenomena in the Independence archive, the suspicion is that this is actually nothing new. What is new is having it documented in writing. This language about the king does not appear in either San Bartolomé or Ocotitlan, but for the fiscalías and cofradías, as the autonomous self-government of neighborhoods, the Church acted as the pivot point of local power.

AGRICULTURE AS COMMUNITY RITUAL

At its essence, land inherited along with saints carried obligatory duties on both household and non-household land. Human labor in the name of the saints complex of ancestors and the community does more than serve patron saints. How did maize-producing plots yield the required candles, incense, and flowers? Inheritors grew maize and maguey cactus, among other plants, to process, sell, and trade.[36] Maize overshadows all others as the predominant crop in the record; at this time, *sembradura de maiz* represents the crop people grow in the name of the household saints.[37]

Such land-use obligations bind inheritors to the community. These symbolic practices require agricultural cultivation within a carefully circumscribed landscape, where land is located in relationship to the other people who work in adjacent plots.[38] Nahuas define boundaries in connection to people.[39] Space remains organized, defined, and allocated to community members with precincts invisible to us, yet they were understood by all; this agricultural work would not be anonymous. In this sense, the agricultural labor itself functions as a ritual not just the proceeds from the harvests. Even if the labor was for saints, the land itself would frequently be identified as belonging to the person who died, and the whole community would see the work being performed. The laborer would be understood to be working to fulfill the wishes of the beloved dead, the ancestor who left them the land to "serve the saints." The labor would not go unnoticed; everyone would know who was working the familiar piece of land, to produce the festivals they all expected.

Imagine yourself in this place: you inherit a piece of land from your grandmother, and she asks you to remember her and/or her saints with this land. You couldn't just cheer then sell it for cash. The whole community would see you work on it or hear about the way you worked the land in her name. In this sense, remembering your grandmother would happen continually; it would start with the cyclical practices of clearing, sowing, watering, and weeding and begin again with the last harvest. This is what it meant to inherit land in the saints complex: daily labor entwined with seasonal celebrations. In protecting the crop, feeding the soil, and gathering the yields, you honor the will of your ancestors. The quotidian work that we perform, and that our community witnesses, fulfills a larger social function of a seemingly private household obligation. Our work not only buys incense and candles but also creates the rituals and reinforces our place in the altepetl. It sustains networks of traded goods while affirming ties to our lineages. This insight gives the saints complex an added dimension: serving the ancestors, serving the saints integrates a network of agricultural obligations that also served the altepetl. This is how something as ordinary and discrete as land inheritance, in the name of household saints, fostered cultural resilience.

In this chapter we encountered the sheer variety of saints to identify the complexity of ritual cycles: people took turns and rarely served the same saints in this multi-altepetl area. Then Feliciana Petrona's many bequests of land to her daughter characterized this process for us; her daughter was expected to work the land to provide for the candles, incense, and flowers for the saints' ritual altars. She then added a personal dimension to this cycle by asking to be remembered herself, "so that they might remember me," specifically instructing her daughter to serve her just like she asks her to serve the saints. Then Dominga Bonifacia offered key evidence that Nahuas are still participating in ritual networks of ancestor veneration at All Saints' Day, the Day of the Dead—all considered at least nominally as part and parcel of the larger saints complex.

The triptych of household saints, ancestors, and altepetl (which in Yancuictlalpan included the king) showed how something as personal as a ritual for one's grandmother was tied to the greater society. Overall, agriculture-as-ritual becomes the bond that reinforces the household and the altepetl simultaneously.

Though as a general rule household ritual practices may not be described in detail within testaments, the Independence archive holds the words of some people who chose to speak out loud about their expectations. Since these practices are almost all spelled out in the testaments Nahua escribanos wrote in Spanish, but not generally in the Nahuatl-language ones, it appears that these practices were assumed before, just not mentioned by the Nahuatl-writing escribanos. In the evolution to Nahuatl-influenced Spanish, they feel the need to spell out exactly what they expected for the land given. In negotiating the transition to Spanish, alongside political change, it is as if in the Spanish-language wills people take things into their own hands and in this small way define cultural birthright.

CONCLUSION

THE FIRST DAY I TRAVELED to meet the municipal historian of San Bartolomé, he never arrived. I waited in his son's little *mercadito*, where stools invite one to sit amidst a riot of candy wrappers. Evening fell and no don Pedro; I arranged a meeting for another day. When we met, I introduced myself, and he listed long grievances against scholars of all stripes who come through asking questions. He didn't like it. People flew through San Bartolomé, promising to send back their work but were never heard from again. I petitioned the kindness beneath his pained expression, sought his blessing and a sense of context, a real connection to a real place. It would not be right for me to write my project in isolation, without having ever known, seen, been shaded by the trees of San Bartolomé. Moved, he agreed to a formal meeting the next morning. What researchers fail to understand is how our work creates ties of kinship and obligation to a pueblo that exists today. Don Pedro has since died; whenever I visit Mexico I call upon his widow, tending the construction of something intangible yet larger than ethnohistorical research.

During our formal meeting don Pedro took me to see his family's *ranchito*. The barranca mentioned in the Independence corpus turned out to be a ravine caused by a little stream that runs west to east, at a slight downward slope from the foothills of the volcano. This stream crosses from San Juan Tilapan into the jurisdiction of Metepec at its western boundary, fed by many tiny potable trickles and *ojos de agua* (springs) seeping from the steep sides of the ravine. The ground is basically wet and frequently disturbed; as we walked along the

FIGURE 31. Don Pedro holding *mostrante*. Photo by Melton-Villanueva.

elevated southern bank of the stream, a young man grazed his two pointed-horn cattle right through the steep bank at our feet. This western area is called El Mostrante, named after the ubiquitous plant of the same name. It looks and smells like mint, which solved another puzzle in the Nahuatl-language texts about what *mostrante* meant.[1]

FIGURE 32. The santísima cruz now overlooks the barranca. Note the difference in stone texture at the sites of the repair. Photo by Melton-Villanueva.

We cemented our friendship because we both speak plants. He taught me the ones he knew. I showed him how to touch nettles, which he called chichicaztle.[2] He was surprised I knew the plant, used it as medicine, and could pick it by hand. And I was surprised he knew its Nahuatl name, but I didn't say so. If the archive taught me anything, it's that Nahuatl profoundly influenced the evolution of Mexican Spanish.

It was here, at his ranchito atop the barranca, that I met the *santísima cruz* (holy cross) that used to grace the center of the church grounds.[3] He said that about forty years ago builders broke the stone cross, knocked it down, and replaced it with a new cross at the north gate and covered over all the graves of the *antepasados* (ancestors).

Don Pedro didn't offer more details, and I didn't want to ask, but he showed me where they reconstructed the old cross on this land. It looked like it had once broken into at least four different pieces. The stone repaired, the santísima cruz was placed between the land's ojo de agua and the barranca. It now overlooks the chasm, protecting the spring.

When that desecration occurred, people resented the simultaneously imposed rules barring the practice of burying people on church grounds. Don Pedro's son said that their community stirred up trouble when the congregation recently buried their beloved Fray José Quesada Romero. The name caught my attention; Romero is the name of Cipriano Giordiano's father, the Independence escribano. Fray José is buried on the church grounds, right in front of the entryway door (*tlaixpan*, to use the old Nahuatl phrase) where apparently don Pedro's santisima cruz used to stand. The grave was fresh, with the wet soil still mounded. He was one of their own, from San Bartolomé, and they wanted him to stay on church grounds, even if it upset the authorities who came with armed guards and orders to exhume. Father Quesada Romero was born in San Bartolomé and lived a life of love and devotion to his town, said don Pedro. The feeling was mutual; there was no more fitting place for him to rest. The people of San Bartolomé continue to resist laws that don't make sense to them. Even if the very stones are torn down, their hands collect, repair, and rebuild them.

RESILIENT STRUCTURES

The Aztecs live on today. They have not disappeared; they occupy an integral part of the social fabric and represent the most progressive streams of Mexican identity, regardless of being demeaned for their civil expectations. Each community lives according to its own needs and opportunities. Irrespective of identification as Aztecs, Nahuas, Macehualli, or Mexicans, some communities still speak Nahuatl while others do not. Where Nahuatl remains current, the language has evolved in the way of all living tongues; Nahuatl speakers cannot readily understand texts in the Independence archive, in much the same way English speakers cannot readily understand Old English. Where Spanish has become the norm, it retains much Nahuatl vocabulary and structure. It is this trajectory into the present time that points to the need for more research connecting older and modern Nahuatl. Kelly McDonough's research offers this effort at wholeness, repairing the path to knowledge acquisition alongside Nahua intellectuals of the past and present: "Nahua intellectuals writing Mexican modernity."[4]

John Sullivan's indigenous language institute in Zacatecas (Zacatecas Institute for Teaching and Research in Ethnology, IDIEZ) trains native speakers to participate in the creation of their own history. As both students and teachers, Delfina and Abelardo Cruz de la Cruz and their cohort partner with international teams of researchers to interpret their own heritage, travel abroad to conferences, and present concepts forged from a living, ongoing connection to what it means to be a native speaker, scholar, leader.

In recent years Native American intellectuals such as Elizabeth Hoover have transgressed national boundaries, working north and south, finding again our territories of health and power in things as simple as saving a seed and as complex as reuniting local producers into regional cultural economies based on community health.[5] Food sovereignty connects people to well-being, the ancestral evidence in dirt, the energy integrity in clean water. In this sense, we are returning to a Nahua understanding of agriculture as the ongoing ritual of weaving the frayed strands of memory into civic wealth and identity.

Intimate moments at death converge; Nahuas' own words tell of the startling tenacity found in the Independence archive. Culture-making, the main theme, forged by regular people through the daily work of self-organization, found structure and identity in horizontal networks of ritual, leadership, and associations that largely remained unknown to colonial and national gate keepers. These hidden-in-plain-sight structures fed local civil society, affording the tensile resilience highlighted in the following summary of findings.

CELLULAR ORGANIZATION

Persistent stereotypes about indigenous groups envision a lone hereditary male ruler, easily corrupted in exchange for the land and labor of his community: a chief, king, or boss with ultimate authority.[6] Certainly, these characters enter the legal record.[7] Litigation reveals the "complex web of alliance and conflict" that existed between leadership bodies.[8] But looking at the Independence archive of San Bartolomé, we also find diversity and complex structures. Instead of a single hereditary leader, or the oligarchic power of a select few, we see a majority of Nahua men each serving a one-year term in San Bartolomé's fiscalía.

Rotation and strict one-year term limits did more than prevent Church officials from monopolizing power. Head officers worked with assistants and worked as a cohort; when taken in sum over three decades, the officer corps represents a large labor pool of men who were trained in self-government. It becomes clear that durable indigenous cellular structures such as the fiscalía allowed altepetl like San Bartolomé to retain, adapt, and participate in Nahua intellectual and ritual traditions, while responding to the challenges of their community. Numerous, widely shared opportunities for political/ritual status supported social formation. These are not just isolated ranks: we saw the existence of "cohorts" of leadership. Even the supposed "lowest" fiscalía official advanced in career progression. Further, the topile, the only fiscalía title with a Nahuatl word in the national period, continues to exist today. The topile remains a position of honor in the fiscalía of San Bartolomé; the different fiscalía officers (from Independence) are now all called fiscales, with the exception of the topile, who retains his Nahuatl title.

Voting results of the well-known cabildo in San Bartolomé differentiated the careers of Church officers. By compiling the names of these other officers "de la santa iglesia" over time and comparing them to the cabildo, the fiscalía was identified. Comparing these lists to census data, it appears that nearly every adult man in San Bartolomé must have served in the fiscalía at some point in his life. Combined with the fact that officeholding did not happen in rapid succession if they served in more than one position, then most of their careers were necessarily spent outside official positions of the cabildo and fiscalía. This led me to analyze terms used for executors as well as the timing of honorary and official titles, offering a small glimpse into the inner workings of the altepetl. One marvels at the sight—order, structure, long-term planning, and teamwork—a far cry from the ignorant peasants, the powerless and violent indistinguishable masses described in histories based on Spanish records and still portrayed today. The civic world described here barely grasps the surface of a complex representative culture still in dialog with Nahuatl.

The parish fostered local control. The Church, as the jurisdiction of the fiscalía, supported and recognized the local Nahua officials and ritual producers central to each altepetl's civic life. The political and religious spheres remained married, and they should not be severed to facilitate analysis; while this study attempts wholeness, it wavers, yielding to ease of compartmentalization between chapters. Thus the first half of the book, chapters 1 through 4, describe Nahua officials, while the second half, chapters 5 through 7, describes more informal roles for culture makers. In reality, civic and religious traditions, male and female spheres, are experienced as a continuum; please forgive.

Adopting Spanish coincides with the destabilization of the Church happening on a larger scale. Yet the local parish continued to serve as the heart of the altepetl at Independence, affording self-organized Nahua groups such as fiscalía escribanos protection. A great irony surfaces in this timing, throwing off Spanish colonial rule while at the same time finally adopting the colonizer's tongue, yet it accords with the many contradictions inherent in narratives of nation-building.[9] Concurrent with striking cultural continuity, the homogenizing goals that come with the Mexican national project succeed in a way that the decentralized colonial project did not. Simultaneously, the early nineteenth century saw the Church continue to house and recognize the native, local leaders central to indigenous political life in Ocotitlan and in the well-documented altepetl of San Bartolomé.

The transition to Spanish happened in the framework of long-standing Nahua social concepts. Along with the shift to writing in Spanish, the fact that the role of tepantlato gets erased from the record with the transition to Spanish points to a change in indigenous ranks. Since tepantlato was more associated with high-ranking officers, a supplanting with the Spanish concept of executor in written records indicates a subtle destabilizing of the full role expected from Nahua civil service. This does not mean that in practice the social significance of tepantlato eroded completely in this last generation of escribanos (customs go underground, visible only to the community), but evidence points to a change that undermines the not yet understood concept of intercessor as associated at this time with Nahua leadership.

Cellular organizations guarantee a dispersal of power, a check and balance mitigating the consolidation of status and influence by one individual.[10] Oxford's Archie Brown describes a contemporary dichotomy of personal vs. collective power that deserves our attention with the aim to understanding this dynamic.[11] Cary Miller takes us solidly in this direction of indigenous ethnohistorians beginning to articulate an internal Anishinaabeg perspective on leadership whose purpose was "directed community action"; imagine a world where politicians serve to unite and energize a society, to engage communities.[12] Shared decision-making creates fewer mistakes in judgments because people are encouraged to critique given plans; creating space for constructive disputes makes the outcomes better. This makes for better planning, incorporating diverse points of view in each situation.[13] Unlike quick top-down decisions that people (whose opinions were not considered) may not fully support, shared decisions are slower to achieve, but their projects *get done* faster because everyone unites in purpose. This line of thought, combined with the survival of cellular civic structures, uncovers our need to shift our early colonial focus from a leadership of elites, to address questions surrounding the decline of hereditary rulers by looking at how exactly altepetl were being led, reproduced, and organized.

THE CULTURE OF WRITING

The Aztecs grouped themselves using the term Mexica in the colonial period, and many scholars who study this ethnic group's language, as written during the colonial period, call them Nahua. It gets interesting when groups use words in different ways. The Independence archive demonstrates how Nahua's Spanish words can illustrate indigenous ideas about things not yet understood. It is through Spanish-language manuscripts we find that *criollos* meant "locals," not "Spanish descent"—as Mexican historians use the word—but a Mexican identity. In this sense, Nahua texts challenge our thinking of Mexican identity because *criollo* means those with indigenous ancestry. In the case of Spanish written by indigenous escribanos, we approached understandings that otherwise remained opaque in the Nahuatl.

Colonialities, our different experiences with ongoing colonial processes, encompass local meanings not shared by the dominant culture. Thus, not all colonialities are imposed; many represent survivance strategies, internal responses to

outside mandates. Evidence from different altepetl demonstrates that the transition to Spanish happened on local terms, on timelines that differed among
neighbors. This is how it can be said that the Spanish used by escribanos was
derived more from indigenous peers within their altepetl lineages than from
Spanish speakers: the form varied geographically by altepetl. The texts reveal local variation from their neighbors' written and cultural traditions. Thus, change
happened locally. Culture-making unique to each community continued to find
expression in writing because each escribano who took up the pen held a deep
appreciation for his people, for what they considered important. Adherence to
local writing standards, as opposed to regional ones, demonstrates the autonomy
of escribanos at the level of the altepetl.

Autonomy surfaced as a significant factor for culture makers. Nahua escribanos persisted in their work over the centuries by replicating not just formulas
but also lineages, training, and community advocacy. Thus this study expands
our understanding of escribanos' roles within local communities. Interstitial
people, negotiating legal requirements for their local altepetl, escribanos became
members of overlapping cellular organizations, participating in self-governance.
Notaries, managers, and bureaucrats have been understood as keepers of empire
in far reaches of the world; in the Nahua world they were also the keepers of
Nahuatl, in all the expanded meanings of a vibrant ethnic identity that values
every word.

Biographical career data found escribanos could move from secular to ecclesiastical organizations. After being elected to write for their altepetl, as escribano de república (in the cabildo), they moved to escribano de la santa iglesia (in
the fiscalía) in San Bartolomé and Ocotitlan. In contrast, for Yancuictlalpan,
the escribano de república wrote down people's last wills, further blurring the
already fluid division of secular and ecclesiastical offices. As complex arrangements not yet well understood, governing bodies follow a cellular arrangement,
allowing for creation and destruction of separate entities (tlaxilacalli becoming
altepetl, for example) according to need, without the decline of the whole.

In the face of Nahua escribanos who transition to writing in Spanish by
retaining Nahuatl structure, cross-cultural assumptions about social decline are
sorely challenged. Some scholars-escribanos writing Spanish-language texts
are fully bilingual, writing in both Spanish and Nahuatl.[14] In San Bartolomé,
Mariano de la Merced served as the model escribano for decoding the Spanish-
language material of the Independence archive, but his writing also represents
ideas and traditions specific to his altepetl. Escribanos in Yancuictlalpan did

not even begin to use Spanish until 1823. Isidro de la Trinidad, the escribano who wrote the only Spanish-language will yet known for Yancuictlalpan, also wrote most of the Nahuatl-language wills. In Ocotitlan escribanos move to Spanish definitively after the typhoid epidemic of 1813. Pablo Leonardo wrote not only the largest number of Spanish wills, half of the sample, but also one of the Nahuatl-language wills. His altepetl's escribano culture conforms to a more conservative Nahuatl structure (when writing in Spanish!) than San Bartolomé, where escribanos wrote in Spanish much *less* often. The intensity of this scholarly precedent astonishes; yet indigenous intonations in Spanish are today inexplicably used by comedians to mean "ignorant." This disconnect from scholarly reality to common mythology represents cultural pain, a people shamed for the very words, the indigenous patrimony, of being Mexican.

Escribanos trained, worked, and substituted for each other and kept a strong esprit de corps within altepetl, as seen in their devotion to their local forms. The variety of paths, cultural resources, and sheer number of writers speaks to deeply rooted institutions that supported escribanos. Father to son, neighbor to neighbor, differences mark notarial identity between altepetl, despite the close contact of adjacent communities with active escribanos. Writing was not a shallow tradition that relied on one single person, or a traveling escribano, to document altepetl transactions. Put in perspective, the parish priests traveled to San Bartolomé rather than living on parish grounds.[15] One way to think about the sweep of writers over time is to remember that *precolonial* Nahua communities functioned as bureaucratic centers, developed as a brand of a colonialism they themselves once imposed on others. In this light, the retention of Nahuatl as the basis for a long-standing written tradition may contradict assumptions of cultural simplification for this late period. But it also makes sense, in the context of groups that facilitated their own bureaucratic conquest, being able to serve in a similar supporting role during a second colonialism that imposed Spanish instead of Nahuatl.

LESS DOCUMENTED LIVES

Paintings of the Last Supper imagine a European Jesus surrounded by other men. Scholars and artists have engaged the question of how cultural dominance creates new realities, why women are not imagined as integral to a Passover Seder where women participate in drinking, cooking, eating, and recounting the

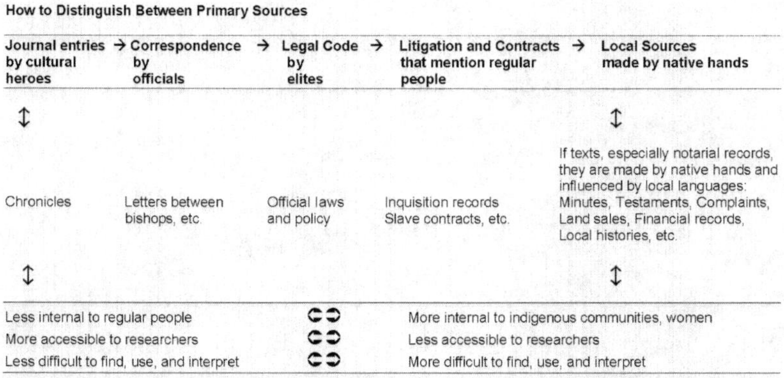

How to Distinguish Between Primary Sources

Journal entries → by cultural heroes	Correspondence → by officials	Legal Code → by elites	Litigation and Contracts → that mention regular people	Local Sources made by native hands
↕				↕
				If texts, especially notarial records, they are made by native hands and influenced by local languages:
Chronicles	Letters between bishops, etc.	Official laws and policy	Inquisition records Slave contracts, etc.	Minutes, Testaments, Complaints, Land sales, Financial records, Local histories, etc.
↕				↕

Less internal to regular people	⟳	More internal to indigenous communities, women
More accessible to researchers	⟳	Less accessible to researchers
Less difficult to find, use, and interpret	⟳	More difficult to find, use, and interpret

FIGURE 33. Method to analyze primary sources: How to include ordinary people in history. This chart helps students identify different points of view in primary documents and understand the social consequences of choosing local sources.

Exodus story and where women initiate the ceremony by lighting the Passover candles.[16] In crafting history, it is not good practice to discount cultural context or women's presence. Even if exiled from men's records, women did exist; we have an obligation to incorporate women into today's written records. Further, including women, children, and elders gives a fuller picture of life stories, grounds events in the sounds of the room.[17] But this goal requires great effort.

Integration poses a methodological problem for historians who focus on time before the contemporary period. Commonly used sources are the least internal to the social lives of regular people: heroes' stories, official correspondence, and legal code.[18] These categories of primary manuscripts may challenge; yet written in dominant languages, they are relatively easy to interpret, compared to local indigenous sources (see figure 33). And the former types of external sources, records cared for by royal bureaucracies, were deposited in central archives, revered and copied and made accessible. Local sources can be pottery, paintings, or other materials analyzed by archaeologists in place or written records *created in and for a community*.[19] I found that for texts, the key is the person doing the writing.[20] When an escribano hails from the community for which he works, the documents reach beyond a simple understanding of the language of his clients: he recognized their status, desires, and affiliations and thought it of value to record them. Without these records, there is no book. Though internal to the local community, local sources don't easily convey the cohesive narrative of a chronicle, making interpretation painstaking; like pulling on loose threads, you can end up with broken, disconnected strands.

Searching for records from indigenous communities and other underrepresented groups, one can attempt to represent more fully the arc of history. The great advantage of the Independence archive came in the sheer numbers of indigenous records from just a few altepetl over three decades. The fragmented details more readily formed a full cloth, representative of whole communities from a concentrated period of time: a mother's will linked the father to his son, both escribanos. These were not records kept by the Crown in central archives but fiscalía records housed in a local parish. The Independence archive continues to offer much promise; I look forward to presenting a broader analysis of land tenure (here limited to ritual use) and kinship. Yet these sources are not unique to what is narrowly considered Latin America; testaments from early periods (called variously notarial or parish records) are found in abundance everywhere Spanish, French, or Portuguese groups reached into the Americas, including large areas now part of the United States.[21] Notarial archives, a generally untapped resource, await historians. Louisiana houses records in Spanish, French, and English—filled with people who have not yet entered the historical record of the United States.

The rewards of these methods are many; in this study I describe significant roles for Nahua women in chapter 6. Women predominated as testament issuers and land bequeathers. Further, looking at the number of properties reported in their wills, women also owned the majority of land. Women sponsored the most elaborate rites at church, established time limits for their Masses to be performed by priests, and actively participated in cofradía-style subunits. In long-standing ritual traditions within the Church, encompassing local religion, women predominated in the ritual landscape, fully participating in the development of new traditions while simultaneously holding to traditional practices. I argue that women's participation all through the colonial period remained strong, and though surprising, the Independence-era numbers do not represent a strong deviation but rather a new lens through which we can examine the participation and importance of indigenous women in the making of Mexican culture.

Where we find women, we also find the men not usually documented: the most local strata of people who lived, day in and day out, outside the gaze of dominating power structures. Men and women served saint images in their households and participated in nominally Christian ancestor veneration as described in chapter 7. Analyzing the way they inherited land with strict orders to serve the saints complex allowed us to see the flowers, incense, and candles in the household—and differentiate from these same rites in the name of ancestors. Devotions unique to households made it appear that they all took turns producing celebrations for their diverse pantheon. As leaders and facilitators, regular people stepped up to produce the celebrations for specific saints that rarely overlapped households, or even neighboring altepetl, encouraging the survival of distinct group identities as evidenced in the strong differentiation of cults. Whether next-door neighbors or adjacent altepetl, all people preferred distinct saints and burial traditions. In the three main altepetl, Nahuas saw their land as a space in relationship to their neighbors, reinforcing this study's identification of a broad and stable civil society, in this case via enduring land allocation systems recognized within their own communities.

As people created meaning within ongoing celebrations of their life, death became a moment of continuity. In the work required to feed the saints, to remember the ancestors, and to weave connections in the community, social obligations were passed on and received by the next generation. Ordinary land, bequeathed to benefit the saints and ancestors in the household, became what connected inheritors to larger networks. In this sense, agricultural labor can be understood as ritual work for the household that also helped establish one's place in the community. Intricately interwoven into ritual land use, these simultaneously collapsing and enlarging relationships, groups, symbols, and agricultural practices nourished the society within which Nahuas inherited land. Whether people used the Nahuatl *tequipanoa* or the Spanish *servir*, life in Nahua homes still required images, incense, flowers, and burning candles. Inheriting land thus meant inheriting a vast array of social, economic, and ritual obligations. People's labor in the name of the saints, ancestors, and community did more than serve patron saints—it bound individuals to their larger community, ultimately fostering cultural resilience by joining individuals, households, and neighboring altepetl in a shared purpose beyond the scope of one lifetime. Daily chores, in corporate agricultural landscapes, became rites of remembering.

EPILOGUE

METHODOLOGY IMPACTS THE EXCLUSION of underrepresented people from the historical narrative: the words we choose to study have lasting impact, build the identity of national and world citizens. Simply put, local sources express the point of view of ordinary people, those of us who have to work for a living. While nonexperts might think that the Aztecs disappeared, and loud voices dehumanize Mexican bodies, I entreat the reader to imagine contemporary meanings in old ideas, how Nahua concepts give light to our modern problems. This humble book provides a nineteenth-century link between the builders of Tenochtitlan's city on the lake as described by astonished Iberians, and contemporary Nahua communities. We have much to learn from the living architecture still spoken in Nahuatl. It is not an accident that political upheaval, and its potential for cultural renewal, springs from indigenous Mexico, areas that retain preexisting collective identities and expectations of representative government, buen gobierno.[1] In action, this means decolonizing our daily hours into a foreseeable future of tightly knit neighborhoods filled with people-centered fun. From grandmothers and musicians to cisterns and gray water and the delicate ceremony of plant guilds, decisions need to be made, in concert. Caucus, an alien concept to the Europeans who ventured into the Americas, allows people to sit down as equals, in shared leadership.[2] So take that bike or bus, and take over the road. Make it yours, make it ours, make it so. Conquerors enslaved, racialized, murdered, and brutalized vast populations of the Americas, but ritual, writing/painting/poetry, and civil society survive. These are the limits to hatred. We hold fast to the words of our ancestors, whispered in pride, naming the embroidered symbol of our shared patrimony. *Ánimo.*

APPENDIX 1

TESTAMENT LISTS FROM THE INDEPENDENCE ARCHIVE WITH REFERENCE CODES

The Independence archive of testaments remains preserved in the Convento de San Juan Bautista in Metepec, State of Mexico. The material is uncataloged, *sin foliar* in Caja 40; thus the code numbers assigned here reflect my own organization and are not indicated in the archive. Footnotes throughout this book lead to these lists.

1. SAN BARTOLOMÉ TLATELOLCO'S TESTAMENTS, 1799–1832

In this list the notaries' names are abbreviated.

BM	Basilio Martín
CG	Cipriano Gordiano
dFNR	don Francisco Nicolás Romero
FNM	Félix Nabor Mulia
JDdlC	Juan Domingo de la Cruz
JGC	José Guadalupe Camacho
JM	José María
JMM	Juan Máximo Mejía
MC	Máximo Calisto
MdlM	Mariano de la Merced

PA   Pedro Agustín
RF   Rufino Faustino
SC   Santiago Cristóbal

Some numbers are missing because of duplications I discovered, and one, 62A, was added. This was to make sure my numbers remained correlated with the photographic index. The list numbers go to 119; the actual total is 116.

WILL #	DATE	TESTATOR	NOTARY	LANGUAGE (NAHUATL UNLESS NOTED)
1	1799	Apolonia Felipa	JDdlC	
2	1803	Dominga Efigenia	BM	
3	1803	Marcela Martina	PA	
4	1806	María Josefa	PA	
5	1809	Victoriana María	dFNR	
6	1809	Tiburcia Valenciana	dFNR	
7	1809	José Abdon	dFNR	
8	1809	María Josefa	dFNR	
9	1810	Pascuala Eleuteria	CG	
10	1810	Manuela Lugarda	CG	
11	1810	Lucaria Crisóstoma	CG	
12	1810	Bernabela Antonia	CG	
13	1810	Lauriano Rafael	CG	
14	1809	Nicolás George	dFNR	
15	1811	Rosa María	CG	
16	1811	Juana María	CG	
17	1811	doña Simona María	CG	
18	1811	Petrona Martina	CG	
19	1811	don Juan de los Santos	CG	

(continued)

WILL #	DATE	TESTATOR	NOTARY	LANGUAGE (NAHUATL UNLESS NOTED)
20	1811	Francisca Javiera	CG	
22	1811	Margarita María	CG	
23	1811	Francisca Javiera	CG	
24	1811	Valentina María	CG	
25	1811	María Francisca	CG	
26	1811	doña Lucaria María	CG	
27	1812	Dominga María	CG	
28	1812	Simona María	CG	
29	1812	María Josefa	CG	
30	1812	Bernardino Antonio	CG	
31	1812	Diego de la Cruz	CG	
32	1812	Florenciana María	CG	
33	1812	Basilia Antonia	CG	
34	1813	Dominga María	CG	
35	1813	Miguel Antonio	CG	
36	1813	Teresa Calista	CG	
37	1813	doña Fausta María	CG	
39	1813	Martina María	CG	
40	1813	Valentina María	MdlM	Spanish
41	1813	Brígida Dionisia	CG	
42	1813	Margarita María	CG	
43	1813	Cristina Sinforosa	CG	
44	1813	Leonarda María	CG (nominal)	
45	1813	Secundina Andrea	CG	
46	1813	don Félix Bernabé	CG	

continued

(continued)

WILL #	DATE	TESTATOR	NOTARY	LANGUAGE (NAHUATL UNLESS NOTED)
47	1813	Manuela María	CG	
48	1813	Fausta Rufina	CG (nominal)	
49	1813	Paula María	MM	
50	1813	Rosa María	CG	
51	1813	Ciriaca Cayetana	CG	
52	1813	Guadalupe María	CG	
53	1813	Vicenta Isidora	CG	
54	1813	Bartolomé Felipe	CG	
55	1813	Melchor Antonio	CG	
56	1813	Ignacia Petrona	CG	
57	1813	Vicente Antonio	CG	
58	1813	Victoria María	CG	
59	1813	Luciano Guadalupe	CG	
60	1813	Luisa Trinidad	MdlM	
61	1813	don Andrés Antonio	CG (nominal)	
62	1813	Felipe de la Cruz	MdlM	Spanish
62A	1813	Marina Cayetana	CG	
63	1813	Juan de los Santos	CG	
64	1814	María Bernardina	CG	
65	1814	Aparicia Feliciana	CG	
66	1814	Margarita María	CG	
67	1815	Lucaria María	RF	
68	1816	Candelaria Martina	CG	
70	1817	Asencia Pascuala	JMM	Spanish
71	1817	Alejandro Justo	JMM	Spanish

continued

(continued)

WILL #	DATE	TESTATOR	NOTARY	LANGUAGE (NAHUATL UNLESS NOTED)
72	1817	Sebastiana Fabiana	JMM	Spanish
73	1818	Bartolomé Luis	CG	
74	1818	Santos Venancio	CG	
75	1818	Petrona Francisca	CG	
76	1818	Bernardinao Gregorio	CG	
77	1819	Domingo Manuel	CG	
78	1819	Lucas Florentino	CG (nominal)	
79	1820	Sebastián Isidoro	RF	
80	1821	Estefania María	RF	
81	1821	Eleuteria Severiana	MC	Spanish
82	1821	Tiburcio Valentín	MC	Spanish
83	1821	Clara María	MC	Spanish
84	1821	Juan Gregorio	MC	Spanish
85	1822	Tomasa Martina	CG	
86	1822	Mariano Rafael	CG	
87	1822	Lugarda María	CG	
88	1822	Gerónima Antonia	CG	
89	1822	Joaquín Benito	CG	
90	1823	Dionisia Jacinta (Casilda)	CG	
91	1823	don Miguel Aparicio	CG	
92	1823	Esteban Ramón	CG	
93	1823	María Albina	CG	
94	1823	Margarita Feliciana	CG	
95	1823	don Hilario Dionisio	CG	
96	1823	Eugenia Gertrudis	CG	

continued

(continued)

WILL #	DATE	TESTATOR	NOTARY	LANGUAGE (NAHUATL UNLESS NOTED)
97	1823	Martín Gordiano	CG	
98	1823	Cipriana Faustina	CG (nominal)	
99	1823	Concepciona María	CG	
100	1823	Perfecto Martín	CG	
101	1823	Simón Marcelino	CG	
102	1823	Alejandro de la Cruz	CG	
103	1823	don Pedro Esteban	CG	
104	1823	Lorenzo Bernardino	CG	
105	1823	Juana Apolonia	CG	
106	1823	Juana Ignacia	CG	
107	1823	Alejandra María	CG	
108	1823	Juan Esteban	CG	
110	1823	Petrona Luciana	CG (nominal)	Spanish
111	1823	Lázaro Martín	CG (nominal)	Spanish
112	1824	Isidra Estefania	JM	Spanish
113	1824	Ascencia María	?	Spanish
114	1824	Martina Bonifacia	FNM	Spanish
115	1824	Dominga Bonifacia	SC	Spanish
116	1824	Alejandro Marcos	JM	Spanish
117	1825	María Josefa	JM	Spanish
118	1825	Mauricio Mateo	JM	Spanish
119	1832	Carmen de la Cruz	JGC	Spanish
			Totals:	95 Nahuatl
				21 Spanish

2. OCOTITLAN'S TESTAMENTS, 1801–1820

WILL #	DATE	TESTATOR	NOTARY	LANGUAGE
1	1801	Ana María	Santos Alberto	Nahuatl
2	1809	Ana María	José Sebastián	Spanish
3	1809	Hilaria María	José Sebastián	Spanish
4	1809	Luisa María	Santiago Cristóbal	Spanish
5	1810	Salvador Miguel	Juan Félix Mejía	Spanish
6	1810	Jacobo Santiago	Sebastián Fabián López	Nahuatl
7	1811	Francisca María	Santiago Cristóbal	Spanish
8	1812	Antonio Francisco	Marcos Alejandro	Spanish
9	1812	Teresa Quiteria	Santiago Cristóbal	Spanish
10	1813	Basilio Julián	Pablo Leonardo	Spanish
11	1813	Diega Gertrudis	Pablo Leonardo	Spanish
12	1813	José Anastasio	Pablo Leonardo	Spanish
13	1813	Juan José	Pablo Leonardo	Spanish
14	1813	Juana Anastasia	Pablo Leonardo	Spanish
15	1813	Juana María	Pablo Leonardo	Spanish
16	1813	Luisa Gervasia	Pablo Leonardo	Spanish
17	1813	Manuela Antonia	Pablo Leonardo	Spanish
18	1813	María Gerónima	Pablo Leonardo	Spanish
19	1813	Martín Pedro	Pablo Leonardo	Spanish
20	1813	Pablo de Santiago	Pablo Leonardo	Spanish
21	1813	Rafael Antonio	Pablo Leonardo	Spanish
22	1813	Ramona María	Pablo Leonardo	Nahuatl
23	1814	María Antonia	José Toribio	Spanish
24	1816	Feliciana Petrona	Toribio Antonio	Spanish
25	1817	Juan de los Santos	Ponciano Guadalupe	Spanish
26	1819	Paulino Santiago	José Sebastián	Spanish
27	1820	Anastasia de la Cruz	Pedro José	Spanish

3. YANCUICTLALPAN'S TESTAMENTS, 1809–1825

WILL #	DATE	TESTATOR	NOTARY	LANGUAGE
1	1809	María Petrona	Marcos Antonio	Nahuatl
2	1810	Margarita María	Marcos Antonio	Nahuatl
3	1810	Juana Nepomucena	Marcos Antonio	Nahuatl
4	1812	Florentina Evangelista	Isidro de la Trinidad	Nahuatl
5	1819	Dionisio Calisto	Isidro de la Trinidad	Nahuatl
6	1820	Nicolasa Bárbara	Isidro de la Trinidad	Nahuatl
7	1821	Lucas Pedro	Isidro de la Trinidad	Nahuatl
8	1821	Mariano Domingo	Isidro de la Trinidad	Nahuatl
9	1823	Juliana Viviana	Isidro de la Trinidad	Spanish
10	1824	Bárbara Manuela	Isidro de la Trinidad	Nahuatl
11	1825	María Bernardina	Isidro de la Trinidad	Nahuatl
12	1825	Francisca Antonia	Isidro de la Trinidad	Nahuatl

4. TOTOCUITLAPILCO'S TESTAMENTS, 1815 AND 1826

WILL #	DATE	TESTATOR	NOTARY	LANGUAGE
1	1826	Petra Angelina	Antonio Ambrosio	Spanish
2	1815	Ana María	Rufino Faustino	Nahuatl
(also SBT#67)				

APPENDIX 2

NOTARIES OF THE INDEPENDENCE ARCHIVE BY ALTEPETL

(N) after a name indicates that the notary worked in Nahuatl; (Sp) indicates that he worked in Spanish.

1. NOTARIES IN SAN BARTOLOMÉ, 1799–1832

	NAME	ABBREVIATION	TESTAMENTS
1	Juan Domingo de la Cruz (N)	JDdlC	SBT#1, 1799
2	Basilio Martín (N)	BM	SBT#2, 1803
3	Pedro Agustín (N)	PA	SBT#3, 1803–1806 SBT#4
4	don Francisco Nicolás Romero (N)	dFNR	SBT#5, 1809 SBT#6 SBT#7 SBT#8 SBT#14

(continued)

	NAME	ABBREVIATION	TESTAMENTS
5	Cipriano Gordiano (N)	CG	SBT#9 and many more, 1810–1823
6	Mariano de la Merced (N and Sp)	MdlM	SBT#49, N; SBT#40, 60, 62, Sp; may have written under the name of CG; all in 1813
7	Rufino Faustino (N)	RF	SBT#79, 80; also possibly 78 for CG, 1819–1820 (spacing and hand different and formulas are considerably different than Toto#2/SBT#67)
		another RF	Toto#2 (also SBT#67) (testator from Toto), 1815
8	Juan Máximo Mejía (Sp)	JMM	SBT#70, 1817 71 72, 1817
9	Máximo Calisto (Sp)	MC	SBT#81, 1821 SBT#82 SBT#83 SBT#84
10	José María (Sp)	JM	SBT#112, 1824–1825 SBT#116 SBT#117 SBT#118
11	Félix Nabor [Mulia?] (Sp)	FN	SBT#114, 1824
12	Santiago Cristóbal (Sp)	SC	SBT#115, 1824; also Oco#4, 1809–1812 Oco#7 Oco#9
13	José Guadalupe Camacho (Sp)	JGC	SBT#119, 1832

2. NOTARIES IN OCOTITLAN, 1801–1820

	NAME	ABBREVIATION	TESTAMENTS
1	Santos Alberto (N)	SA	Oco#1, 1801
2	José Sebastián (Sp)	JS	Oco#2, 1809–1819 Oco#3 Oco#26
3	Santiago Cristóbal (Sp)	SC	Oco#4, 1809–1812 Oco#7 Oco#9 also SBT#115
4	Juan Félix Mejía (Sp)	JFM	Oco#5, 1810
5	Sebastián Fabián López (N)	SFL	Oco#6, 1810
6	Marcos Alejandro (Sp)	MA	Oco#8, 1812
7	Pablo Leonardo (Sp and N)	PL	Oco#10 through 21 (Sp), Oco#22 (N), all 1813
8	José Toribio (Sp)	JT	Oco#23, 1814
9	Toribio Antonio (Sp)	PG	Oco#24, 1816
10	Ponciano Guadalupe (Sp)	PG	Oco#25, 1817
11	Pedro José (Sp)	PJ	Oco#27, 1820

3. NOTARIES IN YANCUICTLALPAN, 1809–1825

	NAME	ABBREVIATION	TESTAMENTS
1	Marcos Antonio (N)	MA	Yan#1, 1809–1810 Yan#2 Yan#3
2	Isidro de la Trinidad (N and Sp)	IT	Yan#4 through 8, 10 through 12 (N), 1812–1824; Yan#9 (Sp), 1823

4. NOTARIES IN TOTOCUITLAPILCO, 1815 AND 1826

	NAME	ABBREVIATION	TESTAMENTS
1	Antonio Ambrosio (Sp)	AA	Toto#1, 1826
2	Rufino Faustino (N)	RF	Toto#2 (also SBT#67), 1815. Two notaries with the name RF; see list no. 1.

APPENDIX 3

SAMPLE TESTAMENTS

Since the corpus of Nahuatl- and Spanish-language testaments on which this study is based is so new, unavailable in published form, and referred to constantly in the body of the study, I provide here full samples of the texts. I have chosen three items, two in Nahuatl and one in Spanish. In making the choices, it became clear that a few samples cannot adequately represent the gender distribution, the years of production, the terminology, and the styles, but at least each item represents some of these things, with the aim of giving the reader a better sense of the Independence archive. I look forward to making the whole corpus of documents available in the future, inviting further research.

Each sample includes a full transcription from the original language, followed by a full translation. For ease of use, I separated the different entries and bequests more visibly than they are often spaced in the originals, and successive numbers are added at the beginning of each entry, to identify words and passages readily. To be clear, the originals contain no such numbers. Each document is preceded by a brief introduction about each text, also not in the original sources. The Spanish-language texts are translated too, which, given the expected readership of this study, may seem superfluous, but the Spanish is so influenced by Nahuatl that it can use interpretation. Of course, translation is an art. In some cases I cannot ascertain exactly what the writers meant, and the Nahuatl-language texts also are often nonstandard; some of these features are discussed.* The following three testament samples follow: 1. Testament of Lugarda María, San Bartolomé Tlatelolco, 1822 (Nahuatl); 2. Testament of Feliciana Petrona, Santa María Magdalena Ocotitlan, 1816 (Spanish); 3. Testament of Margarita María, Santa María de la Rosa Yancuictlalpan, 1810 (Nahuatl).

1. TESTAMENT OF LUGARDA MARÍA, SAN BARTOLOMÉ TLATELOLCO, 1822

NOTARY CIPRIANO GORDIANO (ROMERO) (SBT#87)

This sample represents Cipriano Gordiano's late career. We see his unusual approach to ideas of body and soul. Here (¶4) the soul completely escapes mention; the body is sick all right, but then he says that is as God wishes it for the testator, which usually applies to the healthy soul. On death (¶5) the testator is to belong entirely in the hands of Santa María de la Asunción, with God left unmentioned; this is not the normal thing at all and provided early indications that I was actually looking at the place in the formula that mentions a local church guild, their cofradía. In this will, daughters are called -chpoch and a son is called -coneuh, though the plural of sons is -telpochhuan, using the traditional word applied to grown sons.

In ¶3, persunasa with an extra a at the end is probably more than just a mistake; like many writers of the Toluca Valley, Cipriano sometimes adds a vowel after a final consonant to keep it pronounceable. The form muChia here leaves out hu in the phrase ma in mochihua, "may it be done." In ¶7, tlatzitliConpa (standard tlatzintlancopa; toward the lower part), the second i should be a. A very similar substitution repeats in ¶10. Conas and conas have a syllable missing from conanaz: (she is to take it). This "mistake" is so common in Nahuatl writing that it could almost be considered a convention. In ¶8, milteCon has an initial y or i missing and represents standard imiltenc: (at the edge of . . .). The same thing happens again in ¶10. Also in ¶10, quimopanisque lacks tla and represents quimotlapanizque (they will divide it between themselves). In ¶11, quimalia has ni missing and represents standard quimanilia (he takes it).

---

*A great many aspects of the corpus are shared with eighteenth-century Toluca Valley writing in Nahuatl, and the reader can find much guidance in Pizzigoni, *Testaments of Toluca*, especially pp. 35–39.

In ¶12, *nofiCal* is missing an *s* in standard *nofiscal* (my fiscal). In the form *Gordano*, Cipriano Gordiano varies the spelling of his own name.

===

1. Agosto 23/822
   San Bartolomé
   Lugarda Maria
   Viuda de
   Pedro Pasqual
   Misa resada
2. Jesus Maria Josepe
3. Ca niCa ninoMaChiutia yCa ytlasuMahuistoCatzi Dios tetatzi ynhua Dios yntlasumahuispiltzi ynhua Dios espirito santu lle persunasa [*sic*] ce huel neli teutzitli Dios Ma y muChia [*sic*] Ame Jesus y maria y Jose =
4. Ca niCa nicpehualtia notestameto Nahuatli notoCa Lugarda Maria nonamictzi metztiCapCa difoto ytoCatzi Dn pedro pasqual Ca niCa tiChaneque ypa yn illaltepetzi notlasumahuitatzi santo sn Bartolome tlatelulCo Ca seCa mo-ConCotiCa setetle noCuerpotzi que nehmotlanequilis tto Dios
5. yntla ninomiquilis Ca yseMactziCo nipohuis notlasuMahuinatzi santa maria Asupocio ynhua nopanpa tzilinis Capanatzi neltis notlatol ynhua niquitohua nosepultora lles ynahuactziCo nonamictzi metztiCaPCa yc Calvario neltis notlatol =
6. ynhua notlasuteupixCatzi nehmutloColis setetli Misa resada para ypalehuiluCa lles no-Animatzi mochictzinos neltis notlatol =
7. ynhua niquitohua se sularito yno utehmoCahuililitiquisque notlasutiutzi Manuel Jose uquimoCahuilitiquis notlasutatzi metztiCaPca Julia de santiago AxCa nehuatli unehmoCahuili axca niccahuiliti umeti nohpoChhua se ytoCa Maria de la LoZ oc se ytoCa Bartola Lohuisa quimotlapanisque nepatla de travesado yc tlatzitliConpa [*sic*] Conas [*sic*] Maria de la loz yc tlacpacConpa conas [*sic*] Bartola Luisa neltis notlatol mochihuas notlanahuatil =
8. ynhua niquitohua se tlali de nahui tomipa Ca tepatitla Ca milteCon [*sic*] Dn Martin gregorio AxCa nicCahuiliti noConetzi Manuel siriCo Connanas Amo Aqui tle quitos mostla huipitla neltis notlatol muChihuas notlatol =
9. ynhua niquitohua oc se tlali Ca saCamoli sano de nahui tomipa Ca ymilteco Juan de la Cruz Axca nicCahuiliti oc se noConetzi yntoCa reymodo Julia Conanas neltis notlatol mochihuas notlanahuatil =

10. ynhua niquitohua oc se tlali de se pssupa Ca milteCo [sic] Juan Alverto yc tlatzintliCopa [sic] unehmoCahuiliquis nonamictzin metztiCaCCa yno tlali de nahui tomipa AxCa niquiCahuiliti umeti notelpoChohua Conanasque uome tomipa Conanas noCone Manuel siriaCo yc toloCaConpa oc ume tomipa Conanas oc se noCone ytoCa Reymodo julia yc CalimallaConpa Conanas nepatla quimopanisque [sic] yllermanito neltis moChihuas notlanahuatil =

11. ynhua niquitohua yno oc nahui tomipa lle quimalia [sic] llehuatzin nosubrinotzi Dn Martin gregorio neltis notlatol =

12. ynhua niquitohua notepatlatoCatzin moChictzinos noAlvasia Ca llehuatzin Dn tomas Julia ytla quali quimoChilis Ca tto Dios quimoxtlahuilis nopanpa Ca llonictzoquixti notestameto ymixpatzinCo nofiCal [sic] Mallor de la sata Madre yglesia Dn Rafel Agel fisCal menor Juan Antonio Alhuasil Mallor vicente ferel yhua Essno de la sata madre yglesia sipriano Gordano [sic] Romerro

AxCan Lunes 19 de AGosto de 1822 ayños [sic]

1. August 23, 1822.
   San Bartolomé.
   Lugarda María,
   widow of
   Pedro Pascual.
   Low mass.

2. Jesus, Mary, and Joseph.

3. Here I sign myself with the precious revered name of God the father, God his precious revered son, and God the Holy Spirit, three persons but one very true deity God. May it be done, amen. Jesus, Mary, and Joseph. =

4. I named Lugarda María here begin my testament. My late husband was named don Pedro Pascual, deceased; we are citizens here in the altepetl of my precious revered father San Bartolomé Tlatelolco. My whole body is very ill, as my lord God would wish it for me.

5. If I die, I am to belong entirely in the hands of my precious revered Santa María de la Asunción, and the bells are to ring on my behalf. My statement is to be carried out. And I say that my grave is to be close to my late husband at the Calvario. My statement is to be carried out. =

6. And my precious priest is to favor me with a low mass in order to be the help of my soul. My statement is to be executed and carried out. =

7. And I say that as to that little solar that my precious uncle Manuel José left us on death, that he left to my precious late father Julián de Santiago, and that now my father left to me, now I am leaving it to two daughters of mine. One is named María de la Luz, and the other is named Bartola Luisa; they are to divide it in half, sideways. María de la Luz is to take the lower part; Bartola Luisa is to take the upper part. My statement is to be carried out, my order executed. =

8. And I say that as to another piece of land, in Tepantitlan, of 4 reales, at the edge of a field of don Martín Gregorio, now I am leaving it to my son Manuel Siriaco; he is to take it. No one is to say anything in the future, my statement is to be carried out, my statement is to be executed. =

9. And I say that as to another piece of land, newly cleared, likewise of 4 reales, at the edge of a field of Juan de la Cruz, now I am leaving it to another son of mine named Raimundo Julián; he is to take it. My statement is to be carried out, my order is to be executed. =

10. And I say that as to another piece of land of 1 peso, at the edge of a field of Juan Alberto, my late husband left me the lower part; that land is of 4 reales. Now I am leaving 2 reales to my two sons; they are each to take 2 reales. My son Manuel Siriaco is to take the part toward Toluca; my other son named Raimundo Julián is to take the other 2 reales, toward Calimaya. He [Manuel Siriaco] and his younger brother are to divide it equally. My command is to be carried out and executed. =

11. And I say that my nephew don Martín Gregorio is to take those other 4 reales. My statement is to be carried out. =

12. And I say that the one who is to become my intercessor and executor is don Tomás Julián; if he does it well, our lord God will reward him on my behalf. I have concluded my testament in the presence of my fiscal mayor of the holy mother church don Rafael Angel, fiscal menor Juan Antonio, alguacil mayor Vicente Ferrer, and notary of the holy mother church Cipriano Gordiano Romero.

Today Monday the 19th of August of the year 1822.

2. TESTAMENT OF FELICIANA PETRONA, SANTA MARÍA MAGDALENA OCOTITLAN, 1816

NOTARY TORIBIO ANTONIO (OCO#24)

This is one of the best developed testaments in Spanish to be found in the entire Independence-era archive. It shows a larger Spanish vocabulary and fluency than others. Yet the escribano still varies standard Spanish, mastering it at times. If he usually understands the use of Spanish *a*, as in "se la dexo a mi nieta" (I leave it to my granddaughter), which many Nahuatl speakers did not (¶9), he is still capable of writing "Se la dexo mi hija" (I leave it to my daughter) but omitting the necessary *a*. Most of the time adjectives and articles agree with nouns in gender here, a difficult point because Nahuatl had no grammatical gender, but at times we see violations, as in "Se la dexo al mimo mi hija" (I leave it to my same daughter; article and *same* are masculine), with a mixture of masculine and feminine. Even the daughter's second name appears as both Crisanta and Crisanto. (It was common for notaries to vary the ever-repeating names of their clients.) The grammatical number of verbs was also a problem for the writer, probably because, coming from Nahuatl, he hardly pronounced the *n* that creates so many plurals. Thus an *n* is missing in the passage (¶15) "les Ruego A mis alBaseas para que able por mi" (I implore my executors to speak for me); *able* is for *hablen*. Throughout, the writer uses a Nahuatl word order as in "difunto mi marido" (deceased my husband) instead of *mi difunto marido* or *mi marido difunto*.

Some of the escribano's vocabulary is truly impressive, but he did not always use the Spanish words that he had acquired in a standard way. In "esta casa hubicada de adove" (¶9), the writer means "this house built of adobe," but the word *ubicado* technically means *located*, not *built*. The phrase "compone quarenta y Sinco varas" means "measures forty-five *varas*," but the verb *componer* is not comfortable here for a Spanish speaker. In ¶4, it is hard to know what to make of the phrase "nadie eche a perder delante." It occurs in the sequence where a Nahuatl-language will says *aquen ca* or *catqui*, that there is nothing wrong with the spirit and soul, that it is undamaged; thus, I tentatively posit this is the approximate intention of this passage. Nahuas also varied the *ie* found in many Spanish words; they would write just *e*, or just *i*, and having become aware of the diphthong, they would write it where it didn't belong. Both things happen here: *quin* (¶9) and *quen* (¶10) for *quien* (who) and *Siembradura* (¶10) for *sembra-*

dura (seed). In ¶9 and repeatedly, the writer uses "mañana u otro dia," a literal translation from Nahuatl, taken from *moztla huiptla* (literally, tomorrow [or] the day after tomorrow, with the meaning "in the future, in the coming time"). Much more could be said on the language of this document. It illustrates many of the points discussed in treating testaments in Spanish in chapter 2.

Household saints are featured here, with Guadalupe the first of three named, and there are more, called images, a minority phenomenon in the Toluca Valley and the Nahua world generally, but seen sometimes in the Metepec area specifically, as also happens in the next source, sample 3. Though *imagen* was always part of the vocabulary of Spanish priests, the word here is probably a back translation of Nahuatl *ixiptlatl*. The testator here bequeaths land with the order that it be used to produce rites in her own memory, attaching that condition to two pieces, one to the granddaughter and one to the daughter. Heirs don't simply inherit land, but work the land in order to fund and produce ongoing rituals in ancestors' memory, as described in chapter 6; with candles, flowers, and incense.

———

1. Mayo 25/816.
   Ocotitlan
   Feliciana Petra
   Viuda de Miguel
   de la Cruz.
   Misa rezada.
2. Jesus Maria y Jose
3. Oy dia Miercoles A dies y siete de Abril del Año de mil ochosientos dies y seis haora me percigno en el Nombre de Dios padre Dios hijo y Dios espiritu Santo tres personas distintas y hun Solo Dios Berdadero Creo en el misterio de la Santisima trinidad —
4. haora pongo y comienso Mi testamento para que lo Sepa quantos lo Biere este testamento como yo me llamo Felisiana petrona fui casado con difunto mi marido Miguel de la cruz Somos criollos y nasidos de este pueblo Santa Maria Magdalena S.r de ocotitlan Digo que Se halla enfermo mi cuerpo en cama pero mi alma y corazon Se halla mui contenta nadie eche a perder delante—esperando la muerte y Si Dios Se acordara de mi y me dara la muerte que en Sus manos pongo mi alma que es Su echura y lo Redimio Con Su preSio Sisima Sangre y le

Ruego a mi padre eterno que me llebe a gosar de Su Dulse compania a gosar en Su Santa Gloria pero mi cuerpo lo mando en tierra de que fue formado —

5. y lo primero digo que Se dara medio Real a los santos lugares de Jerusalem que Se cumpla lo que mando

6. y digo que mi mortaxa Dios lo hallara —

7. y digo que honde Se sepultara mi cuerpo halla en la yglesia en el Siminterio honde esta enterrado difunto mi marido haga lo que mando —

8. y Digo para el Sufragio de mi alma Se me dira huna miSa Rresada dentro de veinte dias que se Cumpla mi palabra —

9. y digo y declaro que esta casa hubicada de adove Con la mitad del Solar que Compone quarenta y Sinco baras al lado de Norte que me dexo difun [sic] Mi Marido haora Se la dexo A mi hija Simona Crisanta y Su Marido polonio Basilio que ellos Se queda en la casa para que le Sirba ha Mi madre Nuestra Señora de Guadalupe y S.or San Nicolas y Santo Ni-ño y todos lo himagenes No les falta belas Saumerio los pasquas Grandes No hayga quin les Diga Nada mañana u otro dia que Se Cumpla lo que mando —

10. y Digo que otro pedaso de Solar al lado de Sur que compone diez y ocho varas hasta onde esta el texoxote y hasta honde linda con el Solar de Visente ferrel haora Se la dexo a mi nieta antonia trinidad para que ponga su casa No haiga quen [Se] le diga nada mañana u otro dia que Se cumpla lo que mando

11. yten Mas Digo y declaro que otra tierra Se halla Junto la tierra de difunto Juan Serrano que cave una quartilla de Siembradura de mais que me dexo difunto mi marido Miguel de la cruz ahora Se la dexo mi hija Simona Cristina y Su marido polonio Basilio para que dia Sacara las belas y flores que Se cumpla lo que mando —

12. yten y declaro que otro tierra que esta en el llano Junto la tierra de marcial ugenio que me dexo difunto mi marido ahora Se la dexo al mimo mi hija Simona Crisanta y Su marido polonio Basilio que Se cumpla mi palabra —

13. yten mas Digo y deClaro que otro pedaso de tierra de media quartilla Se la dexo a mi nieta antonia trinidad No haya quin le diga nada mañana u otro dia que Se cumpla lo que mando y Se acordara de mi —

14. yten mas Digo y declaro que otra tierra que me dexo difunto mi padre Juan Luis que Se halla en Frente del Calbario Junto la tierra de D.ña Maria ySoja Viuda al lado de norte y por el Sur linda con la tierra difunto Visente Gusman haora Se la dexo a mi hija Simona Crisanto y Su marido polonio Basilio los que se nombraro arriba para que Se acuerde de mi los dias pasquas Grandes que Se cumpla lo que mando —

15. y Digo que lla cumpli lo que me mando Difunto mi marido no tengo Mas que poner y les Ruego A mis alBaseas para que able por mi que es D.n Jose lionardo y Rafael Antonio y Si asi lo hara que de Dios tendra el premio —

16. Y Nosotros hisimos el testamento como testigos yo el fiscal mayor de la Santa Madre yglesia D.n Martin Diego fiscal teniente Jose Antonio tupile mayor Manuel trinidad Es.no de la Santa yglesia Toribio - Antonio

━━━━━━━━━━

1. May 25, 1816.
   Ocotitlan.
   Feliciana Petra,
   widow of Miguel
   de la Cruz.
   Low mass.

2. Jesus, Mary, and Joseph.

3. Today Wednesday the 17th of April of the year of 1816, I sign myself in the name of God the father, God the son, and God the Holy Spirit, three different persons and a single true God; I believe in the mystery of the most holy Trinity. —

4. Now I issue and begin my testament so that all who should see this testament should know that I am named Feliciana Petrona; I was married to my deceased husband Miguel de la Cruz; we are criollos and natives of this pueblo of Santa María Magdalena and the Señor of Ocotitlan. I say that my body is sick and in bed, but my soul and heart are very content [and undamaged?], awaiting death. If God should remember me and bring about my death, in his hands I place my soul, which is of his making, and he redeemed it with his precious blood; and I implore my eternal father to take me to enjoy his sweet company in his holy paradise, but my body I send to the earth of which it was made. —

5. First I say that half a real is to be given to the holy places of Jerusalem. Let what I order be carried out.

6. And I say that God will provide my shroud. —

7. And I say that where my body will be buried is at the church, in the cemetery, where my deceased husband is buried. Let what I order be carried out. —

8. And I say that for the aid of my soul a low mass is to be said for me within twenty days. Let my word be carried out.

9. And I say and declare that as to this house [built] of adobe, with half of the solar, which measures 45 varas on the north side, that my deceased husband

left me, now I am leaving it to my daughter Simona Crisanta and her husband Apolonio Basilio that they may remain in the house to serve my mother our lady of Guadalupe and lord San Nicolás and the Santo Niño and all the images. They are not to lack candles and incense on the great religious festivities [likely somehow corresponding to Christian High Holidays]. No one is to say anything to them in the future; let what I order be carried out.—

10. And I say that as to another piece of the solar, on the south side, measuring 18 varas as far as where the tejojote is and where it borders on the solar of Vicente Ferrer, now I leave it to my granddaughter Antonia Trinidad to put her house there. No one is to say anything to them in the future; let what I order be carried out.

11. Item, I say and declare that as to another piece of land located next to a piece of land of the deceased Juan Serrano, where a cuartilla of maize seed fits, that my deceased husband Miguel de la Cruz left me, now I leave it to my daughter Simona Cristina [sic] and her husband Apolonio Basilio so that from there she will extract the candles and flowers. May my order be carried out. —

12. Item, I declare that as to another piece of land that is on the plain, next to a piece of land of Marcial Eugenio, that my deceased husband left me, now I leave it to my same daughter Simona Crisanta and her husband Apolonio Basilio. Let my word be carried out. —

13. Item, I say and declare that I leave another piece of land of half a cuartilla to my granddaughter Antonio Trinidad. No one is to say anything to her in the future; let what I order be carried out. And she is to remember me. —

14. Item, I say and declare that as to another piece of land that my deceased father Juan Luis left me, that is located in front of the Calvario, next to a piece of land of doña María [Hinojosa?] on the north side and bordering on the south with a piece of land of the deceased Vicente Guzmán, now I leave it to my abovementioned daughter Simona Crisanta and her husband Apolonio Basilio, so that she will remember me on the High Holidays [literally, days of the great religious festivities]. May my order be carried out. —

15. I say that I have carried out what my deceased husband ordered me; I have no more to dispose. And I implore my executors, who are don José Leonardo and Rafael Antonio, to speak for me, and if they do, they will have their reward from God. —

16. And we made the testament as witnesses, I the fiscal mayor of the holy mother church don Martín Diego, and the fiscal teniente, José Antonio; the chief topile, Manuel Trinidad; and the notary of the holy church, Toribio Antonio.

3. TESTAMENT OF MARGARITA MARÍA, SANTA MARÍA DE LA ROSA YANCUICTLALPAN, 1810

NOTARY MARCOS ANTONIO (YAN#2)

This sample testament retains the Nahuatl metaphor for the home complex, "house, solar, and saints." Here in ¶9 the wording is "yni Caltzintli Much ica solar Yhuan xiptlallotzitzihua Dios santos Yhuan santas" (this house together with the solar and the images of God, the male and female saints), keeping the feminine form. The now rare word *images* is of note. Here the form *xiptlallotzitzinhua Dios* lacks the necessary possessive prefix; the standard form would be *ixiptlayotzitzinhuan Dios* (the images of God). In Yancuictlalpan bequests, heirs were sometimes directed to serve the altepetl and the king with their land inheritances, as described in chapter 6. Such a statement is made here in ¶10.

Margarita María functioned as owner of bequests from her husband's lineage but keeps his family's land separate from her own property. Thus, she makes bequests of land she owns independently while also acting as a custodian of bequests from her husband.

Witnesses for the people making testaments in Yancuictlalpan represent a set of officials of the local municipality (cabildo) not the fiscalía officials used in this capacity in San Bartolomé and Ocotitlan. The alcalde, two regidores (mayor and segundo), alguacil mayor, topile, and the notary make up the bulk of the local municipal officials present. Note that the fiscal of the Church appears too, but without a full and independent fiscalía contingent. Even the escribano, for example, is clearly described as the municipal notary, not the notary of the Church, the divide described in chapter 1.

The escribano reverses some letters, especially the ending *-tl*. Thus in ¶3 *xihuitl* (year), appears as *xiuhilt*, and the same thing happens in ¶4 with *nehhualt* for *nehuatl* (I); in ¶9 *Caltemiilt* is for *caltemitl* (entryway), and in ¶10 *Yehhualt* is for *yehuatl* (that). In ¶8 *sentl* is for *centetl* (one; often *sentel* in the corpus.) Throughout, Marcos Antonio often uses *ll* as the equivalent of *y*, as in *lles* for *yez* (it will be), though sometimes he means a true Nahuatl double *l*, as in *tlapohualli* (count). He also frequently indicates what was traditionally a glottal stop by *h*, as in *niquihtua* for *niquitoa* (I say), where a glottal stop came before the *t*. In the last line of ¶4, in the phrase "yhuan noanimantzin quenin Can que San huel pactica" (and as to how my soul is, it is very sound), the *que* seems to be a loan of the Spanish conjunction, something rare and late in the story of language contact phenomena in Nahuatl.

In ¶10, the form *tiilhuia* remains a puzzle. It comes just before reference to the road to Calimaya. Often one sees an expression such as *inic tihui Calimaya* (by which we go to Calimaya), and perhaps something like that was the intention. Or there was an expression *tiquilhuia* (that we call), and the intention might be "what we call the Calimaya road."

———————

1. Julio 18 de 1810.
   Yancuitlalpan
   Margarita Maria Viuda de
   Juan Gregorio
   Misa Resada
2. Jesus Maria y Jose
3. Axcan Martes Ypan Caxtoli tonalli mani Metztli de Mallo Yhuan xiuhilt tlapohualli 1810 Ninomachiotia Yca Yn itlazonmahuistohCahtzi Yn Dios tetahtzi Dios ytlazonpiltzin Yhuan Dios Espiritu Santo Ma mochihuan Amen Jesus —
4. Ma quimatica muchinti Ynn aquihque quitasque Yni Nomemorial testamento nehhualt notuca Margarita Maria viuda nonamictzin Ytoca Juan Gregorio Difunto niCah tichanihque Ypan Yaltepetzi noSenquiscanantzin Santa Maria de la Rosa natibitas llanquictlalpa Niquintus Ca huel mococua notlalo nosoquio Yhuan noanimantzin quenin Can que San huel pactica
5. intlan mustla noso huiptla nehmonochilis Yn totecullo Dios Ca Ysenmactzinco nicnoCahuililia nolloliantzin Yhuan noanimantzin Ca nitlachihualtzin Yhua nitlamaquixtiltzin ni-nochihuas mostla huiptla
6. Yhuan huel ahato niquihtua Ca nichuenchiuhtia Melio para los Santos lugares de Jerusalen motemaCas neltis mochihuas notlanahuatil
7. Yhuan niquihtua noquimiliuhca lles Ca Dios quimonextilis Y niquihtua Campa tuctos notlalo nosoquio Ca ompa teopa ittualco nehmotlaocolilisque neltis mochihuas notlanahuatil —
8. Yhuan niquihtuan Ypalehuloca lles noanimantzin Can sentle Misa Rezada nopan mihtus Ypan Se Metztli neltis mochihuas notlanahutil —
9. Yhuan niquihtua Yni Caltzintli Much ica solar Yhuan xiptlallotzitzihua Dios santos Yhuan Santas unCa moCauhtzinoa Ypan ithuali Yhuan Caltemiilt ni-

quinnoCahulilitia notelpoh fran.co Juaquin Yhuan Ysihua Ytoca Maria Casimira Para quihmotequipanilhuisque

10. Yhuan niquihtua oc se lali ōnca ōnoc mani tiilhuia [?] Calimalla ohtli de Sentlaxelloli tlaoli nicYnCahuilihtia Sanno Yehhualt notelpoh franco Juaquin Yhuan YSihua Maria Casimira para tlatequipanosq.e Ypan Yaltepetzin tuSenquiscanantzin Yhua quimotequipanilhuisque tutlahtohCatzin Rey ma D.s quimopiele Campa moezttica neltis mochihuas notlanahuatil —

11. Yhuan niquihtua ōc se tlali ōnCa ōnoc mani huelli ōhtli Yteh Yehui tlahco tlaxelloli tlaoli titumilnamique nosobrinohtzi Serafin Mariano nicquihCahuililitia se nohpoh Ytoca franca tomasa Yhuan Ynamictzin Ytoca Andres Dionicio nicneltilia tlen ōmotlanahuatilihtia Difunto nonamictzi metzticatca para Ypan tlatequipanosque neltis mochihuas notlanahuatil —

12. Yhuan niquihtua nohpoh fran.ca tomasa nicnocahulilitia nosenquiscatahtzin S,r S.n felipe de Jesus neltis mochihuas notlanahuatil amaquin tlen quihtus mustla huiptla

13. Yhuan niquihtua Ca Sann ixquih onicmachioti ixpantzinco Dios Yhuan llenhuatintzitzin noAlbaseas mochiuhtzinoa YCa huel niquinotlatlauhtilia lle nopa motlahtoltisque mostla huiptla Ca tla quali quimochihuilisque Ca Dios quimotlaxtlahuilmaquilis Ca Yehuatzi Dn Andres Dionicio Yhuan Yehhuatzi D.n Serafin Mariano

14. Yni ye ōnicchiuh Yni nomemorial testamento nehhualt Ca mochintintzitzin imixpantzinco noS.res oficial de Rep.ca S.r Al.de Actual D,n Cesario matias Re.dor Ma,or D,n S.tos cesario Redor Seg.o Mateo de la Cruz Alg.sil Ma,or Anastacio pedro topile Jose Ramon S.r fiscal de la S.ta Yglecia D.n Juan fran,co El Escrino de Rep.ca MarCos Antonio

────────────

1. July 18, 1810.
   Yancuictlalpan.
   Margarita María, widow of
   Juan Gregorio.
   Low mass.

2. Jesus, Mary, and Joseph.

3. Today Tuesday on the 15th day of the month of May and the year count 1810, I take as my sign the precious revered name of God the father, God his precious son, and God the Holy Spirit. May it be done, amen. Jesus. —

4. May all those who see this my memorandum of testament know that my name is Margarita María, widow; my deceased husband's name was Juan Gregorio. We are citizens here in the altepetl of my consummate mother Santa María de la Rosa de Nativitas, Yancuictlalpan. I say that my earthly body is very sick, and as to how my soul is, it is very sound.

5. If in the future our lord God calls me, I leave my spirit and soul entirely in his hands, for I was made by him and will be saved by him in the future.

6. And first of all I say that I am making an offering of half a real for the Santos Lugares de Jerusalen; it is to be provided. My order is to be realized and carried out.

7. And I say that God will provide what is to be my shroud. And I say that as to where my earthly body is to lie buried, they will favor me with a place in the churchyard. My order is to be realized and carried out. —

8. And I say that the help of my soul will be that a low mass will be said for me within a month. My order is to be realized and carried out. —

9. And I say that as to this house together with the solar and the images of God, the male and female saints, they are to stay in the house compound; I leave it to my son Francisco Joaquín and his wife named María Casimira to serve [the saints].

10. And I say that another piece of land lies on the road [going to?] Calimaya, of one cuartilla of maize; I leave it likewise to my son Francisco Joaquín and his wife María Casimira to [serve] in the altepetl of our consummate mother. And they are to serve our ruler the king; may God keep him where he is. My order is to be realized and carried out. —

11. And I say that another piece of land lies on the highway; half a cuartilla of maize fits in it. It borders on a field of my nephew Serafín Mariano. I am leaving it to a daughter of mine named Francisca Tomasa and her husband named Andrés Dionisio. I am carrying out what my late deceased husband left ordered. It is so that they will serve on it. My order is to be realized and carried out. —

12. And I say that I am leaving to my daughter Francisca Tomasa our consummate father lord San Felipe de Jesús. My order is to be realized and carried out. No one is to say anything in the future.

13. And I say that that is all that I have recorded before God and those who are becoming my executors, so that I greatly implore them to speak for me in the future. If they do it well, God will give them their reward. They are don Andrés Dionisio and don Serafín Mariano.

14. I have made this my memorandum of testament before all my lords officers of the municipality, the lord present alcalde don Cesario Matías; regidor mayor don Santos Cesario; regidor segundo Mateo de la Cruz; alguacil mayor, Anastasio Pedro; topile, José Ramón; fiscal de la santa iglesia, don Juan Francisco. The notary of the municipality, Marcos Antonio.

NOTES

INTRODUCTION

1. Vizenor sees indigeneity as cues to modernity, which circumvents much of the static gaze that attempts to categorize culture in the past-tense. Vizenor, *Manifest Manners*.

2. Altepetl names, hereafter referred to in brief as indicated in italics, reflect an editorial truncation of the full altepetl name found in the sources. Of note, Yancuictlalpan is the only pueblo that today is not commonly recognized by its Nahuatl name. The elders I spoke to in San Bartolomé Tlatelolco only know the town as "Nativitas." Appendix 3 offers sample transcriptions from three altepetl (from the three largest collections of testaments) in the Independence archive.

3. Circa 1500 BCE. For a comparison of archaeological stages in Toluca and Mexico Valleys, see cuadro 1 in Sugiura Yamamota, "Caminando El Valle de Toluca" and Hernández Rodríguez, *El Valle de Toluca*. In the latter, see figure 5 for a preclassic figurine from Lomas Altas, Toluca.

4. For the ongoing political strategy of intermarriage, see also the marriage of princess Azcatlxochitl in Torquemada I as quoted in p. 27, Hernández Rodríguez, *El Valle de Toluca*.

5. Metepec, Ocoyoacac, Atlapulco, Mimiapan, Capulhuac, Xiquipilco, Cacalomacan, Atenco, Michimaloya, Xocotitlan, Totocuitlapilco, and Ocelotepec are

named as Chichimec settlements; from Códice García Granados in García Castro, *Indios, territorio y poder*, 64. See Hernández Rodríguez, *El Valle de Toluca*, 31. García Castro found four references of Metepec considered as Otomí territory: Sahagún, Códice Mendoza, Anales Cuauhtitlan, and Chimalpahin.

6. Hernández Rodríguez, "Los pueblos prehispanics del Valle de Toluca," 220.

7. Horn offers myriad archival references to Otomí in not only altepetl records (where Otomí formed their own tlaxilacalli in Coyoacan) but also visitas, litigation, and land surveys, including reference to apparently ubiquitous Otomí interpreters. Horn also cites the linguistic evidence for Otomí influence on Tepaneca, an influence that predates Tepaneca settlement in the Valley of Mexico. For these specific examples, see Horn, *Postconquest Coyoacan*, 23. See also Pedro Carrasco's study that shows that Azcapotzalco was not an anomaly: in Tlacopan, Nahuatl, Otomí, Matlatzinca, Mazahua, Chocho, and Chichimec were spoken. Carrasco Pizana, *Tenochca Empire of Ancient Mexico*, 177.

8. A much smaller fifth group is also represented in colonial manuscripts, the Ocuilteca, who lived at the southern edge of the valley toward Malinalco. See Wood, "Corporate Adjustments," 12.

9. "1664 Libro de Difuntos" (Metepec, State of Mexico, n.d.), uncatalogued material, Archivo del Ex-Convento de San Juan Bautista. The precise term notwithstanding, it can still be argued that the ethnic terms in this parish record were constructed as a translation for an outside regime. However, the writer appears to use this as a self-designation within this colonial context.

10. In the 1590s, various complaints by the principal Lucas de San Miguel make it clear that Spanish meddling with indigenous boundaries was unwelcome; in documentation of the altepetl's point of view, they say that Matlazinta land was divided among the faithful Mexican altepetl: "[Axayácatl] repartió las tierras del dicho valle desta manera al pueblo de Tltelulco, que en el tiempo de la infidelidad era cabecera de México . . . Se pobló el pueblo de Totocuytlapilco que después que vinieron los españoles a esta nueva España se llama San Miguel Totocuytlapilco y ansi mismo se pobló el pueblo de Tlatelulco." (In this way [Axayácatl] divided that lands in said valley to the *pueblo* Tltelulco, that at the time of infidelity was a *cabecera* of México . . . Totocuitlapilco was founded, after which the Spanish came to New Spain it was called San Miguel Totocuitlapilco, and similarly was the pueblo of Tlatelolco founded.) Hernández Rodríguez, *El Valle de Toluca*, 101–9, 120–1. See also cuadro 3 on p. 63 for a corroborating list of "tierras repartidas por los mexica" in which both San Bartolomé Tlatelulco ([*sic*], this spelling is used today) and San Miguel

Totocuitlpa [*sic*] are considered "tierras dadas a los aliados." Bornemann, *Del señorío a la república de indios.*

11. Commonly referred to as "the Lockhart School," many important scholars did not work directly with James Lockhart yet are considered part of the same intellectual family of Nahuatl fans, and many have expanded the field beyond the Nahuas to study Maya, Mixtecs, and Zapotec society.

12. See García Castro, *Indios, territorio y poder*, 23. Of note, the Matlatzinca word for city-state was *inpuhetzi*; excuse my oversimplification for the sake of clarity.

13. I refer to an excerpt of the transcription in note 11: "[Axayacatl] repartió las tierras del dicho valle desta manera al pueblo de Tltelulco, que en el tiempo de la infidelidad *era cabecera* de México" [emphasis added]. According to Fray Diego Durán, the Mexica phase in Toluca is described as one of relative autonomy (before the rebellion against Axayácatl, with three powerful altepetl vying for land: Toluca, Matlatzinco, and Tenantzinco). See Hernández Rodríguez, *El Valle de Toluca*, 42.

14. García Hernández, *Matlatzincas*, 7.

15. Very early on, the Toluca Valley region became part of Hernando Cortés's Marquesado, under his title for the Valley of Oaxaca, given by King Carlos V in a *cédula* (document) from Barcelona July 6, 1529. Alanís Boyso, *Elecciones de República*, 455.

16. Lienzo de Tlaxcala, plate 40.

17. Chapter 3 quotes a pastoral and an *edicto* (edict) from the eighteenth century. In this contradiction, between official aims and local practice, the story unfolds.

18. The last Nahuatl-language and Spanish-language sources in this study date from 1825 and 1832, respectively; Yan#12, Nahuatl-language testament of Francisca Antonia, 1825, and SBT#119, Spanish-language testament of Carmen de la Cruz, 1832.

19. Viceroy Revillagigedo is known among historians for instituting the most comprehensive early census of New Spain. See Mairot, *Mexican Provincial Society*, 228–29 and table 4.2, "Hispanic Population of Pueblos in Toluca's Jurisdiction," 1791.

20. Ibid., 228.

21. Ibid., 232. Of course a census count that prioritizes the politically dominant ethnic class would skew the reality of demographically dominant indigenous identities and should be used with caution.

22. Justinya Olko presented a source in alphabetic Nahuatl she found that dates from 1543, the earliest known (she estimates Morelos censuses are from the 1530s, but those are not dated).

23. Huitzilopochtli, patron of the Mexica, in one creation myth is described as being born miraculously by Coatlicue, his mother. In this account he was born fully armed and ready for battle. González Torres and Ruiz Guadalajara, *Diccionario de mitología*, 86.

24. This term means that the pictography "conveys meaning directly to the reader without usually having to form words." Boone, *Stories in Red and Black*, 31.

25. Boone describes Aztec writing as a mix of different kinds of writing approaches: abstract and phonetic elements join the pictography "to form a composite system that could function across linguistic boundaries." Ibid., 32.

26. Boone notes that the Aztec system is considered part of the horizon style that "spread over the central portion of Mexico in the post classic period (C.E. 900-1520)." Ibid.

27. In 1568, chapter XCII, Bernal Díaz says, "I must also mention human excrements, which were exposed for sale in canoes lying in the canals near this square, and is used for the tanning of leather; for, according to the assurances of the Mexicans, it is impossible to tan well without it. I can easily imagine that many of my readers will laugh at this; however, what I have stated is a fact, and, as further proof of this, I must acquaint the reader that along every road accommodations were built of reeds, straw, or grass, by which those who made use of them were hidden from the view of the passers-by, so that great care was taken that none of the last-mentioned treasures should be lost." Diaz del Castillo, *Memoirs*.

28. Coe identifies the edible algae species as *Spirulina geitleri*, grown with aquaculture. Coe, *America's First Cuisines*, 100.

29. Charles Gibson quotes Motolinía: "It is well known that Montezuma gave tasks to Indians with no other purpose than to entertain them. . . . Labor in the towns or in the town subdivisions, as for the construction or repair of community buildings, was required of the able-bodied inhabitants . . . local Indian rulers depended upon groups of workers to perform communal tasks, with minimal individual assignments. What impressed the Spanish oidor Alonso de Zorita concerning Indian labor in the early sixteenth century was the sense of contribution, the 'merriment' and 'great rejoicing' that attended it . . . in Europe unskilled mass labor carried implications of coercion or enslavement. In the Indian tradition the same mass labor, if not too onerous,

might be considered rewarding as a shared and pleasurable experience." Gibson, *Aztecs Under Spanish Rule*, 220–21.

30. See English translations available online of the *Requerimiento* for a fascinating window into the legal reasoning for conquest, distilled into not much more than a paragraph.

31. Extensive literature on the Independence period describes the multifaceted life of the priest Miguel Hidalgo y Costilla.

32. Wood, *Transcending Conquest*, 22.

33. Given the known corpus, other parts of the Toluca Valley transitioned to Spanish decades earlier, but until all extant texts have been discovered, the matter remains in doubt. Now Nahuatl-language texts, "anomalous" for their lateness, can be reconsidered as part of the Independence generation of escribanos who negotiated the transition to Spanish with great consciousness and grace, continuing their craft and adapting it.

34. The word *indio* carries problematic and offensive meanings and therefore is not commonly used in Mexican scholarship. Indigenous communities continue to identify themselves by their civic community, not by a continental identity. Unlike the English-speaking experience, native people in Latin America do not generally accept the word *Indian*. Mexican intellectuals mainly focused on the history of the advanced indigenous civilizations that existed precontact; scholars of the nineteenth-century Porfiriato extolled the virtues of Mexican indigenous ancestors while simultaneously considering contemporary indigenous communities a detriment to modernity.

35. Lockhart's description of the "cycle of sources" describes the way historians moved over time, by necessity, toward finding new sources, and marks the foundation of my methodology. In Lockhart, "Social History of Early Latin America," 30.

36. Cook and Simpson, *Population of Central Mexico in the Sixteenth Century*.

37. Cook and Borah, *Indian Population of Central Mexico*, 1.

38. Dahlgren doubled the Cook-Simpson estimate of the Mixteca. See Dahlgren de Jordán, *La Mixteca*, 27–36. Cited in Cook and Borah, *Indian Population of Central Mexico*, 2.

39. The authors consulted the editors of a forthcoming study by Scholes and Adams, *Sobre el modo de tributar*, 25–26, 100. As cited by Cook and Borah, *Indian Population of Central Mexico*, 2.

40. The demographic collapse of America was not well understood until this study, proving that earlier population estimates were exponentially underestimated.

In a move away from uncritical assessments of governmental and ecclesiastical figures, Borah and Cook started counting—literally—indigenous people, initiating the first generation of "Berkeley Demographers." They bring to the fore the importance, in terms of sheer numbers, of indigenous populations.

41. Gibson in his conclusion about Tlaxcala appears to apologize for his focus on the "physical survival of its native inhabitants." Gibson is conscious of the way he expands the methodological boundary of his time by contrasting his historical investigation with its "almost ethnological character." Gibson, *Tlaxcala in the Sixteenth Century*, 190.

42. Osowski, *Indigenous Miracles*, 12.

43. Foundational microhistories continue to inspire, as in Ginzburg, *Cheese and the Worms*.

44. A brief overview of scholars contributing to the trend to use indigenous sources: Bernardino and María, *Relación breve*; Gibson, *Tlaxcala in the Sixteenth Century*; Gibson, *Aztecs Under Spanish Rule*; Chance, *Race and Class in Colonial Oaxaca*; Anderson, Berdan, and Lockhart, *Beyond the Codices*; Karttunen and Lockhart, *Nahuatl in the Middle Years*; Wood, "Corporate Adjustments"; Cline and León-Portilla, *Testaments of Culhuacan*; Burkhart, *Slippery Earth*; Lockhart, *Nahuas and Spaniards*; Lockhart, *Nahuas After the Conquest*; Lockhart, Berdan, and Anderson, *Tlaxcalan Actas*; Haskett, *Indigenous Rulers*; Horn, *Postconquest Coyoacan*; Schroeder, Wood, and Haskett, *Indian Women of Early Mexico*; Kellogg, *Dead Giveaways*; Restall, *Maya World*; Terraciano, *Mixtecs of Colonial Oaxaca*; Offutt, *Saltillo*; León-Portilla, *Literaturas indígenas de México*; Kellogg, *Law and the Transformation of Aztec Culture*; Restall, Sousa, and Terraciano, *Mesoamerican Voices*; Lockhart, Schroeder, and Namala, *Annals of His Time*; Pizzigoni, *Testaments of Toluca*; Yannakakis, *The Art of Being In-Between*; Townsend, *Here in This Year*; Osowski, *Indigenous Miracles*; Schwaller, *Language of Empire*; Pizzigoni, *Life Within*; Christensen, *Nahua and Maya Catholicisms*; Christensen, *Translated Christianities*; and Ramos and Yannakakis, *Indigenous Intellectuals*.

45. Generally, Nahua-language documents fall into the category of local notarial records, but other categories, like Memorias, also survive. New fruitful genres of sources continue to emerge, like annals, "produced by Nahuas for Nahuas." Townsend, *Here in This Year*, 2.

46. Understanding when and how Spanish replaced written Nahuatl has marked important discussions. See Lockhart, "Language Transition in Eighteenth-Century Mexico." My argument corroborates Robert Haskett's conclusion about the persistence of precolonial ruling traditions. See the conclusion in Haskett, *Indigenous Rulers*, 199.

47. Formative works include Ricard, *La "conquète spirituelle" du Mexique*; Zavala, *New Viewpoints*; Chevalier, *Land and Society in Colonial Mexico*; Brading, *Haciendas and Ranchos*; Hanke, *Spanish Struggle for Justice*; Haring, *Spanish Empire in America*; Prescott and Jay I. Kislak Reference Collection, *History of the Conquest of Mexico*.

48. Using municipal treasury accounts, Ladurie followed the yearly rise of wages and found nursing women who worked for a wage essentially did not get a pay increase for about a century, from 1480 to 1563, which translates into a severe pauperization of women. Ladurie, *Peasants of Languedoc*, 111–12.

    Mary Elizabeth Perry notes that in 1604 royal correspondence bemoaned the fact that of the six hundred women who migrated from Seville to the New World only fifty of them were licensed to do so. Perry, *Crime and Society in Early Modern Seville*, 215.

    Bronislaw Geremek set out to synthesize a macro- and micro-history of marginal people in medieval Paris, and women pop up because he used archival sources. That is how we learn that, in addition to the specific streets where women worked (by implication) as shoemakers and coopers, women also had their own street of gendered work: laundresses. Later, even the used clothes dealers organized. Geremek and Schmitt, *Margins of Society*.

    For a synthesis of material from the Roman period, see Torjesen, *When Women Were Priests*, 18–20, 101–3. Council records in the city of Syros show they voted to recognize Berenice for her work as magistrate, priestess, and mother; surviving inscriptions describe women's leadership roles in synagogues.

    The search for women's sources in archives extends beyond the "old days"; see the cross-cultural approach to finding women in archives in Chaudhuri, Katz, and Perry, *Contesting Archives*.

49. In foundational ethnohistories, glossaries omit *cacica* (female indigenous leader); later ones suggest *cacica* meant the wife of a male indigenous ruler.

50. The study of women, in part because of political attacks on funding earmarked for women's studies, expanded into the study of gender and sexuality, many times centering research on men. For formative studies of Latin American women see Arrom, *Women of Mexico City*; Gonzalbo, *Las mujeres en la nueva españa*; Lavrín, *Sexuality and Marriage*. Formative studies of indigenous women are treated in chapter 5.

51. Worldwide, other subfields and disciplines take advantage of notarial records, with similar results: it is at this local level of record-making that regular people, not just elites, enter the historical record regarding their daily lives (without a skewed judicial-criminal context).

I thank Lauren (Robin) Derby for pointing me in the direction of Le-Grand's paper with Corso, a methodical look at notarial records from one of her project sites, with useful references to scholarship on notaries outside the Americas (LeGrand and Corso, *Los archivos notariales*). See also Burns, *Into the Archive*. I find Burns's concept of repositioning literacy as a dual archive particularly useful in teaching history.

52. No comparable set this late is yet known. The records come from smaller settlements in the Metepec orbit: San Bartolomé Tlatelolco with the majority and Ocotitlan and Yancuictlalpan with significant sets.

53. Nahuatl-language texts become scarce by 1770, to the point that James Lockhart, the father of my field, summarizing various remarks made elsewhere, declared that mundane texts subside after that date. Lockhart, "Background and Course of the New Philology," 19.

54. Originally, James Lockhart did not approve of my including the Spanish-language wills in this analysis.

55. The reason these sources identify the fiscalía, give a sense of their career patterns, or track escribano lineages and ritual practices is because this archive represents people from three main altepetl across three decades.

56. I am indebted to Teresa Jarquín Ortega for her kindness with an inexperienced graduate student on her first research trip. Thanks also to the maestros Marco Aurelio Chávezmaya, Bertha Balestra Aguilar, and Eduardo Osorio for their invaluable introductions in Toluca.

57. Ortega, *Guía del archivo parroquial de Metepec*, 129.

58. Paleography training, studying the handwriting of old texts, in addition to language training proved essential to identifying manuscripts in colonial archives. I thank Kevin Terraciano for the expert Nahuatl and paleography training which allowed me to identify the sources in situ.

59. Rosters are found in Appendix 2 to make the footnotes potentially useful.

60. The practice of maintaining the original formatting preserves visible context for future interpretations but standardizes, removing an interesting aspect of the originals described in chapter 2.

61. I thank James Lockhart and Catherina Pizzigoni for their expertise in Toluca's nonstandard Nahuatl and invaluable help developing the first model testaments.

62. James Lockhart generously double-checked my transcriptions and corrected my translations, but every error remains mine. Eleven samples from Yancuictlalpan and three from Ocotitlan were translated by James Lockhart.

63. Pizzigoni, *Testaments of Toluca*.

64. Pizzigoni, *Life Within.*
65. Rabiela, *Vidas y bienes olvidados,* vols. 1–3.
66. Cline and León-Portilla, *Testaments of Culhuacan.*
67. Alanís Boyso, *Elecciones de República.*
68. Sometimes, teasing out the knots of history is a literal occupation and requires understanding alternative literacies. See Salomon and Niño-Murcia, *Lettered Mountain.*
69. See Document 6, Metepec 1795, in Anderson, Berdan, and Lockhart, *Beyond the Codices.*
70. Klein, *Frontiers of Historical Imagination.*
71. Van Young, "Of Tempests and Teapots," 33.
72. Van Young, *Other Rebellion.*

CHAPTER 1

1. In naming the fiscalía (used contemporaneously to mean the archive of the fiscales), I extend its meaning and identify its political organization. Back in 1960, Cook and Borah mention the "fiscal materials" used as sources. Cook and Borah, *Indian Population of Central Mexico,* 2. More contemporanously, Delia Annunziata Cosentino interviewed the community historian of Tlaxcala, Luis Reyes García, contemporary Nahuatl speaker. For him, the fiscalía is a place, overseen by the fiscal, that continues to house their historical archives; it seemed the perfect word. I use the term to identify the whole administrative body of the parish that generated the documents not just the archive. For a study that quotes the municipal historian, see Consentino, "Nahua Pictorial Genealogies." Today in San Bartolomé they are called *fiscales* as a group, with only topile distinguished with his own title.
2. Chance and Taylor sought "evidence of a community civil hierarchy with rotating officeholders ranked on a ladder of prestige," presented here as a fiscalía, separate from the cabildo. Chance and Taylor, "Cofradías and Cargos," 14–15.
3. Gutierrez Hernandez and Canales Guerrero, "Dos siglos de historia."
4. Ibid.
5. Authors looked at baptismal, marriage, and death records to estimate age. Ibid.
6. Ibid. See p. 157 for discussion of a new model of entry and dispersal.
7. Formative studies on indigenous revolts and Mexican Independence include Taylor, *Drinking, Homicide & Rebellion* and Van Young, *Other Rebellion.*

8. In the eighteenth century, the Spanish Crown instituted bureaucratic and tax reforms. This "Bourbon" period is generally associated with population rise in indigenous communities.

9. People describe their pueblo using the word *altepetl* twenty-eight times, out of a total of ninety-five Nahuatl wills in San Bartolomé; about 30 percent of people still used the word.

10. Recorded deliberations among cabildo members exist. See sections 15 and 21 in Lockhart, Berdan, and Anderson, *Tlaxcalan Actas*, 97–103, 114–18.

11. Lockhart, Terraciano, and Restall presented the political entity for Nahua, Mixtec, and Maya groups, respectively, cited above. For Matlatzinca see García Castro, *Indios, territorio y poder*, 23.

12. Gibson, *Tlaxcala in the Sixteenth Century*.

13. For the groundbreaking discussion of the altepetl and the flexible, replicating nature of its subdivisions, see Lockhart, *Nahuas After the Conquest*.

14. Chimalpahin Cuauhtlehuanitzin et al., *Codex Chimalpahin*, 31.

15. To clarify, *fiscalía* is the term used in this study to identify San Bartolomé's parish administration, to differentiate it from the cabildo.

16. In this instance Horn speaks to the cellular nature of both the Mixtec and Nahua subunits. Horn, "Indigenous Identities in Mesoamerica After the Spanish Conquest," 36.

17. This social organization facilitates self-autonomy not dependent on one central leader. See chapter 1 for a detailed description of the altepetl. Lockhart, *Nahuas After the Conquest*, 15.

18. Alanís Boyso, *Elecciones de República*.

19. Haskett also uses election lists to good result. Haskett, *Indigenous Rulers*.

20. Lockhart suspects the prominence of fiscales in Nahua communities was a colonial strategy: "I have yet to see a fiscal mentioned before 1570." Lockhart, *Nahuas After the Conquest*, 211. On p. 40 he uses the generic term "organization" for the fiscalía's parish officers. When I came across Cline's "of the church" notary as a graduate student in 2007, I made a research note: "need to figure out what that means." Cline, *Colonial Culhuacan*, 21.

21. Pizzigoni, *Life Within*, 202. The alcalde is a member of the indigenous cabildo.

22. This interlocking bureaucracy was not unique to Nahua procedure. In Spanish institutions of this time, the marriage of secular and ecclesiastical bureaucracy, regardless of Bourbon reforms, remained common practice.

23. Gibson first showed that cabildo positions were divided between the administrators of four political subunits that comprised Tlaxcala's altepetl. For exam-

ple, governors, alcaldes, and regidores represented the four *cabeceras* equally in the record from about 1545. Gibson, *Tlaxcala in the Sixteenth Century*, 109–11.

He also identified what he calls "vigesimal subgroups" operating in towns "which were distributed into the four provincial segments according to their geographical location" and were formed by representatives (and representatives of these representatives) of household units, 118–19.

24. For a transcription of San Bartolomé's surviving voting results that were sent to the governor, see Alanís Boyso, *Elecciones de República*, 161–70.

25. Lockhart, *Nahuas After the Conquest*, 40. Parish officers can be seen serving as witnesses in Ocotitlan.

26. I cannot completely rule out that the fiscalía as a body existed in Yancuictlalpan, but they do not enter the record in the same way they do in San Bartolomé or Ocotitlan or even in Robert Haskett's Coyoacan documents that document leaders de la santa iglesia (of the holy church).

27. Data from Ocotitlan show another fiscalía structure based in the parish, as in San Bartolomé. This points to another fiscalía organization still active at Independence, outside San Bartolomé.

28. This pattern carries over to the career pattern of fiscalía escribanos, detailed in the next chapter.

29. Lockhart cites the principle of microethnicity in terms of ubiquitous Nahua cellular self-contained civic structures, and local representation of subunits, as the reason for differentiation or "fragmentation." Lockhart, *Nahuas After the Conquest*, 48.

30. Churches were built by the Nahuas, using their own rotational system of labor, the *tequitl*; see Cline, *Colonial Culhuacan*. Churches were considered communal spaces owned by the community in a fundamental way.

31. Evidence suggests that Ocotitlan also had a powerful fiscalía. This pattern is seen in Ocotitlan but not Yancuictlalpan, suggesting that Yancuictlalpan did not have an active fiscalía.

32. For current questions and hypotheses about the nature of cellular organizations, see the discussion in Pizzigoni. She observes that Metepec and Calimaya/Tepemaxalco both had "entirely separate sets of officials, both secular and ecclesiastical" that shared the town's church and "originally belonged to the same encomienda." Pizzigoni, *Life Within*, 202.

33. Lockhart observes that in the Spanish cabildo alcaldes and regidores generally did not mix; they were chosen from different groups of people. The alcaldes

(judges) did rotate annually, but the regidores (councilmen) held offices for life. Of note is that neither would represent subentities (there is no Spanish equivalent to the tlaxilacalli). In contrast, Mexican rulers generally head subunits. Lockhart, *Nahuas After the Conquest*, 6–12, 36, 92.

34. See Joseph Antonio de Villaseñor Sanchez, *Theatro americano*, 220–22, as quoted by both Alanís Boyso and Mark Mairot. The 1746 census recorded indigenous families, while the 1791 Revillagigedo census did not. But, as mentioned in the introduction, 1971 counted 73 "hispanics" (43 female, 30 male) in San Bartolomé Tlatelolco; see Mairot, *Mexican Provincial Society*, 229, 244.

35. This is meant to be an overestimate of available males; according to Mark Mairot, population growth in pueblos appears slow or negative between 1791 and 1834. Mairot, *Mexican Provincial Society*, 246. In this Toluca City census, it was not uncommon for a "family" to have one member. For comparison, Yancuictlalpan, which had a total of 42 families, counted 134 total people in the 1834 census, which averages out to 3.2 people per household. Due to competing jurisdictions, San Bartolomé and Ocotitlan do not appear in this count. *Padron General de Ciudad de Toluca, pueblos, barrios, haciendas y ranchos.* Photograph of original manuscript collected by Mark Mairot from the Archivo Histórico del Estado de México, Toluca, Mexico.

36. Three seventeenth-century wills exist for San Bartolomé in Pizzigoni, *Testaments of Toluca.*

37. Lockhart, Berdan, and Anderson, *Tlaxcalan Actas*, 153. The Spanish fiscal also handled revenue in Mexico; see the tribute records of the Osuna Codex; the Spanish fiscal receives a significant proportion of goods from the indigenous leadership (only three of the eight listed receive more "bundles").

38. Lockhart, *Nahuas After the Conquest*, 215.

39. *Topile* is literally rendered as "official of justice" in Spanish; see Siméon, *Diccionario de la lengua náhuatl o mexicana*, xliii.

40. Not all offices are attested to in each cabildo election announcement; the exact number may have varied.

41. Delia A. Consentino interviewed the municipal historian of Tlaxcala for "Nahua Pictorial Genealogies."

42. The words *menor* and *mayor* appear not just in the Spanish testaments but also in the Nahuatl as Spanish loanwords. In addition, the less common *teniente* also appears instead of *menor*.

43. Don Luis Isario attests as fiscal teniente in SBT#3, Nahuatl-language testament of Marcela Martina, 1803, and as fiscal mayor in SBT#2, Nahuatl-language testament of Dominga Efigenia, 1803.

44. Don Hilario Dionisio attests as fiscal teniente in SBT#39, Nahuatl-language testament of Martina María, 1813, and SBT#62A, Nahuatl-language testament of Marina Cayetana, 1813. He filled in as fiscal mayor in the following wills from San Bartolomé: SBT#40, Nahuatl-language testament of Valentina María, 1813; #48, Nahuatl-language testament of Fausta Rufina, 1813; #49; Nahuatl-language testament of Paula María, 1813; #60, Nahuatl-language testament of Luisa Trinidad, 1813; and #62, Spanish-language testament of Felipe de la Cruz, 1813.

45. Don Lucas José attests as fiscal teniente in SBT#78, Nahuatl-language testament of Lucas Florentino, 1819, and fills in for don Juan Crisóstomo in SBT#77, Nahuatl-language testament Domingo Manuel, 1819.

46. The *Nahuatl Dictionary* (Wood and Sullivan) carries six attestations.

47. Lockhart, *Nahuas After the Conquest*, 190. Horn found attestation to *teopantopileque* who served as witnesses in a land sale in 1588. Horn, *Postconquest Coyoacan*, 163.

48. Ancient flat stamps from Mexico City depict wooden rattles said to be "used as a cane by the Fire God, often as a symbol of the priests, and marked the rhythm of the dances." Enciso, *Design Motifs of Ancient Mexico*, 141–43.

49. Wood and Sullivan, *Nahuatl Dictionary*.

50. For a Spanish translation of *topile* as "low-ranking Indian official," see Marquez and Ramos Navarro, "Topile."

51. See SBT#67, Nahuatl-language testament of Lucaria María, 1815, for attestation of topile menor.

52. See SBT#77 and SBT#78 for his work as topile mayor and SBT#119, Nahuatl-language testament of Carmen de la Cruz, 1832, for his work as fiscal mayor.

53. See wills by Victoria María, SBT#58, and by Gerónima Antonia, SBT#88.

54. See SBT#10, Nahuatl-language testament of Manuela Lugarda, 1810; #65, Nahuatl-language testament of Aparicia Feliciana, 1814; #80, Nahuatl-language testament of Estefania María, 1821; #117, Nahuatl-language testament of María Josefa, 1825; and #118, Nahuatl-language testament of Mauricio Mateo, 1825, for Mariano's career pattern.

55. See SBT#35, Nahuatl-language testament of Lucaria María, 1813.

56. Individual promotion for don Juan Crisóstomo, into these two-time fiscal mayor positions in 1816 and 1819, also happened relatively fast.

57. See SBT#68, Nahuatl-language testament of Candelaria Martina, 1816, and #78 for don José Lucas's work as fiscal menor and SBT#77 for his work as fiscal mayor.

58. See SBT#68 and #78 for don Juan Crisóstomo's career as fiscal mayor and SBT#64, Nahuatl-language testament of María Bernardina, 1814; #65, Nahuatl-language testament of Aparicia Feliciana, 1814; #66, Nahuatl-language testament of Margarita María, 1814; and #67, Nahuatl-language testament of Lucaria María, 1815, for his career as fiscal menor. The concurrent political upheaval of Independence, though unmentioned, must also be understood as a larger context to both social change and disease.

59. Don Luis Isaurio attested as fiscal mayor in 1802 in SBT#2. In SBT#5, Nahuatl-language testament of Victoriana María, 1809; #6, Nahuatl-language testament of Tiburcia Valenciana, 1809; #7, Nahuatl-language testament of José Abdon, 1809; #8, Nahuatl-language testament of María Josefa, 1809; and #14, Nahuatl-language testament of Nicolás George, 1809, he is attested as fiscal mayor in 1809.

60. To clarify, he is not being promoted. Don Luis Isaurio serves in the same post as the second time—it's the time lapse between the two times he serves that corresponds to expected limits of promotion not the career itself.

61. See SBT#67 for attestation of Mariano José as fiscal mayor and SBT#73, Nahuatl-language testament of Bartolomé Luis, 1818; #74, Nahuatl-language testament of Santos Venancio, 1818; #75, Nahuatl-language testament of Petrona Francisca, 1818; and #76, Nahuatl-language testament of Bernardinao Gregorio, 1818, for him as alguacil mayor.

62. However, until I find more evidence I am not completely ruling out the unlikely scenario.

63. A numerical total of five, a proportional total of one-fifth.

64. See Christensen's table 2.1 summarizing responses from the Descripción del Arzobispado de México, where the Instructors of Doctrine in pueblos are frequently listed as "fiscales." Christensen, *Nahua and Maya Catholicisms*, 77–78.

65. A similar pattern may be suggested in Haskett's count of officers in Cuernavaca. Though both secular and parish officials appear in the count, 70 percent of the officers held multiple types of offices. Haskett, *Indigenous Rulers*, 132.

66. Christensen posits that because Bourbon reforms placed schoolteachers into pueblos to teach *doctrina* (doctrine), it may have played a role in destabilizing local autonomy of fiscales. See Christensen, *Nahua and Maya Catholicisms*, 79–80. Based on analysis of available census data, one schoolteacher lived in San Bartolomé; based on his name, Francisco Arburu, and the fact that he was a native of Metepec, he may have been considered mestizo by Spanish priests. Mairot, *Mexican Provincial Society*, 232. Haskett, *Indigenous Rulers*, 199,

concludes that the Bourbon Reforms' new restrictions simply were ineffective in eradicating precolonial leadership traditions in Cuernavaca.

67. Christensen, *Nahua and Maya Catholicisms*, 77.

68. Christensen notes that fiscales keep religious authority through the colonial period, acting as surrogate priests. Ibid., 76.

69. See Horn for a discussion of how Nahua concept of witness differs from the Spanish. Horn, *Postconquest Coyoacan*, 164.

70. Pizzigoni, *Testaments of Toluca*.

71. SBT#32, Nahuatl-language testament of Florenciana María, 1812, is the only testament that names two executors in San Bartolomé in this period.

72. Over 70 percent of people used both *tepantlato* and *albacea* simultaneously in sixty-seven of ninety-five Nahuatl wills that named an executor. In fourteen wills, people used *albacea* exclusively, and ten times people used *tepantlato* exclusively.

73. See SBT#32 for the testament of Florenciana María.

74. Pizzigoni observes that one executor becomes the norm for eighteenth-century Toluca Valley. Pizzigoni, *Life Within*, 210. Lockhart noticed that Molina's early colonial period "model" testament specified the use of two executors, but does not use the Spanish loanword albacea, even though it was a common term "in all periods." Lockhart, *Nahuas After the Conquest*, 471.

75. One exception, described in the subsequent paragraph, occurs years before the executor became the fiscal mayor.

76. Compared to the rest of the executors, those who were also head officers were more likely to be called tepantlato or a combination of tepantlato and albacea.

77. For the one exception, described in detail in the next paragraph, see SBT#72, Spanish-language testament of Sebastiana Fabiana, 1817, for don Vicente Anastacio and SBT#117 and #118 for don Lucas Florentino, both named as albaceas in Spanish wills.

78. Horn, *Postconquest Coyoacan*, 52.

79. See SBT#119 for the will in which Bernabé Antonio is attested as fiscal mayor in 1832.

80. See SBT#15, Nahuatl-language testament of Rosa María, for the will in which Bernabé Antonio is attested as executor in 1811. The exact usage is "*nalvasia.*"

81. See the lists of elected secular officers sent to Spanish authorities to be formalized in Alanís Boyso, *Elecciones de República*, 161–70.

82. My largest sample, from San Bartolomé Tlatelolco, allows the most definitive conclusions. Ocotitlan also attests officers that were members of the fiscalía.

83. Note that all the witnesses are the same fiscalía officials found in the previous century, as documented in Pizzigoni's previous century's corpus. Pizzigoni, *Testaments of Toluca.*

84. See SBT#1, Nahuatl-language testament of Apolonia Felipa, 1799.

85. Since a deputy topile officer only appears once in the record, this rests on the assumption that none of these men worked as deputy topile, which is as yet unknown.

86. Stage 3 is generally considered after 1650, when Nahuas no longer are just borrowing Spanish nouns but becoming bilingual and integrating a "wide spectrum of Spanish phenomena." Lockhart, *Nahuatl as Written*, 114.

87. According to personal correspondence with James Lockhart, he thought he had never before seen fiscales without the honorary *don*, saying that this was "about the only time I can remember such a thing." He considered the anomaly to be an internal factor, based on the evidence of a different hand, meaning a different notary could have just been sloppy.

88. Two attestations for topile mayor in 1819: SBT#77 and #78.

89. For Hilario Dionisio as fiscal mayor, see SBT#40, #48, #49, #60, and #62. For the same person as fiscal menor, see SBT#39 and #62. Note that #49 and #62A do not attest the *don* honorific title.

90. Chance and Taylor, "Cofradías and Cargos," 15. In chapter 6, I show a widespread participation in funding of ritual festivals, further documenting Chance and Taylor's view of the shift to individual sponsorship in the late colonial period.

91. SBT#30, Nahuatl-language testament of Bernardino Antonio, 1812.

92. The numbers are detailed in the above section describing the fiscalía's rotation and succession.

93. As described above, fiscalía officers rotated yearly through six positions that worked together as a cohort.

94. The description in these paragraphs is based on the fiscalía cohort of 1822.

95. This rotation brings the term *heterarchy* to mind. Diffused to social science by the archaeologist Carole Crumley, it is used by various disciplines to describe a more complex understanding of relationships than "hierarchy" or other dichotomies. Ehrenreich, Crumley, and Levy, *Heterarchy and the Analysis of Complex Societies.* In the Nahua and other contexts, identifying leadership outside vertical terms does not preclude hierarchies; horizontal groups can exist within different vertical, or hierarchical, strata. Alison Rautman speaks to the dissatisfaction with many models of political organization as applied to puebloan so-

cieties which offers a useful discussion. Rautman, "Hierarchy and Heterarchy in the American Southwest." Heterarchy has been shown in various fields to be more efficient than hierarchies in supporting complex interrelatedness and rapid change; this should spur ethnohistorians of the Americas to further develop social evidence to refine "cellular" structures. Many of the meanings of heterarchy can be used within the concept of "cellular" social networks as applied by James Lockhart to Nahua society.

96. See Gibson, *Tlaxcala in the Sixteenth Century*, 107–8. See Rounds, "Dynastic Succession," 75, on consensus in open elections, quoting Sahagún, Durán, and Tezozomoc. See Chimalpahin Cuauhtlehuanitzin et al., *Codex Chimalpahin*, 31, on electoral structure. See Chance, *Conquest of the Sierra*, 12–13, on decentralized horizontal power. Steve J. Stern, *Peru's Indian Peoples*, 9, 25, described Peru's early colonial communal and reciprocal arrangements, founded on the diverse ecology of groups' far-flung plots of land, and noted that "indeed community decisions tended to take the form of a consensus reached among a family of lineages" that had representatives whose lordship rested on "his ability to look after his people's interests." Yannakakis, *The Art of Being In-Between*, 130, describes "principles of contingency, consensus, and reciprocity" articulated in defense of Zapotec autonomy. And note the sweep of time: "*Through the early nineteenth century*, seemingly Spanish-style council elections were actually the result of traditional deliberation and consensus" in Cuernavaca (emphasis mine). Haskett, *Indigenous Rulers*, 198.

97. In an instructive parallel, if Garcilaso de la Vega is right, the Inca recordkeepers numbered in the tens of thousands before colonization. Salomon and Niño-Murcia, *Lettered Mountain*, 75.

CHAPTER 2

1. Personal correspondence with Khodadad Rezakhani, Berlin, 2014. His paper on "transliteration" of early New Persian to the Arabic alphabet develops relevant issues regarding language and writing. See also Khodadad Rezakhani, "Writing Khorasani, Speaking Tehrani," http://www.bbc.com/persian/blogs/2013/10/131014_110_nazeran_farsi_rezakhani.shtml.

2. McDonough challenges us to resist the dominant impulse to preference language "purity" and include in analysis the varied language choices available to Nahua intellectuals, past and present. She observes that language choice

reflects more than one's ethnic identity; it changes according to situation. She analyzes texts in Nahuatl, Latin, and the type of hybrid "Nahuañol" seen here, showing how a chosen language reflects situational factors not limited to one's ethnic identity. McDonough, *The Learned Ones*, 14.

3. The key to documenting this level of geographic differentiation rests on choice of sources and methodology. See the introduction and figure 33, conclusion.

4. Heath, *Telling Tongues*. See p. 220 for the full language of 1770 Edicto XV and p. 207 for the Pastoral V of 1769: "And whereas *the decree that the Indians should learn Castilian*, the language of our sovereign, has been urged on the two dominions and has been one of the most saintedly and justly repeated decrees in the laws of these kingdoms, its execution, instead of being moved forward, *every day seems more impossible*" (emphasis added).

5. Eighty-two percent of people left wills in Nahuatl in San Bartolomé.

6. Evidence for Totocuitlapilco is inconclusive.

7. This approach deserves further study and opens up a new corpus for Mexican ethnohistory.

8. Linguists call this agglutination, where you add suffixes and prefixes on to a root until you get a perhaps ten-syllable group that has a larger meaning than just one root.

9. Reproducing exact spacing requires many arbitrary decisions; in some cases one could hesitate forever whether a division is intended or not.

10. Selected transcriptions are available in appendix 3.

11. For comparison, Spanish-dominant writers standardized spacing before the nineteenth century.

12. SBT#40, Spanish-language testament of Valentina María, 1813.

13. The Spanish silver dollar was worth eight *reales*, hence the term *pieces of eight*.

14. SBT#117, Spanish-language testament of María Josefa, 1825.

15. The Spanish-language texts in the Independence archive fit the general picture given in chapter 6; traits and expressions seen here can be considered widespread, identified for other places and times in Lockhart, *Nahuas and Spaniards*. Robert Haskett (personal correspondence) reports finding Nahuatl-influenced Spanish in Cuernavaca; I expect more to surface in provincial archives. Kelly S. McDonough offers a response to the erasure of indigenous meanings within colonial and contemporary writings: a "re-territorialization" of Nahuas' intellecual trajectories; McDonough, *The Learned Ones*, 204.

16. McDonough describes Nahuas working in several languages over time "including the language of the conqueror" in service of their communities (200) and discusses bilingualism, discrimination, and gendering of language use (177–78);

McDonough, *The Learned Ones*. For how Quechua writing continues to be disadvantaged by state writing standards, see Salomon and Niño-Murcia, *Lettered Mountain*.

17. In his chapter on language transition prepared for the second edition of *Nahuas and Spaniards*, James Lockhart recapped the now standard three-stage framework he had worked out with Karttunen—and added a fourth stage, a hypothesis which the Spanish-language texts in the Independence archive fulfills.

18. The conclusions in this section apply to Totocuitlapilco; however, due to the small sample, I frequently exclude this town's data from conclusions.

19. See figure 7. Spanish-language testaments represent roughly 12 percent of the Independence corpus for San Bartolomé. The names of the known escribanos who wrote in Spanish are Mariano de la Merced, Juan Máximo Mejía, Máximo Calisto, José María, Félix Nabor [Mulia?], Santiago Cristóbal, and José Guadalupe Camacho; see appendix 2.

20. SBT#40, 1813.

21. For clarity, SBT#40 and #49, Nahuatl-language testament of Paula María, 1813, are being compared.

22. It will further be developed in chapter 4 that his Nahuatl-language wills represent a full rendering of the local San Bartolomé model.

23. The implication is that, if used in the same way at this time, criollos such as Hidalgo may have consciously bounded their identity to being native to Mexico in the way Nahuas identify with their local altepetl.

24. Today's Nahua intellectuals at IDIEZ use the word *macehualli* in the same sense. Their identity as members of their respective Nahuatl-speaking communities is dependent on their presence; they are macehualli when they are living within their community. This identity changes when they leave.

25. The second bell tower was added to the community of San Bartolomé when they remodeled it in the late nineteenth century.

26. Mariano de la Merced wrote three Spanish-language testaments: SBT#40; #60, Nahuatl-language testament of Luisa Trinidad, 1813; and #62, Nahuatl-language testament of Felipe de la Cruz, 1813.

27. SBT#111, Spanish-language testament of Lázaro Martín, 1823, was nominally by Cipriano Gordiano but the writer is not yet identified.

28. SBT#115, Spanish-language testament of Dominga Bonifacia, 1824.

29. SBT#118, Spanish-language testament of Mauricio Mateo, 1825.

30. This observation is based on extensive experience in the archives by the father of my field (James Lockhart, personal correspondence, 2010).

31. SBT#72, Spanish-language testament of Sebastiana Fabiana, 1817.

32. Regarding the varied application of Church teachings, especially Marian devotions, see Christensen, *Nahua and Maya Catholicisms*, 125–26 and Burkhart, *Before Guadalupe*.

33. See Yan#9, testament of Juliana Viviana, 1823, for the will he wrote in Spanish. For perspective, that is one Spanish-language testament within a twelve-testament group; the balance are all written in Nahuatl.

34. For examples of linguistic innovations of Spaniards living in Mexico, see Parodi, "Indianization of Spaniards in New Spain."

35. The escribano of SBT#111 also adopts a flowery Spanish credo, quoted in the previous section.

36. Oco#10.

37. In Nahuatl, derived forms of verbs retain prefixes indicating the transitivity, reflexivity, etc., of the verb as it would be in the present-tense indicative.

38. Oco#3, 1809, Spanish-language testament of Hilaria María, 1809, by José Sebastián.

39. SBT#111 was nominally by Cipriano Gordiano, but the escribano is not yet identified. That escribano, despite this small Spanish-style influence, still follows the Nahuatl expectations, overlooking that fact that the verb *creer* must be followed by *en* in standard Spanish.

40. Oco#4, written in 1809 by Santiago Cristóbal, follows the Ocotitlan Nahuatl model perhaps even more closely than the will of Pablo Leonardo discussed here. It is interesting that the phrase "mi cuerpo y lodo," from *notlallo noço-quiyo* (my earth and clay or mud), found in an 1824 San Bartolomé testament as seen above, pops up in Ocotitlan too. These "new" special conventions in Spanish were arising based on literal translations from the Nahuatl and were shared across the whole region.

41. Toto#1, Spanish-language testament of Petra Angelina, 1826.

42. Testaments of Toluca, nos. 37 (1732) and 38 (1737).

43. One of the Nahuatl-language wills from Totocuitlapilco I count as being written in San Bartolomé for this same reason; see the chapter 4 on Nahuatl notarial models.

CHAPTER 3

1. I have not yet found evidence that the escribanos in this study were paid by those dictating their wills; while it may be assumed they charged a fee, I do

not rule out differing institutional expectations. Many reports exist about escribanos bypassing requirements that kept documents in strict chronology—and ethics—for personal gain.

2. Figure 7 charts the testament language totals: 110 Nahuatl, 47 Spanish.

3. For example, María Francisca, Juan de la Cruz, and Francisco Nicolás represent saint names used in pairs. In this Mexican pattern of pairing "first" names, neither was transferred to children as a "family" name.

4. SBT#25, Nahuatl-language testament of María Francisca, 1811.

5. For career patterns in the cabildo, see election lists in Alanís Boyso, *Elecciones de República*, 168–69. The Independence corpus shows Cipriano Gordiano serving as escribano of the fiscalía for the first time in 1810; see SBT#9, Nahuatl-language testament of Pascuala Eleuteria, 1810.

6. For Francisco's career in the cabildo as escribano de republica, see ibid., 165–66.

7. While I do not have evidence of this family's noble title, one does wonder if escribanos perpetuated the lineage of elites in Nahua communities, as described by John Chuchiak for the Maya: "Even when a town's batab was not selected from the traditional elite, a town's escribano continued to be selected from the Maya nobility throughout the colonial period." Chuchiak, "Writing as Resistance," 93.

8. This abbreviation expresses extraordinary conservativism in that he still knew this form at Independence. In this case, it comes at the very end of a line, where it saves space. See testament SBT#14, Nahuatl-language testament of Nicolás George, 1809.

9. Cipriano's lack of a *don* may reflect the temporal sequence of his career, with only two years between the time he served in the cabildo and the fiscalía. As described above, Cipriano's father was elected escribano de republica well before his career within the fiscalía; there was more lag time between that service and service as escribano in the fiscalía.

10. SBT#6, Nahuatl-language testament of Tiburcia Valenciana, 1809.

11. SBT#9, Nahuatl-language testament of Pascuala Eleuteria, 1810.

12. SBT#10, Nahuatl-language testament of Manuela Lugarda, 1810.

13. SBT#16, Nahuatl-language testament of Juana María, 1811.

14. SBT#22, Nahuatl-language testament of Margarita María, 1811.

15. SBT#25, Nahuatl-language testament of María Francisca, 1811.

16. SBT#96, Nahuatl-language testament of Eugenia Gertrudis, 1823.

17. SBT#99, Nahuatl-language testament of Concepciona María, 1823.

18. For the seventeenth- and eighteenth-century Toluca Valley, there are several instances in Pizzigoni, *Testaments of Toluca*.

19. See document 41, Cline and León-Portilla, *Testaments of Culhuacan*.

20. This confusion could lead a reader in many illusory directions. Was he implying something about the ethics of someone whose soul he called sick? Could it be a sly witty jab only his assistant would notice, and laugh about later?

21. See SBT#41, Nahuatl-language testament of Brígida Dionisia, 1813.

22. Compelling arguments exist for the continuity of noble lineage in notarial lines as a strategy to retain power within families through the colonial period. Chuchiak identifies families within Maya communities that held on to notarial positions. Chuchiak, "Writing as Resistance," 99.

23. That escribanos did not rotate in the way of other officers can also be considered a continutity from the earliest colonial record. Lockhart, Berdan, and Anderson, *Tlaxcalan Actas*, 73.

24. See SBT#3, Nahuatl-language testament of Marcela Martina, 1803, and SBT#4, Nahuatl-language testament of María Josefa, 1806, for the two wills Pedro Agustín penned.

25. For election lists, see Alanís Boyso, *Elecciones de República*.

26. SBT#3. As written by Pedro Augustín, 1803: "ca cenca huel mococotica notlalnacayo auh noanimantzin ca san pactica quen quimonequiltitzinoz in Dios" (My earthly body is very sick indeed, but my soul is sound, as God would want it).

27. SBT#4, Nahuatl-language testament of María Josefa, 1806.

28. SBT#67, Nahuatl-language testament of Lucaria María, 1815.

29. SBT#67. James Lockhart in personal correspondence proposed that this nonstandard spelling probably reflects the use of vocative (standard *totecuiyoe*) instead of the declarative, something that often happened in Nahuatl.

30. See SBT#67 for don Juan Crisóstomo as fiscal menor in 1815 and #68, Nahuatl-language testament of Candelaria Martina, 1816, for San Bartolomé's fiscal mayor in 1816. Two other wills, #79, Nahuatl-language testament of Sebastián Isidoro, 1820, and #80, Nahuatl-language testament of Estefania María, 1821, bear Rufino Faustino's name, but everything about them shows that either there was another Rufino Faustino or someone else did a testament in his name. In these examples the soul/body statement is orthodox. For a closer discussion see below.

31. Because *naming* the witnesses dodges the more common declaration that the testament is said *before* (in the presence of) witnesses, the mystery about place cannot be completely settled and leaves open the possibility that the will was made with witnesses in absentia.

32. See SBT#79 and #80 for Rufino Faustino's nominal wills.

33. SBT#67, Nahuatl-language testament of Lucaria María, 1815.

34. Casas, *In Defense of the Indians*, 44.

35. Example from Rufino #2, SBT#80.

36. The one nominally by Cipriano is SBT#78, Nahuatl-language testament of Lucas Florentino, 1819; the other two are #79 and #80. Traits making it possible to establish that #78 is by the same person who wrote #79 and #80 include the unusual spelling *ytuaca* for the usual *ytoca* (his name), the insertion of an *o* after *-chpoch* (one's daughter), and the use of a long pair of lines, one over the other, to separate sections.

37. SBT#1, Nahuatl-language testament of Apolonia Felipa, 1799.

38. Alanís Boyso, *Elecciones de República*.

39. SBT#2, Nahuatl-language testament of Dominga Efigenia, 1803.

40. Mariano wrote in Nahuatl in his own name during the epidemic: once in Nahuatl, SBT#49, and three times in Spanish, SBT#40, Spanish-language testament of Valentina María, 1813; #60, Nahuatl-language testament of Luisa Trinidad, 1813; and #62, Spanish-language testament of Felipe de la Cruz, 1813.

41. My body is really very sick, and my soul is sound, as our lord God would want it.

42. See SBT#44, Nahuatl-language testament of Leonarda María, 1813; #48, Nahuatl-language testament of Fausta Rufina, 1813; and #61, Nahuatl-language testament of don Andrés Antonio, 1813, for wills nominally written by Cipriano but actually penned by Mariano de la Merced.

43. See SBT#49, Nahuatl-language testament of Paula María, 1813, for the Nahuatl-language will signed by Mariano; "huel cenca mococoa nocuerpo ihuan noanimantzin ca çan pactica quen quimo-nequiltiz yn toteco de Dios."

44. James Lockhart insisted that I use the word *Lord* as the translation of *totecuiyo*, for the sake of continuity in the field. However, it should be noted that for the Nahuas themselves this term for the divine was not gendered male, unlike *Lord* that reflects a colonial Spanish political and male-gendered concept of power. Therefore, I propose we visit this issue in the future, for translations like this one make it appear that Nahuas conceived of the divine as male authority that operated in a feudal context, and this is not the case. Potentially, this could cause problems, further obscuring Nahua political structures by imposing a feudal European political concept on a Nahuatl word that does not actually carry this gendered political meaning.

CHAPTER 4

1. In the section of this chapter on the Nahuatl-language testaments of San Bartolomé, I revised pages of my 2008 *Ethnohistory* article (Melton-Villaneuva and Pizzigoni, "Late Nahuatl Testaments from the Toluca Valley"), with much material added.

2. Head calpixque (*hueycalpixqui*) may have had a say in governance. García Castro, *Indios, territorio y poder*, 92.

3. Back in the mid-1500s, this town had already spent one hundred years as the bureaucratic seat of calpixque (tax collectors). Administrators and accountants, calpixque imposed Nahuatl as the official language among a native population that spoke in distinct tongues. Hernández Rodríguez, *El Valle de Toluca*, 42.

4. See the introduction for a discussion of Mexican writing systems.

5. For research on the technical processes of early colonial escribanos, with analysis of inks as well as the working groups, see Magaloni Kerpel, *Colors of the New World*, 21–30, 35–40.

6. Wood could have been chosen for the dual purpose of physical protection and chemical deterrence; the collection shows no sign of beetle larva or mold. Only one will (from Ocotitlan) shows a dark-brown stain in this well-preserved collection.

7. For the topic of tracing change with contact stages, see the section, "The Nature of Nahua Testaments in Spanish," in chapter 2.

8. The formulas for the previous century are extrapolated from nos. 22, 23, and 24 in the collection of Pizzigoni, *Testaments of Toluca*. In both templates, material in brackets means it is sometimes omitted. Material in parentheses is always present, but either is formulated generally instead of the specific words that would be used in a given testament or specifies the Nahuatl word or phrase that is used. I thank James Lockhart, with his vast experience with notarial records in the Toluca Valley, for his assistance with contrasting these templates to earlier Toluca material.

9. Sometimes the statement of conclusion comes before mention of the executors.

10. The Spanish-language testaments of the Independence archive confirm this meaning.

11. James Lockhart, personal correspondence (March 3, 2011).

12. For these quotes and many examples of how these standards were applied throughout the Nahuatl-language region, see Sell et al., *Nahuatl Theater*, 45–47.

13. Christensen, *Nahua and Maya Catholicisms*, 239. My findings support Christensen's careful study of preambles; each town developed their own basic formula and worked from there. See chapter 7, "Voices from the Dust."

14. SBT#118, Mauricio Mateo's testament in Spanish, 1825, says the following: "Que mi curpo y Mi alma Se alla mui enfermo si mi Dios se acordar de Mi. Soy Confradia de Mi madre Santisma La lipian comsepcion" (I am [of] the confraternity of my mother, the saintly Immaculate Conception).

15. Here I am following the same strategy I used for standardizing a model will for escribanos in San Bartolomé; material in brackets is sometimes omitted in actual wills. Material in parentheses is always present, but either is formulated generally instead of the specific words that would be used in a given testament or specifies the Nahuatl word or phrase that is used.

16. Compare with the sixteenth-century testaments of Culhuacan for a stark contrast. Household items such as chests or ink or fabric at Independence are no longer mentioned. Cline and León-Portilla, *Testaments of Culhuacan*.

17. A note on methodology: decades-worth of altepetl-based sources demonstrate these local altepetl customs, practices not discerned in studies based on regional groupings of wills and stretched over longer periods of time.

18. For a discussion of tracing change with contact stages, also mentioned in the beginning of this chapter, see the section, "The Nature of Nahua Testaments in Spanish," in chapter 2.

19. A comparison with sources in Pizzigoni's Toluca collection shows that escribanos also wrote the date at the start of testaments in the previous century, perhaps the most common form throughout the valley in the eighteenth century.

20. The comparison with Yancuictlalpan and Ocotitlan detects a traditional notarial practice in San Bartolomé that may open up these escribanos to questionable practices like adding bequests, but without further evidence, I leave the question open.

21. Here Spanish nouns are coupled by Nahua escribanos. Applying the definition of *difrasismo*, this apparently Nahuatl phrasing may indicate the two nouns were perceived to have, on some level, different meanings that may in their juxtaposition mean something greater than the two. It leaves one with the sense that the notary may have considered the Spanish loanwords to mean something slightly different, so both are used in order to render the full sense.

22. The meaning of having God provide the shroud requires further study; it may similarly point to the function of a cofradía. This point remains an open question.

23. Though inconclusive, this may hint at the unique autonomy and relationship with the priest of the fiscalía in San Bartolomé.

24. See chapter 1 for a presentation of the fiscalía, as an altepetl governing body distinct from the cabildo.

25. Yan#9, Spanish-language testament of Juliana Viviana, 1823.

26. For more detail on the topic of his Spanish wills, see chapter 2.

27. Oco#1, Nahuatl-language testament of Ana María, 1801; Nahuatl-language testament of Jacobo Santiago, 1810, #6; and #22, Nahuatl-language testament of Ramona María, 1813.

28. As noted before, the Spanish silver dollar was worth eight *reales*.

29. Oco#1 escribano Santos Alberto uses *anima*.

30. The Independence archive carries one eighteenth-century example, so few that I cannot make generalizations.

CHAPTER 5

1. Melton-Villaneuva and Pizzigoni, "Late Nahuatl Testaments from the Toluca Valley."

2. An identical proportion appears in San Bartolomé with the addition of the Spanish-language texts. Including the Spanish-language wills with those in Nahuatl, the seventy-six women to forty men results in a nearly identical ratio, with women again marking 66 percent of the total testators. In Yancuictlalpan the ratio increases, with women representing 75 percent of all testators. Of all people in Ocotitlan who left wills, women recorded 63 percent. In Totocuitlapilco, the sample of two is too small to be reliable, but for comparison it also shows women in the majority as testators, with no men represented.

3. Pizzigoni, *Testaments of Toluca*, 7–8.

4. Rabiela, *Vidas y bienes olvidados*, 1:59–60. Overall numbers: in volume I women make up 37% of testators; in volume II 29% are by women; and in volume III 38% of testaments are women's.

5. Pizzigoni, *Testaments of Toluca*, 7–8.

6. Sousa, "Women and Crime in Colonial Oaxaca," 75.

7. Pizzigoni, *Life Within*.

8. Ana Xoco is listed both as a witness and with the title cihuatepixque in document 38 from the sixteenth-century testament collection from Culhuacan. Cline also mentions that Duran interpreted this position as officials in charge of

female citizens (cited as Duran 1967, I:186). Cline and León-Portilla, *Testaments of Culhuacan*.

9. Cline, *Colonial Culhuacan*, 130–31, 133, 135.

10. See chapter 4, fn. 46 in Cline, *Colonial Culhuacan* for the reference to Susan Schroeder's 1984a paper presented at the American Society for Ethnohistory, "Chimalpahin and the Role of Cihua." See "Women also figure among the elders or *huehuetque* as *ilamatque* (old women), *tonanhuan*, and *tocihuan* (mothers, grandmothers, ancestors), surely among the keepers of the *huehuetlatolli* (ancient histories, oral traditions) of their people." Schroeder, "Noblewomen of Chalco," 53–54.

11. "Even when institutions survived, like markets, the formal roles for women in positions of authority began to disappear. For example, control of the large markets in Mexico City passed from Mexica to Spanish hands after the 1530s as Spanish aguaciles, always male, took over the duties of the *tianquizpan tlaiacanque*." Kellogg, "From Parallel and Equivalent to Separate but Unequal," 123.

12. Horn, *Postconquest Coyoacan*, 163. This phenomenon is not limited to the Nahuas; see Sousa, "Women and Crime in Colonial Oaxaca." Sousa documents indigenous women serving as plaintiffs, defendants, and witnesses in Oaxaca.

13. Osowski, *Indigenous Miracles*, 112.

14. Though Spanish women rarely performed the role of witness in the Spanish setting, Nahuas saw no problem in using Spanish women to witness their land sales; see Horn, *Postconquest Coyoacan*, 163. In Spanish legal framework, the *Siete Partidas* explicitly excludes female witnesses, but Nahua practice does not follow this stricture in the early colonial period; see Cline, *Colonial Culhuacan*, 28–32. This exclusion, more successful as time passes, continues in force at Independence, a moment when roles as witnesses are performed exclusively by men.

15. The overall numbers follow.

16. See Wakild's research. I saw her present on the effect of aridity on the historical trees in Mexico City (Environmental History Conference, Portland, Oregon, 2010). Wakild, *Revolutionary Parks*.

17. See document nos. 22 (Ambrosio Lorenzo, 1715) and 23 (Gregorio Juan, 1731); Pizzigoni, *Testaments of Toluca*.

18. "Incense made from the sap of the copal tree was offered at nearly all ritual occasions." M. Smith, *Aztecs*, 220.

19. The number of trees of each species that lived at this time is not defined; Nahuatl does not mark the plural of inanimate nouns. However, if seventeen

people requested to be buried near this species of tree, and we know that there had been such requests for at least a hundred years, it would follow that there was more than one tree. With cypresses, people described them with specificity, as large and small. In 1811, two people described their grave as near a large and a small cypress, respectively (SBT#15, Nahuatl-language testament of Rosa María, 1811; and #20, Nahuatl-language testament of Francisca Javiera, 1811). And in 1822 and 1823, three different people described their resting places as either near a small cypress or a big one (SBT#85, Nahuatl-language testament of Tomasa Martina, 1822; #83, Nahuatl-language testament of María Albina, 1823, #93; #103, Nahuatl-language testament of don Pedro Esteban, 1823). The copal trees appear well established (no mention of small ones), and the cypresses apparently were added later, either mixed intergenerational stands or separate areas of older and newer plantings, which fits with the increase of cypresses being requested in this time period.

20. "*S. molle* is known in parts of Mexico and the Philippines as *el Peru´* or *Peruil* to this day." Goldstein and Coleman, "Schinus Molle L. (Anacardiaceae) Chicha Production," 524–25.

21. Ibid.

22. Burial outdoors was nearly universal in Ocotitlan. For the one exception, see Oco#2, Spanish-language testament of Ana María, 1809, where Ana María asked to be buried indoors, "dentro de la yglecia." In the remaining Spanish-language testaments, all except one use the Spanish word for cemetery. Various spellings of *sementerio* appear, and the word is often paired with *patio*, appearing in the odd construction "patio del sementerio." See Oco#1, Spanish-language testament of Ana María, 1801, and Oco#6, Spanish-language testament of Jacobo Santiago, 1810, for two Nahuatl-language wills of Ocotitlan that use *teopan ithualco* (churchyard). It is of note that the Nahuatl-language testaments do not use the Spanish loanword for *cemetery* despite the word's near-universality in Spanish, appearing as early as 1809.

In Yancuictlalpan, an outdoor churchyard burial also became nearly universal; one asked to be buried in the churchyard, generally using the Nahuatl phrase *teopan ythualco*. See Yan#12, the Nahuatl-language testament of Francisca Antonia, 1825, the only one to use the Spanish loanword for *cemetery*. It does not replace the Nahuatl word for *churchyard*; rather, the terms are used together, in Nahautl methaphoric form. She put it in visual terms, saying, "Ompa teopa ythualco yxpan tiopan ythualco ytiqui Siminterio" (In the church courtyard, facing the church courtyard inside the cemetery).

23. In the previous century, burial inside the church greatly outweighs burial outside for cases where the site is specified. Since many wills do not specify the site, some uncertainty remains. Pizzigoni, *Testaments of Toluca*, 16.

24. See SBT#70, Spanish-language testament of Asencia Pascuala and #72, Spanish-language testament of Sebastiana Fabiana for the testaments from 1817. For 1824, see SBT#112, #115, and #116; the latter is quoted.

25. My thanks to John Chuchiak for this insight. For a discussion on the concept of cemetery in relation to illness and the *real cédula* from April 3, 1787, establishing the legal foundation for cemeteries distant from the hospitals in Mexico City, Puebla, and Veracruz at the turn of the nineteenth century, see Cuesta and Cuesta, "Muerte e ilustracion," 136–37.

26. These conclusions are based on a comparison with the general picture in the Toluca Valley not just the San Bartolomé records in Pizzigoni, *Testaments of Toluca*.

27. Of the total, seventy-three are women and forty-one are men, and one comes from outside the community and is not counted here.

28. Responsos came from thirty-four women and twenty-four men.

29. Women outnumber men thirty-nine to seventeen in choosing Masses in San Bartolomé.

30. When men predominate this is somehow not considered to reflect a bias of the record. This study points to the need to change this assessment.

31. Of twenty-seven total wills in Ocotitlan.

32. Seven people left responsory prayers: four were women and three were men in Ocotitlan.

33. Thirteen women and five men asked for Masses in Ocotitlan.

34. Oco#23, Spanish-language testament of María Antonia, 1814.

35. Of eighteen people that set a timetable in Ocotitlan, thirteen are women and five are men. Of the nine people that do not set timetables, six are men.

36. Oco#1; because the date of the notation is unclear, it could even say '02!

37. Chimpalpahin says Fray Gerónimo de Zárate "took all the great duties of justice upon himself" and sold houses that belonged to true heirs in the name of Masses that were never said; Lockhart, Schroeder, and Namala, *Annals of His Time*, 197. Cline suggests friars felt competition with heirs over inheritances; Cline, *Colonial Culhuacan*, 22. Notaries have also been implicated in unethical practices; see Burns, "Notaries, Truth, and Consequences."

38. In Ocotitlan, of the nine people who asked for completion in a twenty-day period, six were women.

39. Oco#24, Spanish-language testament of Feliciana Petrona, 1816.

40. Ocotitlan counts eighteen Masses and seven responsos, two with no request for a Church rite.

41. Yan#9, Spanish-language testament of Juliana Viviana, 1823.

42. The stamps date from 1937.

43. My forthcoming manuscript treats kinship and land patterns, describing the nuances of this process for the Independence period. Generally, Nahua naming patterns familiar for the early colonial period continue into the nineteenth century.

44. Don Pedro said that at one point the laws changed, and they were no longer allowed to donate/inherit land. You had to show that it was purchased. So these wills were drawn to prove ancestral lands were subsequently purchased and therefore legally owned, even if the price was only one peso or was never expected to be paid. Similar to colonial-period *composiciones* (compositions), this harkens back to the reasoning that ancestral possession needed to be formalized beyond the act of inheritance. Without further study on how legal reforms impacted San Bartolomé, I can say that the sheer fact that private ownership might be questioned (and must be plainly described) shows that the altepetl retained a strong notion of corporate identity into the mid-twentieth century.

45. Pizzigoni, *Testaments of Toluca.*

46. His original verse: "las campanas de mi tierra / son voces del corazón / y su eco todo encierra / sentimientos de ilusión." English translation by the author.

47. For a European example of male and female bell formulas, see Campaneros, http://www.oficiostradicionales.net/es/urbanos/campaneros/segura.asp, for attestations (in 1929 and 1935) of the whole death toll cycle being run twice for women and three times for men in the Parish of Nuestra Señora de la Asunción de Segura in Segura, Guipúzcoa, Spain posted in 2011 in the section "Oficios Tradicionales" by the Departamento para la Innovación y la Sociedad del Conocimiento. For new scholarship around the acoustic context of social life, see Niall Atkinson's *The Noisy Renaissance.*

48. It is still not entirely certain whether some communities actually lacked the tradition of ringing bells for the dead or whether they merely lacked the convention for recording it.

49. An interesting comparison can be made in specific words used. Near the city of Toluca people tended to use the old Nahuatl word for bell, *miccatepoztli* (dead-person iron) or just *tepoztli*; in San Bartolomé only the loanword *cam-*

pana was used. See nos. 22 (1715) and 23 (1731, 1724, 1737, and passim). Pizzigoni, *Testaments of Toluca.*

50. Wood specifically cites Ricard in this regard. I continue to see women excluded from even the newest studies of cofradías being presented at conferences.

51. SBT#118, Spanish-language testament of Mauricio Mateo, 1825.

52. SBT#30, Nahuatl-language testament of Bernardino Antonio, 1812.

53. SBT#88, Nahuatl-language testament of Gerónima Antonia, 1822.

54. SBT#48, Nahuatl-language testament of Fausta Rufina, 1813.

55. SBT#30, Nahuatl-language testament of Bernardino Antonio, 1812. The exact wording is "nephew don Mariano de la Merced, for he is a son of my precious father señor San José [i.e., belongs to that cofradía]."

56. I will not rule out the possibility that these guilds are not formal cofradías but rather a parallel or cellular indigenous institution based on the vigesimal system; Gibson notes especially family working groups of twenty and one hundred mentioned in notices. Of note, Gibson also observed the ratio of one fiscalía per barrio (using the terms alguacil, fiscal, or topil de la iglesia) in the earliest times. Gibson, *Aztecs Under Spanish Rule*, 182–84.

57. To quote: "Mauricio Mateo's words in Spanish reveal in 1825 that the Virgin also represents a cofradía dedicated to her. Or more specifically, the Virgin represents two cofradías dedicated to Asunción or to Limpia Concepción, two different aspects of her. A possible implication of the use of the future tense is that the testator expects to enter the cofradía at death."

58. Thirteen asked for Masses and eight for responsory prayers.

59. Forty Masses and forty-four responsory prayers.

60. Aside from a long career as a teacher and administrator, she, a longtime family friend, notably founded a bilingual program for elementary-age students. Monica is not her real name.

61. Hermandad, literally brotherhood, corresponds with cofradía, or lay church guild.

62. Monica, a longtime resident of Los Angeles, has learned to "translate" Peruvian tradition by more commonly familiar Mexican analogy.

CHAPTER 6

1. Studies based on regional sampling obscure differences among altepetl.

2. Pizzigoni, *Testaments of Toluca.*

3. Christensen, *Nahua and Maya Catholicisms*.

4. Lockhart, *Nahuas After the Conquest*; Wood, "Adopted Saints"; Pizzigoni, *Life Within*. See also Pizzigoni, *Testaments of Toluca*, 22–25 and passim.

5. In this instance, Margarita María spoke using the older Nahuatl terminology, where the household's land, the house structure, and the saints define an interrelated unit. She called her house *caltzintli* and her lot *solar*, and she joined these two with *xiptlallotzitzihua* for images (standard *ixiptlayotzitzinhuan*) in the description of her household. "Yni Caltzintli Much ica solar Yhuan xiptlallotzitzihua Dios santos Yhuan Santas unCa moCauhtzinoa Ypan ithuali Yhuan Caltemiilt niquinnoCahulilitia notelpoh fran.co Juaquin Yhuan Ysihua Ytoca Maria Casimira Para quihmotequipanilhuisque."

Lorenzo Bernardino uses similar phrasing as late as 1823, leaving it along with the lot (*nosularito*) and the house (caltzitli), to serve the saints "santo sa Manuel yhua san Marcos" (SBT#104.2, Nahuatl-language testament of Lorenzo Bernardino, 1823).

6. Pizzigoni, "Region and Subregion in Central Mexican Ethnohistory," 87.

7. "The Virgin Mary was the most popular" saint. Wood, "Adopted Saints," 278.

8. Wood lists Virgin Mary, Mary Magdalene, and Ann.

9. Taylor, "The Virgin of Guadalupe in New Spain," 19.

10. Asunción, Dolores, and Guadalupe are the exceptions to this rule, seen more than once.

11. Terraciano, *Mixtecs of Colonial Oaxaca*, 307.

12. Osowski, *Indigenous Miracles*, 10.

13. Ruiz, Teofilo F., *A King Travels: festive traditions in late medieval and early modern Spain*, Princeton University Press, 2012.

14. Oco#11.2, Spanish-language testament of Diega Gertrudis, 1813.

15. Chance and Taylor, "Cofradías and Cargos," 21. The early colonial testaments of Culhuacan, for example, do not attest to land use in the support of saints, only in support of ancestors (see discussion of Day of the Dead later in this chapter).

16. Cofradía groups were comprised of women as well as men; for data about individuals' service to confraternities, see Pizzigoni, *Life Within*, 177–81.

17. People who traveled with saints to collect alms connected people from different communities; Osowski, *Indigenous Miracles*, 11, 100–31.

18. Independence data on saints, culled from people's bequests of saints at death, may underestimate the actual number served in households. In terms of methodological bias, figure 30 gives a probable undercount; it does not include

general references to *santos y santas*. Further, it is possible, as in inheritance of land, that people transferred sponsorship of their household saints well before death, bypassing the testamentary record.

19. See table 1.1, Pizzigoni, *Life Within*, 41.

20. The question remains how gender parallelism functioned at this time.

21. The Independence archive supports Pizzigoni, *Life Within*, in the distinction between household and distant, or non-household, land. In this, Feliciana Petrona's third bequest, she leaves one non-household parcel issuing from her husband's estate, a piece of land she held in custody for her daughter. Oco#24, Spanish-language testament of Feliciana Petrona, 1816, third bequest.

22. Oco#12, Spanish-language testament of José Anastasio, 1813.

23. Oco#11.3, third bequest in Nahuatl-language testament of Diega Gertrudis, 1813.

24. SBT#115, Spanish-language testament of Dominga Bonifacia, 1824.

25. Tavarez, "Autonomy, Honor, and the Ancestors," 132.

26. SBT#12, Nahuatl-language testament of Bernabela Antonia, 1810, second bequest.

27. Cline and León-Portilla, *Testaments of Culhuacan*, document 52 in which Ana Tlaco (1581) bequeaths land to her little brother, saying, "Perhaps he will favor me with some candles on the feast of the dead [miccailhuitl]." See also document 53 in which María Tiacapan (no exact date) says, "I put my husband Mateo Opan in charge of seeing to it that on the day of the dead [miccailhuitl] he remember me before God and bring candles each year. Let him not forget me." In document 73 Agustín Tepanecatl (158?) clearly links land use to ancestor worship, bequeathing his children land with which "there they will produce its tribute when I have died, the tribute of the dead."

   University of Oregon's Nahuatl Library gives attestation of "great feast of the dead," *huei miccailhuitl*, in Berhorst, *Ballads of the Lords of New Spain*, 35, and *miqueylhuitl* in Tlaxcala 1662–1692, citing Buenaventura Zapata y Mendoza, *Historia cronológica de la noble ciudad de Tlaxcala*, 360–61.

28. In a representative critique of Claudio Lomnitz-Adler, Pamela Voelkel said, "Lomnitz is wont to use evidence from the recent past to support claims about earlier centuries." Lomnitz-Adler, *Death and the Idea of Mexico*; Voekel, "Book Review."

29. Sabina Cruz de la Cruz describes Xantolo [Day of the Dead] and Lavamanos still being practiced in her community, "These are things we do today just as we did long ago, and this to me is an indication that our culture is alive." McDonough, *Learned Ones*, 158.

30. Many describe the central role of women in protests. Osowski describes how women "aggressively defended" community rites. Osowski, *Indigenous Miracles*, 115.
31. Kanter, *Hijos del pueblo*, 24.
32. Van Young, *Other Rebellion*. For a strong encapsulation of this "contradiction," see Benton, "No Longer Odd Region Out." See also the discussion in B. Smith, *The Roots of Conservatism in Mexico*, 117.
33. Yan#3, Nahuatl-language testament of Juana Nepomucena, 1810.
34. Yan#2, Nahuatl-language testament of Margarita María, 1810.
35. Yan#8, Nahuatl-language testament of Mariano Domingo, 1810.
36. In addition, it appears that inheritors could hire subcontractors and renters to work the land.
37. This quote from Oco#24, Spanish-language testament of Feliciana Petrona, 1816.
38. In a forthcoming manuscript I present the kinship and land-use data from the Independence archive.
39. Mundy, *Mapping of New Spain*. Pizzigoni shows that people identify land by naming the people associated to adjacent land in the previous century, another continuity with the Independence archive. Pizzigoni, *Life Within*.

CONCLUSION

1. González Rodrigo identifies mostrante or mostranza as *Mentha x rotundifolia*. González Rodrigo, *Santa Catarina del Monte*, 98. Mixtec speaker Julio César del Río Lozano, with Organización de Médicos Indígenas de la Mixteca, identifies chichicaztle as a different plant called *Urtica chamaedryoides*, http://www.cdi.gob.mx/participacion/omima/chichicastle.htm. And the Real Academia contradicts don Pedro, considering mastranzo to be a plant commonly called mint, *hierbabuena*; Real Academia Espanola, *Diccionario de la lengua espanola*, 1209.
2. The Nahuatl word is *chichicaztli*, the same as don Pedro used, except that Spanish changes a final Nahuatl *i* to *e*.
3. Don Pedro said that this cross was the original one referred to in the Independence archive; I cannot be certain.
4. McDonough, *Learned Ones*.
5. See her website for great links. "From Garden Warriors to Good Seeds: Indigenizing the Local Food Movement," https://gardenwarriorsgoodseeds.com.

See also E. Hoover, M. Renauld, M.R. Edelstein, and P. Brown, "Social Science Collaboration with Environmental Health," *Environmetal Health Perspectives* 123, no. 11 (November 2015): 1100–1106.

6. Osowski describes how "today in Mexico *cacique* means a corrupt political boss." Osowski, *Indigenous Miracles.*

7. See Yannakakis's description of Zapotec communities that held fiscales responsible for corruption, removing them from office and punishing them. Yannakakis, *Art of Being In-Between*, 67–69.

8. Ibid., 74.

9. This complexity further supports Van Young's description of indigenous responses in Van Young, *Other Rebellion*. See Derby's many contributions to understanding the tension between popular and state constructions of identity. Derby, *Dictator's Seduction* and "Gringo Chickens with Worms."

10. Haskett anticipates my argument: "The tendency of all members of the ruling group (sometimes including elite women) to participate in many activities, ostensibly the province of elected officers alone, is further evidence for the persistence of indigenous custom." Haskett, *Indigenous Rulers*, 199.

11. Brown, *Myth of the Strong Leader.*

12. Miller, *Ogimaag*, 19.

13. Contemporary decision-making theorists confirm and describe this process. See especially Starhawk, *Empowerment Manual* and also Walls, *Community Organizing* and Sheeran, *Beyond Majority Rule.*

14. Bilingualism as a strategy reminds me of John Chuchiak's account about early Maya use of both pictorial and alphabetic writing systems: "the Maya elite as early as the late 1560s had come to use both written traditions." Chuchiak, "Writing as Resistance," 88. Seen as a continuity, bilingualism is just another in a line of strategic adaptations by indigenous writers, paralleling early graphic pluralism, straddling two worlds.

15. When I interviewed the municipal historian, the priest still only visited San Bartolomé and was not a resident of the parish.

16. Of many who have used the Last Supper trope to great effect, Chicago's was perhaps the most informative. She chose thirteen place settings as a place from which to begin to tell women's history. Chicago, *Dinner Party*, 9.

17. Adding oral histories to the written record has been not only important to documenting the history of indigenous communities but also essential to documenting many women's histories. See Contesting Archives: Finding Women in the Sources, especially Goodwin, "Revealing New Narratives of Women in Las Vegas" and Bauer, *We Were All Like Migrant Workers Here.*

18. The essay that most informed my ethnohistorical methodology describes the evolution of how historians of Latin America have used sources over time. See Lockhart, "Social History of Early Latin America: Evolution and Potential."

19. Much wonderful work has been done in recent years with litigation that represents indigenous people, as it lends exciting narratives; though not always written by and for indigenous people, it does offer rich detail about individuals as they encounter the legal system. The environmental/geological record also informs history based on local sources and deserves more study by ethnohistorians.

20. Mark Christensen has found the same phenomena in analyzing both Nahuatl and Maya religious texts written by indigenous escribanos in the parish setting. See his discussion of category 3 texts. He presents local religious ideas based on what native escribanos choose to include in their own versions of creeds, prayers, commandments, and other ostensibly standardizing doctrine. Christensen, *Nahua and Maya Catholicisms*.

21. These notarial records from the colonial period remain an understudied treasure of sources in the United States.

EPILOGUE

1. Eileen Truax, the journalist, recently observed that representative government remains an expectation of Mexican indigenous communities; see Rojo, Hernandez, and Ramos, *Analysis*. Her latest book is Truax, *Dreamers*.

2. See the discussion about the Algonquian caucus, Iroquois longhouse, Zuni council of papas, Aztec *tlatoani* or representative speakers, and Yaqui elections vs. the European expectation of "relying on a single supreme authority." Weatherford, *Indian Givers*, 122–25.

GLOSSARY

ALGUACIL: Official in the indigenous cabildo and fiscalía.

ALTEPETL: Precolonial Mexica, Aztec, city-state that used Nahuatl as the lingua franca.

ANTEPASADOS: Ancestors.

BARRANCA: Cliff, chasm.

CABILDO: Altepetl officers called "de la republica."

CACICA: Indigenous leader, female.

CACIQUE: Indigenous leader, male.

CALPIXQUES: Nahuatl word for bureaucrats and tax collectors.

CHICHICAZTLE: Nahuatl word for the plant called nettles.

CHICHIMECS: Nahuatl name for nomadic people (and ancestors) north of Tenochtitlan.

ESCRIBANO: Spanish word for notary.

FISCAL: Head official of the indigenous parish and of the fiscalía.

HUITZILOPOCHTLI: The main deity of Mexico Tenochtitlan was born fully formed and ready for battle against his sister.

IBERIANS: People from the Iberian Peninsula; when the Spanish first arrived, they had not yet formed a national identity.

LINGUA FRANCA: The language of trade, in this case Nahuatl.

MATLATZINCA: Most numerous ethnic group in the Matlatzinco Valley.

MATLATZINCO VALLEY: The early name for Toluca Valley, named for the most numerous group.

MAZAHUA: Ethnic group in the Matlatzinco Valley.

MERCADITO: Small "corner" store.

MEXICA: The dominant people in central Mexico at the arrival of Cortés. Their language, Nahuatl, was the language of trade. Also known as the Aztecs.

MOSTRANTE: Mint-like plant.

NAHUAS: The people who spoke Nahuatl (generally refers to postconquest period).

NAHUATL: The language of the Mexica aka Aztecs aka the Nahuas of today.

OCOTITLAN: One of the altepetl recorded in the Independence archive, whose full name is attested as Santa María Magdalena Ocotitlan.

OJO DE AGUA: The source of a spring of water.

OTOMÍ: Ethnic group in the Matlatzinco and Mexico Valleys.

RANCHITO: As used by don Pedro in the conclusion, this term holds the meaning found in the Independence archive, a humble dwelling on the outskirts of town, as opposed to meaning a "ranch" that focuses on animal husbandry.

REAL: One-eighth of a peso.

SAN BARTOLOMÉ: One of the altepetl recorded in the Independence archive, whose full attested name is San Bartolomé Tlatelolco.

SANTÍSIMA CRUZ: The holy cross mentioned in many testaments.

SEMASIOGRAPHIC WRITING: A writing system that conveys whole meanings from graphics, without dividing into words.

TECPAN: Nahuatl word for precolonial government compound.

TLACUILO: Nahuatl word for notary.

TOLUCA: The main city in the Toluca Valley.

TOLUCA VALLEY: Contemporary name of the Matlatzinco Valley.

TOPILE: Official of the indigenous cabildo and fiscalía; a Nahuatl term.

TOTOCUITLAPILCO: One of the altepetl recorded in the Independence archive; full name is attested as San Miguel Totocuitlapilco.

YANCUICTLALPAN: One of the altepetl recorded in the Independence archive; full name is attested as Santa María de la Rosa de Nativitas Yancuictlalpan.

BIBLIOGRAPHY

Note: For ease of use, the primary documents of the Independence archive are listed in the Appendix according to the abbreviations used in the endnotes (for example, SBT#97).

Anonymous. "1664 Libro de Difuntos." Metepec, Edo. de Mexico, n.d. Uncatalogued material. Archivo del ex convento de San Juan Bautista.

Alanís Boyso, José Luis. *Elecciones de República para los pueblos del corregimiento de Toluca, 1729–1811*. Mexico City: Biblioteca Enciclopédica del Estado de México, 1978.

Anderson, Arthur J. O., Frances Berdan, and James Lockhart, eds. *Beyond the Codices: The Nahua View of Colonial Mexico*. UCLA Latin American Studies Series 27. Berkeley: University of California Press, 1976.

Arrom, Silvia Marina. *The Women of Mexico City, 1790–1857*. Stanford, CA: Stanford University Press, 1985.

Atkinson, Niall. *The Noisy Renaissance: Sound, Architecture, and Florentine Urban Life*. University Park: Pennsylvania State University Press, 2016.

Bauer, William J., Jr. *We Were All Like Migrant Workers Here: Work, Community, and Memory on California's Round Valley Reservation, 1850–1941*. Chapel Hill: The University of North Carolina Press, 2009.

Benton, Lauren A. "No Longer Odd Region Out: Repositioning Latin America in World History." *Hispanic American Historical Review* 84, no. 3 (2004): 423–30.

Bernardino, de Sahagún, and Angel María Garibay K. *Relación breve de las fiestas de los dioses.* Cuernavaca, Mexico: Tipografía Indígena, 1947.

Bierhorst, John, transcriber and translator. *Ballads of the Lords of New Spain: The Codex Romances de los Señores de la Nueva España.* Austin: University of Texas Press, 2009.

Boone, Elizabeth Hill. *Stories in Red and Black: Pictorial Histories of the Aztecs and Mixtecs.* Austin: University of Texas Press, 2000.

Brading, David. *Haciendas and ranchos in the Mexican bajío: León 1700–1860.* 1st ed. Cambridge: Cambridge University Press, 1979.

Brown, Archie. *The Myth of the Strong Leader: Political Leadership in Modern Politics.* New York: Basic Books, 2014.

Buenaventura Zapata y Mendoza, Juan. *Historia cronológica de la noble ciudad de Tlaxcala.* Transcripción paleográfica, traducción, presentación y notas por Luis Reyes García y Andrea Martínez Baracs. Tlaxcala, Mexico: Universidad Autónoma de Tlaxcala, Secretaría de Extensión Universitaria y Difusión Cultural; Centro de Investigaciones y Estudios Superiores en Antropología Social, 1995.

Burkhart, Louise M. *Before Guadalupe: The Virgin Mary in Early Colonial Nahuatl Literature.* Albany, NY: Institute for Mesoamerican Studies, University at Albany, 2001.

———. *The Slippery Earth: Nahua-Christian Moral Dialogue in Sixteenth-Century Mexico.* Tucson: University of Arizona Press, 1989.

Burns, Kathryn. *Into the Archive: Writing and Power in Colonial Peru.* Durham, NC: Duke University Press, 2010.

———. "Notaries, Truth, and Consequences." *The American Historical Review* 110, no. 2 (2005): 350–79.

Carrasco Pizana, Pedro. *The Tenochca Empire of Ancient Mexico: The Triple Alliance of Tenochtitlan, Tetzcoco, and Tlacopan.* Norman: University of Oklahoma Press.

Casas, Bartolomé de las. *In Defense of the Indians: The Defense of the Most Reverend Lord, don Fray Bartolomé de las Casas, of the Order of Preachers, Late Bishop of Chiapa, Against the Persecutors and Slanderers of the Peoples of the New World Discovered Across the Seas.* Translated, edited, and annotated by Stafford Poole. DeKalb: Northern Illinois University Press, 1974.

Chance, John K. *Conquest of the Sierra: Spaniards and Indians in Colonial Oaxaca.* Norman: University of Oklahoma Press, 1989.

———. *Race and Class in Colonial Oaxaca.* 1st ed. Stanford, CA: Stanford University Press, 1978.

Chance, John K., and William B. Taylor. "*Cofradías* and Cargos: An Historical Perspective on the Mesoamerican Civil-Religious Hierarchy." *American Ethnologist* 12, no. 1 (1985): 1–26.

Chaudhuri, Nupur, Sherry J. Katz, and Mary Elizabeth Perry. *Contesting Archives: Finding Women in the Sources.* Urbana: University of Illinois Press, 2010.

Chevalier, François. *Land and Society in Colonial Mexico: The Great Hacienda.* Berkeley: University of California Press, 1963.

Chicago, Judy. *The Dinner Party.* New York: Penguin, 1996.

Chimalpahin Cuauhtlehuanitzin, Domingo Francisco de San Antón Muñón, *Codex Chimalpahin: Society and Politics in Mexico Tenochtitlan, Tlatelolco, Texcoco, Culhuacan, and Other Nahua Altepetl in Central Mexico: The Nahuatl and Spanish Annals and Accounts Collected and Recorded by don Domingo de San Antón Muñón Chimalpahin Quauhtlehuanitzin.* Translated and edited by Arthur J. O. Anderson and Susan Schroeder. Norman: University of Oklahoma Press, 1997.

Christensen, Mark Z. *Translated Christianities: Nahuatl and Maya Religious Texts.* University Park: The Pennsylvania State University Press, 2014.

———. *Nahua and Maya Catholicisms: Texts and Religion in Colonial Central Mexico and Yucatan.* Stanford, CA: Stanford University Press; Berkeley, CA: The Academy of American Franciscan History, 2013.

Chuchiak, John F. "Writing as Resistance: Maya Graphic Pluralism and Indigenous Elite Strategies for Survival in Colonial Yucatan, 1550–1750." *Ethnohistory* 57, no. 1 (2010): 87–116.

Cline, S. L. *Colonial Culhuacan, 1580–1600: A Social History of an Aztec Town.* Albuquerque: University of New Mexico Press, 1986.

Cline, S. L., and Miguel León-Portilla, eds. *The Testaments of Culhuacan.* 1st ed. Los Angeles: UCLA Latin American Center Publications, University of California, Los Angeles, 1984.

Consentino, Delia A. "Nahua Pictorial Genealogies." In *Sources and Methods for the Study of Postconquest Mesoamerican Ethnohistory,* edited by James Lockhart, Lisa Sousa, and Stephanie Wood. Eugene: Wired Humanities Projects, University of Oregon, 2007. http://whp.uoregon.edu/Lockhart/index.html.

Coe, Sophie D. *America's First Cuisines.* 1st ed. Austin: University of Texas Press, 1994.

Cook, Sherburne Friend, and Woodrow Wilson Borah. *The Indian Population of Central Mexico, 1531–1610.* Ibero-Americana 44. Berkeley: University of California Press, 1960.

Cook, Sherburne Friend, and Lesley Byrd Simpson. *The Population of Central Mexico in the Sixteenth Century*. Ibero-Americana 31. Berkeley: University of California Press, 1948.

Dahlgren de Jordán, Barbro. *La Mixteca: Su cultura e historia prehispánicas*. Mexico City: Impr. Universitaria, 1954.

Derby, Lauren H. *The Dictator's Seduction: Politics and the Popular Imagination in the Era of Trujillo*. Durham, NC: Duke University Press, 2009.

———. "Gringo Chickens with Worms: Food and Nationalism in the Dominican Republic." In *Close Encounters of Empire: Writing the Cultural History of U.S.-Latin American Relations*, edited by Gilbert Joseph, Catherine C. LeGrand, and Ricardo D. Salvatore, 451–93. Durham, NC: Duke University Press, 1998.

Diaz del Castillo, Bernal. *The Memoirs of the Conquistador Bernal Diaz Del Castillo, Vol 1 (of 2) Written by Himself Containing a True and Full Account of the Discovery and Conquest of Mexico and New Spain*. Translated by John Ingram Lockhart. Project Gutenberg, 1568. http://www.gutenberg.org/3/2/4/7/32474/.

Ehrenreich, Robert M., Carole L. Crumley, and Janet E. Levy. *Heterarchy and the Analysis of Complex Societies*. Arlington, VA: American Anthropological Association, 1995.

Enciso, Jorge. *Design Motifs of Ancient Mexico*. New York: Dover Publications, 1953.

García Castro, René. *Indios, territorio y poder en la provincia Matlatzinca: La negociación del espacio político de los pueblos otomianos, siglos XV–XVII*. Mexico City: CONACULTA-INAH, 1999.

García Hernández, Alma. *Matlatzincas*. Mexico City: Comisión Nacional para el Desarrollo de los Pueblos Indígenas, PNUD México, 2004.

Geremek, Bronislaw, and Jean-Claude Schmitt. *The Margins of Society in Late Medieval Paris*. Translated by Jean Birrell. Cambridge: Cambridge University Press, 1987.

Gibson, Charles. *The Aztecs Under Spanish Rule: A History of the Indians of the Valley of Mexico, 1519–1810*. Stanford, CA: Stanford University Press, 1964.

———. *Tlaxcala in the Sixteenth Century*. 1967th ed. Stanford, CA: Stanford University Press, 1952.

Ginzburg, Carlo. *The Cheese and the Worms: The Cosmos of a Sixteenth-Century Miller*. Baltimore: Johns Hopkins University Press, 1980.

Goldstein, David John, and Robin Christine Coleman. "Schinus Molle L. (Anacardiaceae) Chicha Production in the Central Andes." *Economic Botany* 58, no. 4 (2004): 523–29.

Gonzalbo, Pilar. *Las mujeres en la nueva españa: Educación y vida cotidiana*. Mexico City: Colegio de México, Centro de Estudios Históricos, 1987.

González Rodrigo, José. *Santa Catarina del Monte: Bosques y hongos*. [Mexico City]: Universidad Iberoamericana, 1993.

González Torres, Yólotl, and Juan Carlos Ruiz Guadalajara. *Diccionario de mitología y religión de Mesoamérica*. Madrid: Larousse, 1991.

Goodwin, Joanne L. "Revealing New Narratives of Women in Las Vegas." In *Contesting Archives: Finding Women in the Sources*, edited by Nupur Chaudhuri, Sherry J. Katz, and Mary Elizabeth Perry, 177–91. Urbana: University of Illinois Press, 2010.

Gutierrez Hernandez, Silvia Alejandra, and Pedro Canales Guerrero. "Dos siglos de historia de la poblacion San Mateo Atenco (1654–1840)." In *La proeza historica de un pueblo: San Mateo Atenco en el Valle de Toluca (siglos VIII al XIX)*, edited by René García Castro and María Teresa Jarquín Ortega, 151–60. Toluca, Mexico: El Colegio Mexiquense; Universidad Autónoma del Estado de México, 2006.

Hanke, Lewis. *The Spanish Struggle for Justice in the Conquest of America*. Philadelphia: University of Pennsylvania Press, 1949.

Haring, C. H. *The Spanish Empire in America*. New York: Oxford University Press, 1947.

Haskett, Robert Stephen. *Indigenous Rulers: An Ethnohistory of Town Government in Colonial Cuernavaca*. 1st ed. Albuquerque: University of New Mexico Press, 1991.

Heath, Shirley Brice. *Telling Tongues: Language Policy in Mexico, Colony to Nation*. New York: Teachers College Press, 1972.

Hernández Rodríguez, Rosaura. "Los pueblos prehispanics del Valle de Toluca." In *Estudios de Cultura Náhuatl*, 219–25. Mexico City: Universidad Nacional Autónoma de México, Instituto de Investigaciones Históricas, 1966.

———. *El Valle de Toluca: Epoca prehispánica y siglo XVI*. Toluca, Mexico: Colegio Mexiquense; Ayuntamiento de Toluca, 1988.

Hoover, E., M. Renauld, M. R. Edelstein, and P. Brown. "Social Science Collaboration with Environmental Health." *Environmental Health Perspectives* 123, no. 11 (November 2015): 1100–1106. http://dx.doi.org/10.1289/ehp.1409283.

Horn, Rebecca. "Indigenous Identities in Mesoamerica After the Spanish Conquest." In *Native Diasporas: Indigenous Identities and Settler Colonialism in the Americas*, edited by Gregory D. Smithers and Brooke N. Newman, 31–78. Borderlands and Transcultural Studies. Lincoln: University of Nebraska Press, 2014.

———. *Postconquest Coyoacan: Nahua-Spanish Relations in Central Mexico, 1519–1650*. Stanford, CA: Stanford University Press, 1997.

Jarquín Ortega, Ma. Teresa. *Guía del archivo parroquial de Metepec*. Zinacatepec, Mexico: El Colegio Mexiquense, 1991.

Kanter, Deborah E. *Hijos del pueblo: Gender, Family, and Community in Rural Mexico, 1730–1850.* Austin: University of Texas Press, 2009.

Karttunen, Frances E., and James Lockhart. *Nahuatl in the Middle Years: Language Contact Phenomena in Texts of the Colonial Period.* Berkeley: University of California Press, 1976.

Kellogg, Susan. *Law and the Transformation of Aztec Culture, 1500–1700.* Norman: University of Oklahoma Press, 2005.

———. *Dead Giveaways.* Salt Lake City: University of Utah Press, 1998.

———. "From Parallel and Equivalent to Separate but Unequal: Tenochca Mexica Women, 1500–1700." In *Indian Women of Early Mexico*, edited by Susan Schroeder, Stephanie Wood, and Robert Haskett, 123–43. Norman: University of Oklahoma Press, 1997.

Klein, Kerwin Lee. *Frontiers of Historical Imagination: Narrating the European Conquest of Native America, 1890–1990.* 1st ed. Berkeley: University of California Press, 1997.

Ladurie, Emmanuel Le Roy. *The Peasants of Languedoc.* Translated by John Day. Urbana: University of Illinois Press, 1977.

Lavrín, Asunción. *Sexuality and Marriage in Colonial Latin America.* Lincoln: University of Nebraska Press, 1989.

LeGrand, Catherine, and Adriana Corso. "Los archivos notariales como fuente histórica: Una visión desde la zona bananera del Magdalena." *Anuario Colombiano de Historia Social y de la Cultura* 30:159–208, 2003. http://www.revistas.unal .edu.co/index.php/achsc/article/view/8166.

León-Portilla, Miguel. *Literaturas indígenas de México.* 1st ed. Mexico City: Fondo de Cultura Económica, 2003.

Lienzo de Tlaxcala: Manuscrito pictórico mexicano de mediados del siglo XVI. Mexico City: Librería Anticuaria G.M. Echaniz, [prólogo 1939].

Lockhart, James. "Introduction: Background and Course of the New Philology." In *Sources and Methods for the Study of Postconquest Mesoamerican Ethnohistory*, edited by James Lockhart, Lisa Sousa, and Stephanie Wood. Eugene: Wired Humanities Projects, University of Oregon, 2007. http://whp.uoregon.edu/Lockhart /index.html.

———. *Nahuatl as Written: Lessons in Older Written Nahuatl, with Copious Examples and Texts.* 1st ed. Stanford, CA: Stanford University Press, 2002.

———. "The Social History of Early Latin America: Evolution and Potential." In *Of Things of the Indies: Essays Old and New in Early Latin American History.* Stanford, CA: Stanford University Press, 1999.

———. *The Nahuas After the Conquest: A Social and Cultural History of the Indians of Central Mexico, Sixteenth Through Eighteenth Centuries.* Stanford, CA: Stanford University Press, 1992.

———. "A Language Transition in Eighteenth-Century Mexico: The Change from Nahuatl to Spanish Recordkeeping in the Valley of Toluca." In *Nahuas and Spaniards: Postconquest Central Mexican History and Philology*, edited by James Lockhart. UCLA Latin American Studies 76; Nahuatl Studies Series 3. Stanford, CA: Stanford University Press; Los Angeles: UCLA Latin American Center Publications, University of California, Los Angeles, 1991.

———. *Nahuas and Spaniards: Postconquest Central Mexican History and Philology.* UCLA Latin American Studies 76; Nahuatl Studies Series 3. Stanford, CA: Stanford University Press; Los Angeles: UCLA Latin American Center Publications, University of California, Los Angeles, 1991.

Lockhart, James, Frances Berdan, and Arthur J. O. Anderson. *The Tlaxcalan Actas: A Compendium of the Records of the* cabildo *of Tlaxcala, 1545–1627.* Salt Lake City: University of Utah Press, 1986.

Lockhart, James, Susan Schroeder, and Doris Namala, eds. *Annals of His Time: Don Domingo de San Anton Munon Chimalpahin Quauhtlehuanitzin.* 1st ed. Stanford, CA: Stanford University Press, 2006.

Lomnitz-Adler, Claudio. *Death and the Idea of Mexico.* Brooklyn, NY: Zone Books, 2005.

———. *Los archivos notariales como fuente histórica: Una visión desde la zona bananera del Magdalena.* Bogotá: Universidad Nacional de Colombia, 2004. http://www .revistas.unal.edu.co/index.php/achsc/article/view/8166.

Magaloni Kerpel, Diana. *The Colors of the New World: Artists, Materials, and the Creation of the Florentine Codex.* Los Angeles: The Getty Research Institute, 2014.

Mairot, Mark Joseph. *Mexican Provincial Society During the Age of Revolution: A Social and Economic History of Toluca, 1790–1834.* Los Angeles: University of California, Los Angeles, 2013. http://search.proquest.com/docview/1420357030 ?accountid=14512.

Marquez, Ophelia, and Lillian Ramos Navarro, eds. "Topile." In *Compilation of Colonial Spanish Terms and Document Related Phrases, Based on Usage in Colonial Manuscripts.* Midway City, CA: Society of Hispanic Historical and Ancestral Research Press, 1998. http://www.somosprimos.com/spanishterms/spanishterms .htm.

McDonough, Kelly S. *The Learned Ones: Nahua Intellectuals in Postconquest Mexico.* Tucson: University of Arizona Press, 2014.

Melton-Villanueva, Miriam, and Caterina Pizzigoni. "Late Nahuatl Testaments from the Toluca Valley: Indigenous-Language Ethnohistory in the Mexican Independence Period." *Ethnohistory* 55, no. 3 (2008): 361–91.

Menegus Bornemann, Margarita. *Del señorío a la república de indios: El caso de Toluca, 1500–1600.* Madrid: Ministerio de Agricultura, Pesca y Alimentación, Secretaría General Técnica, 1991.

Miller, Cary. *Ogimaag: Anishinaabeg Leadership, 1760–1845.* Lincoln: University of Nebraska Press, 2010.

Mundy, Barbara E. *The Mapping of New Spain: Indigenous Cartography and the Maps of the Relaciones Geográficas.* Chicago: University of Chicago Press, 1996.

Offutt, Leslie Scott. *Saltillo, 1770–1810: Town and Region in the Mexican North.* Tucson: University of Arizona Press, 2001.

Olko, Justinya, and Agnieszka Brylak. "'The Old Idolatry Is There . . .': Preconquest Religious Practices in the Oldest Known Nahuatl Document from Tlaxcala," panel *Nahuas and Spaniards: New Perspectives on Cross-Cultural Contact, Part I (In Memory of James Lockhart),* American Society for Ethnohistory Annual Conference, Indianapolis, November 10, 2014.

Osowski, Edward W. *Indigenous Miracles: Nahua Authority in Colonial Mexico.* Tucson: University of Arizona Press, 2010.

Osuna Codex. "Painting of the Governor, Mayors, and Rulers of Mexico." 1565. http://www.wdl.org/en/item/7324/.

Parodi, Claudia. "Indianization of Spaniards in New Spain." In *Mexican Indigenous Languages at the Dawn of the Twenty-First Century,* edited by Margarita Hidalgo, 29–52. Berlin: Mouton de Gruyter, 2006.

Perry, Mary Elizabeth. *Crime and Society in Early Modern Seville.* 1st ed. Hanover, NH: UPNE, 1980.

Pizzigoni, Caterina. *The Life Within: Local Indigenous Society in Mexico's Toluca Valley, 1650–1800.* Stanford, CA: Stanford University Press, 2013.

———. "Region and Subregion in Central Mexican Ethnohistory: The Toluca Valley, 1650–1760." *Colonial Latin American Review* 16, no. 1 (2007): 71–92.

———, ed. *Testaments of Toluca.* 1st ed. Stanford, CA: Stanford University Press, 2006.

Prescott, William Hickling. *History of the Conquest of Mexico, and History of the Conquest of Peru.* New York: Modern Library, 1936.

Rabiela, Elsa Leticia Rea López Constantino Medina Lima Teresa Rojas. *Vidas y bienes olvidado.* Vol. 3, *Testamentos indigenas novohispanos.* 1st ed. Mexico City: CIESAS, 2000.

———. *Vidas y bienes olvidados.* Vol. 1, *Testamentos indígenas novohispanos.* Mexico City: CIESAS, 1999.

———. Vidas y bienes olvidados. Vol. 2, *Testamentos indígenas novohispanos*. Mexico City: CIESAS, 1999.

Ramos, Gabriela, and Yanna Yannakakis, eds. *Indigenous Intellectuals: Knowledge, Power, and Colonial Culture in Mexico and the Andes*. Durham, NC: Duke University Press, 2014.

Rautman, Alison E. "Hierarchy and Heterarchy in the American Southwest: A Comment on Mcguire and Saitta." *American Antiquity* 63, no. 2 (April 1, 1998): 325–33. doi:10.2307/2694701.

Real Academia Espanola. *Diccionario de la lengua espanola*. 22nd ed. Madrid: Planeta Publishing, 2002.

Restall, Matthew. *The Maya World: Yucatec Culture and Society, 1550–1850*. 1st ed. Stanford, CA: Stanford University Press, 1999.

Restall, Matthew, Lisa Sousa, and Kevin Terraciano. *Mesoamerican Voices: Native-Language Writings from Colonial Mexico, Oaxaca, Yucatan, and Guatemala*. Cambridge: Cambridge University Press, 2005.

Ricard, Robert. *La "conquète spirituelle" du Mexique*. Paris: Institut d'ethnologie, 1933.

Rojo, Freya, Ricardo Hernandez, and Julio Ramos. "Analysis: Ayotzinapa." Radio interview. *Nuestra Voz*. KPFK, Los Angeles. KPFK Studios, 2014.

Rounds, J. "Dynastic Succession and the Centralization of Power in Tenochtitlan." In *The Inca and Aztec States, 1400–1800: Anthropology and History*, edited by George Allen Collier, Renato Rosaldo, and John D. Wirth, 63–86. New York: Academic Press, 1982.

Ruiz, Teofilo F. *A King Travels: Festive Traditions in Late Medieval and Early Modern Spain*, Princeton, NJ: Princeton University Press, 2012.

Salas Cuesta, Marcela, and Maria Elena Salas Cuesta. "*Muerte e ilustracion: Cementerios extramuros*." In *Homenaje a Jaime Litvak*, edited by Antonio Benavides, Linda Manzanilla, and Lorena Mirambell, 127–42. Mexico City: UNAM, 2004.

Salomon, Frank, and Mercedes Niño-Murcia. *The Lettered Mountain: A Peruvian Village's Way with Writing*. Durham, NC: Duke University Press, 2011.

Scholes, France V., and Eleanor B. Adams. *Sobre el modo de tributar los indios de Nueva España a su majestad, 1561–1564*. Mexico City: J. Porrúa, 1958.

Schroeder, Susan. "The Noblewomen of Chalco." *Estudios de Cultura Nahuatl*, 22 (1992), 45–86.

Schroeder, Susan, Stephanie Gail Wood, and Robert Stephen Haskett. *Indian Women of Early Mexico*. Norman: University of Oklahoma Press, 1997.

Schwaller, Robert C. *A Language of Empire, a Quotidian Tongue: The Uses of Nahuatl in New Spain*. Durham, NC: Duke University Press, 2012.

Sell, Barry D., Louise M. Burkhart, Gregory Spira, and Miguel León Portilla. *Nahuatl Theater.* Vol. 1. Norman: University of Oklahoma Press, 2004.

Sheeran, Michael J. *Beyond Majority Rule: Voteless Decisions in the Religious Society of Friends.* New ed. Philadelphia: Philadelphia Yearly Meeting of Religious Society of Friends, 1983.

Siméon, Rémi. *Diccionario de la lengua náhuatl o mexicana.* Mexico City: Siglo XXI, 1988.

Smith, Benjamin T. *The Roots of Conservatism in Mexico: Catholicism, Society, and Politics in the Mixteca Baja, 1750–1962.* Albuquerque: University of New Mexico Press, 2012.

Smith, Michael E. *The Aztecs.* 2nd ed. Malden, MA: Wiley-Blackwell, 2002.

Sousa, Lisa Mary. "Spinning and Weaving the Threads of Native Women's Lives in Colonial Mexico." In *Contesting Archives: Finding Women in the Sources*, edited by Nupur Chaudhuri, Sherry J. Katz, and Mary Elizabeth Perry, 75–88. Urbana: University of Illinois Press, 2010.

———. "Women and Crime in Colonial Oaxaca: Evidence of Complementary Gender Roles in Mixtec and Zapotec Societies." In *Indian Women of Early Mexico*, edited by Susan Schroeder, Stephanie Gail Wood, and Robert Stephen Haskett, 199–214. Norman: University of Oklahoma Press, 1997.

Starhawk. *The Empowerment Manual: A Guide for Collaborative Groups.* Gabriola Island, BC, Canada: New Society Publishers, 2012.

Stern, Steve J. *Peru's Indian Peoples and the Challenge of Spanish Conquest: Huamanga to 1640.* Madison: University of Wisconsin Press, 1993.

Sugiura Yamamoto, Yoko. "Caminando el Valle de Toluca: Arqueología regional, el legado de William T. Sanders." *Cuicuilco* 16, no. 47 (December 2009): 87–111.

Tavarez, David. "Autonomy, Honor, and the Ancestors: Native Local Religion in Seventeenth-Century Oaxaca." In *Local Religion in Colonial Mexico*, edited by Martin Austin Nesvig, 119–44. Albuquerque: University of New Mexico, 2006.

Taylor, William B. "The Virgin of Guadalupe in New Spain: An Inquiry into the Social History of Marian Devotion." *American Ethnologist* 14, no. 1 (February 1, 1987): 9–33.

———. *Drinking, Homicide & Rebellion in Colonial Mexican Villages.* Stanford, CA: Stanford University Press, 1979.

Terraciano, Kevin. *The Mixtecs of Colonial Oaxaca: Ñudzahui History, Sixteenth Through Eighteenth Centuries.* Stanford, CA: Stanford University Press, 2001.

Torjesen, Karen Jo. *When Women Were Priests: Women's Leadership in the Early Church and the Scandal of Their Subordination in the Rise of Christianity.* 1st ed. San Francisco: HarperSanFrancisco, 1993.

Townsend, Camilla, ed. *Here in This Year: Seventeenth-Century Nahuatl Annals of the Tlaxcala-Puebla Valley*. Stanford, CA: Stanford University Press, 2009.

Truax, Eileen. *Dreamers: An Immigrant Generation's Fight for Their American Dream*. Boston: Beacon Press, 2015.

Van Young, Eric. "Of Tempests and Teapots: Imperial Crisis and Local Conflict in Mexico at the Beginning of the Nineteenth Century." In *Cycles of Conflict, Centuries of Change: Crisis, Reform, and Revolution in Mexico*, edited by Elisa Servín, Leticia Reina, and John Tutino, 23–59. Durham, NC: Duke University Press, 2007.

———. *The Other Rebellion: Popular Violence, Ideology, and the Mexican Struggle for Independence, 1810–1821*. 1st ed. Stanford, CA: Stanford University Press, 2002.

Villaseñor y Sánchez, José Antonio de. *Theatro americano: Descripción general de los reynos, y provincias de la Nueva-España, y sus jurisdicciones*. Mexico City: Editora Nacional, 1952.

Vizenor, Gerald. *Manifest Manners: Narratives on Postindian Survivance*. First Bison Books Printing ed. Lincoln: University of Nebraska Press, 1999.

Voekel, Pamela. "Book Review: Death and the Idea of Mexico." *The American Historical Review* 112, no. 1 (2007): 254–55.

Wakild, Emily. *Revolutionary Parks: Conservation, Social Justice, and Mexico's National Parks, 1910–1940*. Tucson: University of Arizona Press, 2011.

Walls, David S. *Community Organizing*. 1st ed. Cambridge: Polity, 2014.

Weatherford, Jack. *Indian Givers: How the Indians of the Americas Transformed the World*. New York: Ballantine Books, 1989.

Wood, Stephanie G. *Transcending Conquest: Nahua Views of Spanish Colonial Mexico*. Norman: University of Oklahoma Press, 2003.

———. "Adopted Saints: Christian Images in Nahua Testaments of Late Colonial Toluca." *The Americas* 47, no. 3 (January 1, 1991): 259–93. doi:10.2307/1006801.

———. "Corporate Adjustments in Colonial Mexican Indian Towns: Toluca Region, 1550–1810." PhD diss., University of California, Los Angeles, 1984.

Wood, Stephanie, and John Sullivan. *Nahuatl Dictionary*. Eugene, OR: Wired Humanities Projects, University of Oregon, 2007. http://whp.uoregon.edu/dictionaries/nahuatl/.

Yannakakis, Yanna. *The Art of Being In-Between: Native Intermediaries, Indian Identity, and Local Rule in Colonial Oaxaca*. Durham, NC: Duke University Press, 2008.

Zavala, Silvio. *New Viewpoints on the Spanish Colonization of America*. New York: Russell and Russell, 1968.

INDEX

In this index, glossary entries are indicated by page numbers in **bold**. References to charts, graphs, and photographs are in *italics*. Information located in the notes is indicated thus: 203n76, meaning note 76 on page 203.

A note about Nahua names: Most of the individuals referenced here lack family names; people's names typically consist of paired saints' names. These names have been indexed by the first letter of the first name. This includes a few whose saint's name includes a "de la" construction, e.g., Juan Domingo de la Cruz, who appears under *J* for Juan, and not *D* for Domingo or *C* for Cruz.

Spanish names that do not follow this pattern are indexed as usual, e.g., Bartolomé de las Casas, who appears under *C*.

This index does not include references to the specific contents of the sample testaments included in the appendix, beyond those discussed in the main text.

ABOUT THE AUTHOR

Miriam Melton-Villanueva received her PhD in history from the University of California, Los Angeles, in 2012. She is an assistant professor in the Department of History at the University of Nevada, Las Vegas, where her research explores the cultural strategies and status of women and men in colonial Mexico's central highland indigenous communities. Her development of ethnohistorical methods as a way to bring people's voices into history, using archival records such as native-language wills, underpins her analysis. Her work appears in the edited volume *Documenting Latin America: Gender, Race, and Empire* (Prentice Hall, 2011) and the journal *Ethnohistory*. She was Ford Foundation Postdoctoral Fellow in residence at UCLA's Chicano Studies Research Center from 2014 to 2015.